POLITICS IN THE POETRY OF COLERIDGE

POLITICS
IN THE POETRY
OF COLERIDGE

Carl R. Woodring

THE UNIVERSITY OF WISCONSIN PRESS · MADISON, 1961

Published by The University of Wisconsin Press,
430 Sterling Court, Madison 6, Wisconsin

Copyright © 1961 by the Regents of the University of Wisconsin

Printed in the United States of America
by the Vail-Ballou Press, Inc., Binghamton, New York

Library of Congress Catalog Card No. 61–11643

TO MY MOTHER† AND FATHER

Preface

A few economies have been practiced in the documentation of this study. Brief citations are made parenthetically in the text, especially for the works listed in the table of abbreviations that follows this preface. Other notes appear together at the end of the volume. *The Cambridge Bibliography of English Literature* and its *Supplement* of 1957, with the excellent annual bibliographies in the *Philological Quarterly,* have made it possible to omit a full list of sources. Where no intermediate source is specifically cited, I have gone to the manuscript, newspaper, or other document named as the ultimate source; for convenience, I have followed and cited the standard editions when the only discrepancies are in mechanics not significant for the purpose in hand. Ligatures, long *s,* large initial letters, and punctuation under raised letters are ignored in transcriptions. But Coleridge capitalized nouns, partly for emphasis and partly out of habit, after the practice had become unfashionable, and I have retained capitals and small capitals in quoting from him.

The present study began with a student paper on Coleridge's patriotism submitted in 1941 to Professor George W. Whiting of Rice Institute (now Rice University). If he suggested the topic, he has much to answer for. A second volume will contain, I hope, a less detailed examination of politics in the poetry of Wordsworth,

Byron, Shelley, and poets associated with them. The study has since been aided by other teachers and by many generous scholars; by conscientious librarians in two countries; much more often than not by my wife; by three grants from the Research Committee of the Graduate School of the University of Wisconsin; and by the John Simon Guggenheim Memorial Foundation. A fellowship from the Fund for the Advancement of Education enabled me to observe and read politics and political history in the city where Coleridge was chained to journalism. Nearer home, the steady service of Marguerite Christensen has been relieved by the hospitality of Stanley Pargellis and the Newberry Library. In answer to queries, facts have been generously provided by Kathleen Coburn, E. L. Griggs, Lewis Patton, and George Whalley. Whatever its present state, the book has been much simplified, clarified, and improved by suggestions from official readers, and most of all by corrections and criticisms from David V. Erdman.

My chief indebtedness for manuscripts and books is to the British Museum. For permission to quote from manuscripts I am grateful generally to A. H. B. Coleridge, and specifically to William A. Jackson and the Harvard University Library, John D. Gordan and the New York Public Library, Frederick B. Adams, Jr., and the Pierpont Morgan Library, Norman C. Kittermaster and Rugby School, and to the Bollingen Foundation for quotation from a notebook of Coleridge not yet published. All students of Coleridge are indebted to the Oxford University Press for its editions of his poems and his letters.

C.R.W.

Madison, Wisconsin
April, 1961

Abbreviations

Used for Documentation

The following table lists the works signified by abbreviations appearing in the notes and parenthetically in the text. The author of the works starred is Samuel Taylor Coleridge. The place of publication is London unless otherwise indicated. These abbreviations appear throughout in Roman type. Abbreviations in italics, to signify modern periodicals, follow the table that precedes the annual bibliography in *PMLA*, the official journal of the Modern Language Association of America. In citing those among the works below that are paginated successively from one volume to another, the volume number is omitted. Numbers following a colon designate line numbers on the page cited.

BE   *Biographia Epistolaris*, ed. A. Turnbull. 2 vols. 1911.
BL   *Biographia Literaria*, ed. J. Shawcross. 2 vols. 1907.
BP   Lord Byron, *Works: Poetry*, ed. E. H. Coleridge. 7 vols. 1898–1904.
CL   *Collected Letters*, ed. E. L. Griggs. Vol. I, II. 1956. (Volume numbers are given for III and IV, 1959.)
CN   *Notebooks*, ed. K. Coburn. "Volume I" (2 vols.). 1957.
CPW   *Poetical Works*, ed. E. H. Coleridge. 2 vols. 1912.
DJ   Lord Byron, *Don Juan*, ed. T. G. Steffan and W. W.

Pratt. Vols. II, III. Austin, 1957. (Cited by canto and stanza.)

EKC E. K. Chambers, *Samuel Taylor Coleridge*. Oxford, 1950.

EOT *Essays on His Own Times*, ed. Sara Coleridge. 3 vols. 1850.

F *The Friend*, ed. H. N. Coleridge. 3 vols. 1850.

George *Catalogue of Political and Personal Satires . . . in the British Museum*, ed. M. D. George. Vols. VI–X. 1938–52.

HCR *Henry Crabb Robinson on Books and Their Writers*, ed. E. J. Morley. 3 vols. 1938.

IS *Inquiring Spirit*, ed. K. Coburn. 1951.

JDC *Poetical Works*, ed. J. D. Campbell. 1893.

LL Charles Lamb, *Letters*, ed. E. V. Lucas. 3 vols. 1935.

LS *A Lay Sermon Addressed to the Higher and Middle Classes*. 1817.

MC *Morning Chronicle*.

MP *Morning Post*.

SM *The Statesman's Manual*. 1816.

SPJ *The Spirit of the Public Journals*. (Cited for each year as given in the annual title; e.g., SPJ for 1797.)

UL *Unpublished Letters*, ed. E. L. Griggs. 2 vols. 1933.

W *The Watchman*. 1 March–13 May 1796.

WPW William Wordsworth, *Poetical Works*, ed. E. de Selincourt and H. Darbishire. 5 vols. (2nd ed. of Vols. I–III.) 1947–54.

Contents

POLITICS IN THE POETRY OF COLERIDGE

Introduction

> One of the most surprising aspects
> of Coleridge's political activities in
> Bristol in 1795 is the closeness of his
> attachment to the contemporary po-
> litical scene.
>
> —John Colmer, *Coleridge:*
> *Critic of Society,* 1959

Coleridge, of the English Romantic poets, gave most thought to politics. He had, no doubt, the most thought to give. Born with a fertile mind, he fertilized it interminably by reading. But his combination of turbulence and lethargy has kept the produce of this fertility sadly uncollected for more than a century. Out of his voluminous political prose, partly journalistic and occasional, partly theoretic and ideal, sometimes not only orderly but even downright clear, at least one concept grew into originality and significance: his idea of the "clerisy," comprising all those engaged in "the continued and progressive civilisation of the community"; not only the clergy, but also the sages and professors of all the liberal arts and sciences; the *enclesia,* called into the state to redress the overbalance of the commercial and landed interests, as well as the *ecclesia* called out of it. With Wordsworth he broadcast also their new concept of nationalism as national self-determination. Every half-informed graduate, if not every schoolboy, knows of John Stuart Mill's tribute to Coleridge as one of the two seminal minds from which the most important ideas in Victorian England evolved. Coleridge's seminal mind opposed Bentham's Utilitarianism, said Mill, with an idealism that describes society and the state organically and morally. In Coleridge's idea both society and the state are conservers, for all classes and all generations, of everything in the actuality that approaches in goodness the moral idea that informs each part.

Like the other English Romantics, Coleridge emerged from childhood into the excitement of accelerated change in intellectual systems and in social arrangements. Ideas epitomized in the empirical individualism of John Locke had been further codified by the French *philosophes*. In 1790 Cambridge, if not Oxford, talked about the universal equality and freedom of men, the basic rationality and potential goodness of the individual, the right to social contract between ruler and ruled, further natural rights derived from natural law, and the necessity—under reason—of tolerance for every sect and individual. Fraternity, Equality, and other abstractions of the French Revolution seemed at first to represent the explosion of new thought, but intellectually they proved to be Jacobin versions of Enlightenment: rationalistic, mechanistic, utilitarian, expedient, epicurean. Comparing the *ancien régime* of France with the Roman empire, Coleridge found both rotted by the philosophy of Epicurus, "a philosophy which regards man as a mere machine, a sort of living automaton; which teaches that pleasure is the sole good, and a prudent calculation of enjoyment the only virtue." (EOT, 482) [1] Were the Jacobins essentially different?

Rousseauistic sentiment and Wesleyan emotion lie hidden under the premises of William Godwin's *Enquiry concerning Political Justice*, 1793, but Godwin argued with dry logic from universal reason and necessity to anarchy (that is, orderly absence of government) and dispassionate justice for all, sister and stranger alike. He denied the validity of just those prejudicial ties of affection that Coleridge and Wordsworth wished to recommend. Introspective Romantic vitalism could not make peace with such mechanistic rationality as Godwin's, and yet no other intellectual bases were readily available for the social change and humanitarian hope that excited young poets.

Alfred Cobban, in *Edmund Burke and the Revolt against the Eighteenth Century* (1929), has influentially grouped Coleridge, Southey, and Wordsworth with Burke as Romantic because conservative. In this view there is much truth. Caught historically between mechanistic libertarianism and Romantic vitalism, or organicism, Coleridge butted with divided mind against this dilemma most of his life. Not that the division was sharp. The Enlightenment passed along not only its maxim that private pleasures are public benefits, but also the Ciceronian maxim that public liberty depends upon individual and collective virtue. After quoting Milton's *Comus* on the point, the *Political Disquisitions* of James Burgh (which Coleridge borrowed from the Bristol Library and much admired) put succinctly the Roman view that the Romantics were to inherit: ". . . scarcely any woman loses her virtue, no nation its liberties, without their fault." [2] The moral imperative of Coleridge's prose and Wordsworth's poetry assumes an Old Testament *therefore* in several of Coleridge's poems. Unlike the unluxurious ancients, Englishmen have lived sumptuously; "Therefore, evil days Are coming on us, O my countrymen!" It is impolitic to offend "all-avenging Providence." (CPW, 260:123–25) How a political maxim of this sort expanded into other areas of Coleridge's poetry can be glimpsed in a metaphor preserved in the first version of *Religious Musings:* "The Atheist your worst slave." [3] In so far as political morality was inherited along with doctrines of expediency, it helped as much as Napoleon's imperialism in the name of new freedom to bring intellectual crisis. A large problem, of course, was patriotic rejection of ideas regarded as French.

Many students have encountered, and a good many have written about, Coleridge's political ideas; but very few have recognized the variety of ways by which he put political ideas, feelings, and dilemmas to work in his poems. Wordsworth informed younger men how the French Revolution made it bliss in that dawn to be alive; but the bulk of Coleridge's poems present the negative side, discolored by the alarmist policies of Pitt and his fellow ministers: suspension of habeas corpus, gagging of the public press, indictment of patriots for sedition and treason. As a hired journalist, Coleridge produced verse explicitly political in forms related to conventional pasquinades, parodies, odes, and ballads. Even some of his nobler poems, like *France: An Ode,* were produced partly for pay and partly out of a conflict of political impulses. In the chapters that follow, an attempt will be made to identify those impulses in the creation of Coleridge's poems that should be called political. Although the attempt to isolate political elements cannot succeed completely, it should be made. Perhaps *France: An Ode* resulted ultimately from frustrations in the poet's marriage. It certainly resulted in part because Coleridge knew from his reading that palinodes could be written. But he had considerable interest in deciding which political views to retract. And the poem, too, has a biography. We must continue to ask, though the answer may never be forthcoming, what parts the editor Stuart played before and immediately after Coleridge gave *France: An Ode* its original shape. We can suspect that Stuart cared more about what the poem said, about the content that could be paraphrased, than Coleridge did.

In some critical circles it is thought mechanical and undignified to mix politics with poetry. More than once evidence has been distorted to avoid seeing political implications in *Kubla Khan*. I hope to show that Coleridge, like Milton, was at least occasionally of another opinion. Since critical judgments are implicit in the space allotted to particular poems, as well as in the choice of Coleridge rather than, say, Southey or Moore, I include explicit evaluation in the effort to show what difference politics makes to Coleridge's poetry. The word *politics* is here used in a very wide sense, to include not only partisan debate and harangue—which certainly have their innings in Coleridge's poems—but also political assumptions and theory, in the sense of Aristotle's *Politics*. It has been necessary to include in the study the humanitarianism and other impulses that moved this poet very early toward political expression. Because the boundaries of motivation cannot be drawn, and because it seems worth while to show the emotional and aesthetic contexts of political elements in the poems—and thus to show how these political elements are limited—the study reports also on related subjects, especially on feelings associated with politics, whether consciously by Coleridge or demonstrably in his poems.[4]

In general, the variety of ways in which political forces act in his poetry can best be seen, and can be most profitably discriminated, by studying as a group all the poems of each genre to which he gave political content. Later chapters therefore take up Coleridge's different genres, from those directly involved in "local and temporary politics" to the more elevated poems where political impulse is less immediately apparent: from laudatory newspaper sonnets, looser poems of praise, and partisan *jeux d'esprit,* to exalted odes and dramas. Many of the earlier poems, whatever their genre or ostensible subject, reveal ways in which pity, joined by a passion for freedom of the written word, led young Coleridge to fiercely partisan language as well as to utopian visions. Chapters III, IV, and V, therefore, concern terms, phrases, metaphors, and feelings important to politics in Coleridge's poetry, without reference to genre. First, biased toward politics and "intentions," let us begin with the life of the young man who wrote the poems.

CHAPTER II

The Young Man
in His Time

It is very unpleasant to me to be often asked if Coleridge has changed his political sentiments—for I know not properly how to reply—pray furnish me.

—Mrs. Coleridge
to Thomas Poole, 1799

Born thirty months after Wordsworth, Coleridge developed and revealed earlier than Wordsworth a concern with political affairs. It cannot have been long after the most important single event in the relationship of political revolution to the Romantic movement in literature, 14 July 1789, that Coleridge as a bluecoat boy at Christ's Hospital celebrated it by *An Ode on the Destruction of the Bastile.* (CPW, 10) His teachers, the reigning neoclassic poets and the caning pedagogues, had taught him to sing of personified Tyranny, Freedom, and Hope, of "Oppression's band," "Power's blood-stain'd streamers," and, hardly less abstract, "favour'd Britain." Of reading remembered later, he specifies two works: the Whig essays published in 1724 as *Cato's Letters* and Voltaire's dictionary to create and amuse infidels. A classmate who remained also a friend in college, C. V. LeGrice, gave as his example of Coleridge's prodigious memory the recitation of whole paragraphs from the latest pamphlets by Burke. A Grecian, or creamiest boy,

Coleridge won at the beginning of 1791 an exhibition from Christ's Hospital and a sizarship at Jesus College, Cambridge.

In March, at eighteen, before taking up residence at Cambridge in October, he accumulated political images consciously in *A Mathematical Problem*, sent in a letter to his oldest brother. This *tour de force*, acknowledging the Authority of geometric axioms, praised the sides of an equilateral triangle, "Unambitiously join'd in Equality's Band." (CPW, 23:41) The egalitarian triangle illustrates not only "sure alliance" but also the "balance of power." (CPW, 23:54) And so on. This effort may have helped free the poet from temptations to surrender more serious verse to seductive phrases like "natural rights" and "social contract." It may be taken as symbolic that the poem associates such phrases with mathematics. He managed to find at Cambridge an atmosphere decidedly Whiggish, agreeably agitated by breezes from a revolution that would supposedly give Frenchmen the liberties enjoyed by Englishmen since 1688. Set various college exercises that were expected to bring forth metrical sentiments against slavery, Coleridge won the Browne Gold Medal in 1792 for a prize ode in Greek Sapphics on the slave trade, with the Latin motto *"Sors misera Servorum in insulis Indiae occidentalis."* (JDC, 476)

In his life as in his poems, political impulses rose in the midst of other impulses, political passions were enmeshed in other passions. Churning with unrequited love for a sensible Mary Evans, he opened 1793 in a mixture of furious study for further honors and obstructive, hysterical dissipation. Debts engulfed him. He failed, though narrowly, to win the Browne Medal for 1793 and the Craven scholarship. We may assume that Coleridge never gave up for long his "preposterous pursuit" of theological controversy and esoteric mystics and philosophers. (BL, I, 10)

Those were churning times for everybody. The first assumption among readers Whiggishly inclined, that the Revolutionists in France were seeking and achieving liberties similar to those of Englishmen, had been staggering since November, 1790, from the arguments of Edmund Burke's *Reflections on the Revolution in France*. Evidences of irrational fear in Burke had given Thomas Paine several opportunities for successful ridicule in the first part of his *Rights of Man*. The utilitarian rebuttal of Burke in James Mackintosh's *Vindiciae Gallicae*, April, 1791, was more respectable

than Paine's vivid journalism to a Cambridge still subject to
Newton's optimistic rationalism and Locke's empirical and libertarian insistence on the isolation of the individual psychologically
and politically. There were other answerers. But Burke's renunciation in 1791 of his friendship with Charles James Fox, the nominal
head of the Whigs, had sundered the party, and he was bringing
confusion to all groups—except the Tories—by his denunciations
of the abstract rights claimed by the French Jacobins for individual
man. These abstract, theoretical, unreal rights, declared Burke,
were perversely derived from the divinely given social contract of
natural law, "the great primaeval contract of eternal society, link-
ing the lower with the higher natures, connecting the visible and
invisible world, according to a fixed compact sanctioned by the
inviolable oath which holds all physical and all moral natures,
each in their appointed place." [1]

Burke was answering specifically the Rev. Dr. Richard Price,
who had used Nonconformist pulpits and the rostrum of the Society
for the Commemoration of the Revolution in Great Britain (the
"Glorious Revolution" of 1688) to praise the recent events in
France as demonstrations of natural right. As Burke recognized,
religious Dissenters formed the phalanx of reformist and revolutionary opinion in England. Not only did they speak for the urban
middle class barely represented in the unreformed Parliament;
not only had they been driven to establish an educational system
separate from that of the ruling classes; they were men excluded
by law even from municipal office so long as they obeyed their
consciences and avoided the sacraments of the Established Church.
With cries of "Church and State," roused by celebrations of Bastille
Day, 1791, a Birmingham mob destroyed the house, papers, and
scientific apparatus of Price's internationally famed colleague, the
Unitarian Joseph Priestley.

Although Pitt and his domestic opponents would argue end-
lessly over the direct causes of the outbreak, both France and Great
Britain moved frantically through January, 1793, toward inevitable
and immediate war. During the previous year two important associations had joined the revived Society for Constitutional Information with the ultimate aim of reforming Parliament and the
immediate purpose, annoying to the Government, of circulating
Paine's *Rights of Man*. The new associations of 1792 were the

London Corresponding Society, led by the shoemaker Thomas Hardy (the dangerous meaning of its name was correspondence with the Revolutionary leaders in Paris), and the society of Friends of the People, founded by Charles Grey and other high Whigs. Hardy's society marks one of the beginnings of the Chartist movement, for it advocated more democratic reforms to Parliament than the Act of 1832 accomplished.

In defense of uncommitted individual reason, Godwin's *Political Justice*, which appeared unluckily just when war was declared, decried such associations and avoided catch-phrases like "the Majesty of the People," but it defended the right of free speaking against privilege and inequality. In August and September, at Edinburgh, Lord Justice Braxfield, "expert in feudal law," declared the British Constitution perfect, but denied the right of political association under the Constitution to Thomas Fyshe Palmer and Thomas Muir, whom he sentenced to transportation to Botany Bay for twelve and fourteen years respectively. Ministers under Pitt moved toward the suspension of habeas corpus in May, 1794, and the consequent arrest of leaders of the London societies, including Hardy, John Horne Tooke, and John Thelwall. For the prosecution of such "patriots," the Government was to receive aid from counter-patriots like John Reeves, founder of the Association for Preserving Liberty and Property against Levellers and Republicans.

Meanwhile, on the one hand, the Revolution gave further signs of bloodiness after the execution of Louis XVI on 21 January 1793 and gave proofs of blasphemy in November with the worship of Reason at Notre Dame and in some 2,400 Temples of Reason. On the other hand, the second partition of Poland by Russia, Prussia, and Austria hardened the Opposition against Pitt's chief military allies.

There were elements of stability in 1793, not all of them attractive to a volatile young mind. George III, who had "lost the Colonies," was still on the throne. His chief minister, William Pitt, the younger, had assumed his post in 1783 at the age of twenty-five. In the judgment of the Opposition, Billy Pitt was an ancient, unenlightened despot. Even to later judges, the unreformed Parliament represented an oligarchy of land and money. More than one fourth of the members of the House of Commons were either

baronets or the sons of peers, and more than half had been preceded in the House by relatives in the male line. Although George
III had regained less control over the Commons than the Whigs
said and believed, the House was nevertheless well supplied with
courtiers and placemen.[2]

There was stability also in the official curriculum at Cambridge,
which was primarily mathematical and Newtonian. Through truant
reading, Coleridge could discover in the *Observations on Man*, by
David Hartley, an argument for the construction of a complex
love of God out of the multiple associations of simple ideas, themselves made up of elemental sensations; yet Hartley's associational
psychology was more rigidly materialistic than the Cambridge
textbook on which it was founded, Locke's *Essay on the Human
Understanding*. Within the curriculum, Newtonian physics was
carried into other fields by William Paley. *The Principles of Moral
and Political Philosophy*, 1785, proved—by the test of utility—
the moral and social values of expediency and self-interest. In
A View of the Evidences of Christianity, 1794, Paley carried the
standard of utility further toward his argument in *Natural Theol-
ogy*, 1802, that the world was self-evidently created by God because
it is exquisitely fitted to the body and senses of man.

Jeremy Bentham—unconnected with Cambridge—had made
his first public attack on Tory rigidity and clumsy anachronisms in
a *Fragment on Government*, 1776. Although he had not achieved
anything like the general influence he would have after 1830, most
of the Benthamite shibboleths—the ethic of utility, the avoidance
of pain, the greatest happiness for the greatest number, and *laissez
faire*—were readily available in writers as diverse as Hartley,
Hartley's necessitarian explicator Joseph Priestley, and Adam
Smith, whose *Wealth of Nations* appeared in the same year as the
Fragment on Government. Along with his practical day-to-day
battles, for Parliamentary reform and against corrupt practices
in the courts (especially in trials for libeling the Crown), Bentham
was helping to dissolve such rationalistic concepts as those of
natural law, natural right, and social contract. His analyses penetrated and weakened all theories of rational pattern in history,
whether of linear progress or of progressive cycles.[3] Priestley and
Godwin supported his utilitarianism, but he did not support their

necessitarianism; nor did he endorse "perfectibility," Godwin's term for the capacity of man for infinite improvement.

Probably Coleridge had absorbed more than the normal under-graduate amount from the reforming opinions of William Frend, a Unitarian expelled from his fellowship at Jesus for a technical reason that stemmed from his carrying his political and religious opinions closer to Tom Paine and the French than the other Fellows carried theirs. Coleridge applauded conspicuously during Frend's trial before the Vice-Chancellor's court, in May. Conspicuously—but Frend's method of defense indicates what the atmosphere at Cambridge must have been, at least until Burke's arraignments of the Jacobins had general effect, and probably until the declarations of war in January and February, 1793, precipitated such conflicts as Frend's trial. The defendant asked: "Was it a crime, Sir, to rejoice, when the whole nation was of one mind, and this university thought it a duty to impress the sentiment on our young men, by giving them as a proper subject for their talents, the taking of the bastile?" [4] Coleridge could not have become a Unitarian, as at this stage he did, had intellectual freedom not appealed to him; once identified as an extremist among dissenters, he would feel the discrepancy between the newly granted tolerance in Catholic France and the disabilities that could now be imposed on him in Freedom's isle.

He probably now read Voltaire and Helvétius with some analytic detachment. (CL, 78) In his known verses of 1792, 1793, and the first half of 1794, he expresses a conventional, half-orthodox Christian stoicism that renounces "forensic storms"—poems of some political interest because anti-political. (CPW, 33:11) The coming of war brought to his explicit passivism a temporary cessation, until he could use it for partisan attack. Unfortunately, the stoic way did not spread from his verses to his life. He always understood his birthday to be one day earlier than it actually was, but in any event he reached manhood only technically on 21 October. Shortly afterward he attempted unsuccessfully to lessen the burden of his debts by purchasing a lottery ticket. On 2 December 1793 he enlisted in the King's Light Dragoons, for which he chose a *nom de guerre* to signify his unfitness. Professor Griggs believes that Coleridge's brothers, who worked patiently until they secured his release, never knew how Coleridge's inglorious record was closed in the muster roll: "discharged S. T. Comberbach / Insane / 10 Apl." (CL, 76) Where there is so much blame to be assigned, only a small portion can be laid on Cambridge for making him feel social inferiority as a sizar—the sorry cause, according to Elia, when two other scholars up from Christ's Hospital "exchanged their Alma Mater for the camp." [5] By aberrations he at least gained the attention of several of the foremost liberals at Cambridge. He obviously repaid (and compounded) the attention of the several-sided reformer Gilbert Wakefield, and believed that he taught something to the dissentient Dr. Thomas Edwards, whom he therefore the more readily identified for an Oxford friend as "the great Grecian of Cambridge and heterodox Divine." (CL, 118)

Most of Coleridge's verses for the next several months looked back wistfully to the innocence of his childhood. His Unitarian religion and his republicanism united in the aims and language of sympathy, pity, and universal fraternity. But enlightened sympathy could hardly be confined, and certainly not by the undisciplined Coleridge, to non-political humanitarianism. If his own account can be trusted, he had become known in Cambridge as an energetic republican and did little to refute the local view of him as an unrestrained Jacobin. (A "republican" was a confused, seditious fellow who had no respect for hereditary aristocracy and wished the King off the throne; a "Jacobin" was a leveler who would pull him off.) Pausing from a walking tour at Oxford, in June, Coleridge met an eager young bigot named Robert Southey, whom he joined in planning an ideal settlement of twelve couples, on a communistic principle that Coleridge called Pantisocracy. Of the enthusiasts involved, only Southey stirred Coleridge demonstrably. Before the end of August he and Southey had rushed to completion a drama in verse, *The Fall of Robespierre*, to delight and instruct the public by interpreting what seemed the most important news since the fall of the Bastille.

Excited by boundless dreams for himself and society, Coleridge felt shame over the passionate muddle he had made of his years and a compensating exultation over a decision, now forming, to abandon college and all related obligations to his family and his past. He was momentarily unable to evade the stern morality which young Southey sometimes sophisticated for himself but seldom if ever compromised for others. In torment and nostalgia, Coleridge was losing hope of winning Mary Evans. Southey, engaged to a girl with sisters, saw the best beginning toward the new society in marriage between the sisters and his pantisocratic brothers. It was soon easy to convince the affectionate and voluble Coleridge, even easy to remind him, that he had unmistakably proposed to Sara Fricker. Whatever he had said to Sara, we can be sure that Coleridge had not, on this or any other occasion, spoken or acted unmistakably. It was not easy to convince him that he should marry a girl he only occasionally thought he loved, but in December, 1794, he wrote: "Mark you, Southey!—*I will do my Duty.*" (CL, 145) While he saw Southey as inclined to reduce and postpone Pantisocracy in submission to his relatives, who exerted the pressures of execration richly mixed with bribery, Coleridge saw himself as having given up great wealth of all kinds for a cause betrayed. Disordered by intellectual, social, and sexual passion, he was probably guiltier than Southey. (CN, 1605)

In the same months Coleridge began his half-forced engagement and unhappy, broken, but fruitful marriage with political journalism. During 1794 he drew close to Benjamin Flower, a friend of Frend and of the libertarian Baptist, Robert Hall, and the editor and chief owner of the *Cambridge Intelligencer,* one of the few provincial newspapers "virulent" against Pitt and the war. Early in June the *Intelligencer* first carried Coleridge's advertisement for a projected major work, imitations from modern Latin poets, which was to be further advertised—and, like succeeding projects, further promised—in vain. Coleridge seems to have known, when he took *The Fall of Robespierre* in September as a publishing venture for Opposition booksellers in London, that Flower would publish it immediately, as he did, when Coleridge returned with the manuscript to Cambridge. Ten days after his return, and just before the appearance of *Robespierre* in public, the *Intelligencer* contained the first explicitly political verse published by Coleridge. Written in July at an inn once the home of John Kyrle, the famous "Man of Ross," the poem praised Kyrle as "Nobler than Kings, or king-polluted Lords." (CPW, 57:2) Alexander Pope too, in his *Moral Essays,* had praised the humility and rural simplicity of Kyrle's charitable life. Pope had cried, "Blush, Grandeur, blush! proud Courts, withdraw your blaze!" But young Coleridge's phrases concerning royal pollution rashly exceed not only Pope's urbane bow toward rustic life but also any primitivism acceptable among gentlemen in the age of Rousseau. During the weeks before returning to London for concentrated journalism, Coleridge fobbed off on Flower three juvenile poems written or rewritten the previous year; at least two of them, as Professors Griggs and Mayo have separately discovered, had appeared elsewhere during 1793. Making arrangements to write for the *Morning Chronicle*, Coleridge meanwhile "promised" Flower poems by Southey. (CL, 116)

Flower's conservative Unitarianism pleased his young contributor. Later, closing the last number of the *Watchman*, Coleridge recommended that his readers take up the *Intelligencer*, which would continue "fighting fearlessly the good fight against Tyranny, yet never unfaithful to that Religion, 'whose service is perfect Freedom.'" (W, 324) And Flower, kind to his undergraduate contributor, may have known anyway that the contributions had been slightly used. He later reprinted *Parliamentary Oscillators* a week after it appeared in the *Morning Post;* in the autumn of 1800 the *Intelligencer* reprinted at least four poems by Coleridge and Wordsworth. Besides begetting the authoress of *Nearer, My God, to Thee* and spending six months in Newgate prison in the cause of free speech, Flower performed a greater act for poetry by commissioning for the *Intelligencer* in 1796 Coleridge's *Ode on the Departing Year.* Just before sending the ode, Coleridge offered also his scolding lines on the causeless melancholy of Charles Lloyd, in order to round out his contributions to the *Intelligencer* with a concluding disrespect for "the thron'd Murderers of Mankind." (CPW, 158:15; CL, 268) Seldom one to meet commitments, Coleridge was at this time continually conceiving a never-born answer to Godwin; we may wonder if Flower did not receive the two angry and implacable poems of 1796, one in rare fulfillment of commission, for the ironic reason that Coleridge sympathized intensely with Flower in the loss of a child by death.[6]

Of the poems that S. T. C. of Jesus College had entrusted to the *Morning Chronicle* in 1793 (one of them, according to Daniel Stuart, for the high fee of one guinea), not even the prayerful couplets *To Fortune: On Buying a Ticket in the Irish Lottery* had been overtly political. (CPW, 55) Between the appearance of these verses and the next known to be Coleridge's, the editor of the *Chronicle,* James Perry, narrowly escaped conviction for expressing seditious opinions. (Unrepentant, he was not forever to escape the desperation of the Government and the watchfulness of the *Anti-Jacobin.*) One week before further non-political verses by Coleridge appeared anonymously, and just as their confused author was rushing back to Cambridge, the editor announced in the *Chronicle* of 15 September 1794: "We intreat our valued Correspondent, S. T. C. to inform us how we may address a note to him." On 1 December began one of Coleridge's best-known contributions to a newspaper, the series of sonnets on eminent contemporaries. On 17 December he wrote to Southey: "I dined yesterday with Perry, and Grey (the proprietors & Editors of the Morning Chronicle) at their House—and met Holcroft . . . ." (CL, 138) He smoked and drank with Charles Lamb. Most of his sonnets praised "friends of Freedom"; those on Freedom's enemies justified the opening of the stanzas *To S. T. C.* which appeared in the paper on 27 December:

> How the warm soul with indignation glows;—
>   How VIRTUE mingles horror with delight,
> When thy nerv'd Lines seize on thy Country's Foes,
>   And drag the lurking Felons into light!

The stanzas, signed "NOT TO BE MISTAKEN," probably came from Bristol, whence Southey was soon to come in order to reclaim the stray for Sara and for diminished, Welsh Pantisocracy. The stanzas closed with an urgent appeal:

> Then haste thee quickly from thy dark retreat—
> And once again congenial fervour meet!

Coleridge was not yet eager to approach Sara; he was never to return to his patient college. Probably he completed no more sonnets for the present sequence after 17 December. On Christmas Eve he accepted submissively the final rejection from Mary Evans, and may have begun quietly that day the politically unquiet *Religious Musings.* Five days later he admitted surrender: "I am calm, dear Southey! as an Autumnal Day . . . ." He asked as if casually: "I am not, I presume, to attribute some verses addressed to S. T. C. in the M. Chronicle to you—. To whom?—" (CL,

140–46) Out of an adolescent need for funds and bafflement by political and personal alternatives, he had plunged with passionate exhilaration in and out of political journalism.

During the first half of 1795 he delivered two or three series of "Addresses to the People" in Bristol, eloquent messages in which he opposed the slave trade and more immediate Ministerial deviations from hallowed principles of justice and freedom. Although concerned with current policies of the war against the French revolutionists, the known lectures, as represented by amalgamation in the published *Conciones ad Populum,* contain much more on the sources and uses of knowledge and on freedom of thought, speech, and press than the *Watchman* of the next spring. They contain, I think, Coleridge's clearest prose. They give—what the poems give seldom and doubtfully, with imaginative transformation—dated markers in the stream where disillusionment with France brought eddying change to his political principles. They show Coleridge determined to possess reasoned (and even illusioned) faith rather than disillusion. Between March and November, 1795, he dropped from the first of the "addresses to the people" a mitigation of the crash heard in France by Freedom herself— "yet shall she not have heard it unbenefited, if haply the Horrors of that Day shall have made other nations timely wise—if a great people shall from hence become adequately illuminated for a Revolution bloodless, like Poland's." He substituted a passage of three pages explaining how Brissot, Robespierre, and the Terror illustrate the necessity of guarding against the pollution of public opinion by demagoguery.[7] In 1820 Coleridge wrote in a copy presented to the John Morgans, now at Harvard, that except for two or three necessitarian and Unitarian passages and "some flame-colored Epithets," he had little to retract or regret. Earlier, unfortunately, when he reprinted the "Introductory Address" in the *Friend* as evidence of his political constancy, he regretted—or in any event retracted—more than epithets and phrases. The very copy given to the Morgans was marked for the purpose, to get rid of several rather long passages whose epithets fitted their essence, for example a passage on "those despicable adherents to fraud and tyranny, who ironically style themselves Constitutionalists." (p. 15)

Near the last week of November, against Pitt's two bills then passing into oppressive law concerning "Seditious Meetings" and

"Treasonable Practices" (of writing and publishing), Coleridge wrote for delivery two lectures, immediately consolidated and published as *The Plot Discovered*. Despite heady rhetoric, they are hardly more republican than Bolingbroke, whom they frequently quoted (at second hand, through Burgh, but with concurrence). A fragmentary manuscript in the Houghton Library at Harvard shows Coleridge exercising prudence in revision: Principles of Liberty, which were first "being attacked" by Pitt, were on second thought "being endangered." (MS. Eng 947.7) An appeal to Algernon Sydney (itself a change in the manuscript) became in print an appeal to Lord Somers. The published work opens ironically with a sentiment from Bishop Horsley, that the mass of the people have nothing to do with the laws but obey them, and closes with an ironic petition from the people of Denmark for relief from liberty. (EOT, 56–98) But Coleridge entertained his original audience, or planned to, with two still more amusing, imaginative, and bitter sallies. The holograph ends with an address to the "Illustrious Beggars of the Cornish Boroughs," whom it calls on, barbarous, poor, and miserably dependent though they are, to show fortitude, heroism, intelligence, and learning at the ensuing election. The earlier sally begins: "Supposing an honest man to sit in the house of Commons—This would be his Language— Since I have the honor, I should say, the dishonor of sitting in this house, I have been witness to many strange many infamous transactions—"

Except to avoid conviction for "encompassing the life of the king" or other seditious utterance, Coleridge was willing to be known as a republican. If there could have been doubt, he had found by going among democrats that he was no democrat. He wished to abolish private property, but he would retain distinctions of intellect and decency. Communism should begin at home —among a remote Pantisocratic set of enlightened families. In protest against the Hair Powder Tax, which Cottle tells us he lectured against, he wore his uncombed hair unpowdered. As a lecturer, according to a Bristol pamphlet, he was slovenly; friends would have him wear cleaner stockings, and comb his hair.[8] But he thought he did not, like Welsh democrats, stink.

Through 1795, until their severance in November, Coleridge quarreled with Southey over whether his *"Tug* of Brain" gave more to their collaborations than the other's industry of hand, and over the extent to which Southey was accountable to the moral vision of Pantisocracy. (CL, 172) Coleridge had found some personal peace in the certitude of his own loyalty to their dream. Amid sloughs of melancholy, shame, and anxiety, he held more ebulliently than ever, with a religious glow, the necessitarian optimism that had been crude in Hartley and dry in Priestley. He interpreted one expression of "the pious confidence of Optimism" more carefully to the would-be-selfish Southey: "However wickedly you might act, God would make it ULTIMATELY the best." (CL, 168) He first feared and then despised republican spokesmen because of their narrow atheism. He hoped to answer Godwin with a republicanism grounded in personal affection and faith in an all-benevolent God. Increasingly, even more excitedly in his letters than in *Religious Musings*, his anti-materialist, optimistic Unitarianism grew rampantly evangelistic. Already it was inevitable that Coleridge's "inspired Philanthropist" of Galilee, in the *Watchman* essay *On the Slave Trade*, would become the "redeeming Theanthropist" of his marginal correction in the Ashley copy. (W, 108; B.M. Ashley 2842)

On 4 October Samuel married Sara, moved temporarily into rustic retirement, and caught the first calm joy of double husbandry in blank verse finer than any Wordsworth had then written. He won successive heights: tranquil with his bride, tilling the soil, he was spiritually founding Pantisocracy; removed in February nearer to the Bristol library, he stood amid the battle, to proclaim, as he put it in the first prospectus of the *Watchman*, "the State of the Political Atmosphere, and preserve Freedom and her Friends from the attacks of Robbers and Assassins!!" (B.M. Ashley 406) With a distaste for the frequent subsidies to genius received from several friends, disliking journalistic "detention" in London, afraid that tutoring or holding school or a Unitarian pulpit would choke his yearning for fame as a great poet, he had projected a political and literary magazine. The *Watchman*, which began tardily on 1 March 1796, was foredoomed to close no later than 13 May. It was not literary. Coleridge mismanaged every commercial and editorial department by himself. His arguments against Pitt's fiscal policy can be found in other Opposition periodicals; they have some value in supplementing the political themes of his verse, since credit did not seem as poetical a subject to Coleridge as it did to a later poet named Pound. The speeches he quoted at length, staler than when they had appeared in the daily papers, came usually from *The Senator; Or, Clarendon's Parliamentary Chronicle.* We are asked to believe that George Burnett had abridged them in so slovenly a way that Coleridge redid them. (CL, 189) He ransacked many other sources for scraps to imitate, adapt, or plagiarize. The initial calm of his marriage had been dissipated in the search for subscribers. The scramble for copy banished joy, creativity, and honesty. By early 1796 national and international politics, as related to right theory, had secured a place next below the throne of religion in Coleridge's mind. He had dedicated himself in verse to "the bloodless fight Of Science, Freedom, and the Truth in Christ." (CPW, 108:61–62) After the failure of the *Watchman,* and partly as a result of its perversity, the fight was not to be pure again for many years. Coleridge had risen like a phoenix, "slightly damaged," from earlier acts of impetuous folly; the *Watchman* debauched him. Admittedly the truth could not be had simply; throughout the *Watchman,* exculpations of the French alternate with perturbations over their present and future course. The "Remonstrance to the French Legislators," in the eighth number, begins: "GUARDIANS of the LIBERTY of EUROPE!" (W, 229)

The unexpected illness of Sara during the months before the birth of their first child, Hartley, kept Coleridge in pained awe. He had endured, with some help from opium, his own racking illnesses. Frequent sickness in a growing family multiplied his agonies for several years. On the day the *Watchman* died, he began a series of inquiries concerning a situation as tutor; a few days later the Royal Literary Fund voted him ten guineas; he accepted funds and occupational advice from hopeful friends, whom he played off group against group for optimum security with maximum freedom. One tutorial plan attempted, the taking into his cottage of the treacherously neurotic Charles Lloyd, was to result in a bitter if temporary division from Lamb and other friends. When the sub-editor of the *Morning Chronicle* died, Coleridge accepted "in general terms" an offer of the post from Perry, but somehow this like other commitments collapsed. (CL, 219–40, esp. 233, 236) Uneasy about political journalism, with its distortions, concealments, and lampoons, if not quite as shy as he claimed, he wrote to his Unitarian friend Estlin in July: "... local and temporary Politics are my aversion—they narrow the understanding, they narrow the heart, they fret the temper." To Thomas Poole he wrote almost the same words. (CL, 222, 227) In October he declared "politicians and politics," inescapable in cities, "a set of men and a kind of study which I deem highly unfavourable to all Christian graces." (CL, 240) Succeeding letters reiterate the theme. Praise for politics during the same months is meant only for metapolitical theorizing, not for action or current events.

Against London and all full-time, narrow tasks he must cry: "If I go, farewell Philosophy! Farewell, the Muse! Farewell, my literary Fame!—" (CL, 227) He assured Charles Lloyd senior in November: "I might have a situation as a Unitarian minister, I might have lucrative offices as an active Politician . . . ." But why confine and prostitute his powers? Although not at the hub in London, from his place of retirement near Bristol he could give instruction through the daily press. "Shall I not be an Agriculturist, an Husband, a Father, and a *Priest* after the order of *Peace?* an *hireless* Priest?" (CL, 255) As Coleridge took pleasure in putting it, applying to himself the denunciation of Priestley in Gibbon's autobiography, he had laid aside his squeaking baby-trumpet of sedition. On 13 December he went further: "My poetic Vanity & my political Furore have been exhaled; and I would rather be an expert, self-maintaining Gardener than a Milton, if I could not unite both." Four days later, to the democratic lecturer John Thelwall, he revealed his hope to unite both: "I am not *fit* for *public* Life; yet the Light shall stream to a far distance from the taper in my cottage window." (CL, 275, 277) In journalistic fact, he was earning an occasional guinea toward his family's bread and cheese by reviewing novels and miscellaneous works for George Gregory's *Critical Review.*

Only one sentence in the Preface to his *Poems on Various Subjects,* 1796, referred to politics: "Some of the verses allude to an intended emigration to America on the scheme of an abandonment of individual property." (CPW, 1137) He was silent on the political views expressed in some of the poems, not because they were occasionally "local and temporary," but because their unconventionality might reduce his poetic fame among the unawak-

ened. Except for *Religious Musings*, which was irreparably
prophetic, he hoped to make the second edition, of 1797, still less
republican and less political, but even in this hamper of "my
choicest fish, pick'd, gutted, and clean'd," other political prophecies
remained. (CL, 312) He had intended to give first place in the
volume to a prophetic poem tentatively titled "The Progress of
Liberty, or the Visions of the Maid of Orleans." With this poem
unfinished, he substituted instead the politically inflamed *Ode on
the Departing Year*, and author or printer failed to snuff its political flames by calling it, in the table of contents, "Ode to the New
Year." But the poems no longer openly called all monarchs scoun-
drels, and the sonnets in praise and blame of current notables
were excluded.

Coleridge's *annus mirabilis*, 1797–98, has been always so called
because no fitter name has been found for it: William and Dorothy
Wordsworth's removal to Somerset evoked the best of Wordsworth
and the superlative Coleridge of *The Ancient Mariner*, the first
of the two completed parts of *Christabel*, his most sinewy blank
verse, the non-Wordsworthian *France: An Ode*, and probably (although several recent scholars have followed Elisabeth Schneider
in arguing for a later date) *Kubla Khan*. Coleridge's tragedy,
Osorio, later to be revised and performed as *Remorse*, carried its
humanitarian and libertarian conflicts to a more Elizabethan
altitude than Wordsworth's *The Borderers*, which examined more
intimately the political dilemma on which both poets were caught.
Coleridge thought Wordsworth the greatest man alive, and himself possibly second. Wordsworth in effect concurred. From their
letters I conclude that Wordsworth gave Coleridge a living image
of greatness, so great that he could not admit emulating it. The
sense of his own power was nourished less by Wordsworth than
by Thomas Poole, for whom Coleridge probably felt more personal
affection than for any other man, and by other provincial friends
who offered more love than genius. Unfortunately he felt a direct
responsibility to repay with Miltonic performance the trust that
friends made concrete by patronage in cash. Always, the more
grandiosely Coleridge aspired, the more frantic and ineffective
he became. His frequent apology a few years later, that comparison
of himself with Wordsworth taught him he was no poet, and
helped dry his fount, does not excuse all, but it should be taken

seriously. Meanwhile, he had choices to make. The name Berkeley, given in May, 1798, to the second son, may be taken as the most prominent signpost on the crooked road from necessitarianism to Neoplatonism. Reluctant to choose among the proffered vocations of journalism, Unitarian ministry, and tutoring, the poet was saved in January, 1798, from complete bondage to Daniel Stuart's *Morning Post,* and other fates worse than transportation, by an annuity of £150 from Josiah and Thomas Wedgwood.

The first-fruits of the arrangement made in November through Stuart's brother-in-law, James Mackintosh, had been the first of the weekly guineas in Coleridge's hungry pocket and some pitying lines on a fallen woman in the *Post* for 7 December 1797. The poem, admired at least by Coleridge, had gone homeless since March. (CL, 312–14, 359–60; CPW, 171) Thereafter, occasionally drawn toward London to be near the political dogfighting, Coleridge wrote in 1798, 1799, on through 1803 when Stuart relinquished major control, the best editorials and political lead-articles in the *Post,* and published his liveliest political verse there. Usually on a weekly salary, he whittled indifferent paragraphs, translated and adapted epigrams and squibs, rewrote some of Wordsworth's juvenile poems, and variously suffered to meet the requirements of small type. In 1800, he tried Parliamentary reporting, and once thereby notoriously improved the language of Pitt. The struggle to extract copy from him was more successful than Stuart later remembered. In after years, hurt into rebuttal by Coleridge's extravagant claims, Stuart denied that Coleridge had either proved irreplaceable or determined the political policies of the paper. He nonetheless granted that Coleridge had raised both the literary quality and the circulation.

For the *Morning Post,* or at least with the paper as one eductive force, Coleridge wrote *France: An Ode; Ode to the Duchess of Devonshire; The Devil's Thoughts* (with Southey); *Fire, Famine, and Slaughter; Parliamentary Oscillators; Recantation: Illustrated in the Story of the Mad Ox; A Christmas Carol; Talleyrand to Lord Grenville;* and other political poems and light sallies. Among previously unrecorded contributions recently pointed out by David V. Erdman, Coleridge provided 148 lines of "The Visions of the Maid of Orleans" the day after Christmas, 1797. Repeated emotional turmoil, to which political dilemmas and journalism contributed, helped give imaginative unity, and greatness, to some of his newspaper poems. The poems, in turn, have objective uses. They, and Coleridge's footnotes clarifying their mysteries, show the souring effect on him of the Directory's rupture of negotiations for peace and the appointment of Bonaparte to lead an army into England in the autumn of 1797. Purges, demagoguery, and apparent yearnings toward imperial expansion, with the blind and blasphemous Feasts of Reason, had troubled his original view of France as the embodiment of man's hope; the invasion of Switzerland by Bonaparte early in 1798 ended uncertainty, or at least laid down a line concerning France that the vacillating writer never quite recrossed. Beginning with *France: An Ode* (first titled "Recantation"), the poems trace the march of Bonaparte and Sieyès into Coleridge's jungle of black beasts, where Pitt, Dundas, and Grenville still prowled. As all the brains had previously seemed to be on the revolutionary and oppositionist side, the satiric skill of writers for the new *Anti-Jacobin* jolted Coleridge toward retrenchment and ambiguity early in 1798. Its prospectus had promised to expose falsehoods in four named papers, but actually the *Anti-Jacobin* had been reprinting "Lies" and "Misrepresentations" almost altogether from the *Morning Chronicle* and *Morning Post*. Southey had been a favorite butt. On 7 April the *Post* examined in return "Ministerial Candour" as practiced by Anti-Jacobins. Then, just when Coleridge and the *Post* exercised greater caution, the *Anti-Jacobin* satirists, and specifically the caricaturist Gillray, depicted him so graphically as the ass-eared among Jacobins that further caution would have been tardy and therefore useless. He now oscillated more erratically than ever.

Wordsworth had already rejected the Revolution, never to praise again that blissful dawn. He may not have talked much with Coleridge of his disillusioning experiences in 1792 near the center of the Revolution. But he had affirmations to make. Although he did not quite convince Coleridge that the truest human dignity lay in the lower and rural orders, Wordsworth certainly taught, more clearly than Coleridge had previously learned, that Nature held healing balm for imaginations impaired by too much agonizing thought on political affairs. We think customarily of Wordsworth and Coleridge as republicans turning Tory together, perhaps suddenly out of moral shock, as *The Prelude* has it, or, in Browning's phrase, just for a handful of silver; or perhaps gradually and steadily from experience and reflection. But the change gradually apparent grew only partly from fearful observation of events in France and patriotic forgiveness of England for declaring war against freedom; even more the change grew out of the intellectual and spiritual crisis of Romantic beliefs that found no correlative among the Jacobinical generalizations concerning abstract rights based on equality of reason among men. It was partly the search for a way out of passive materialism that made Coleridge move politically like a crab.

Studious months in Germany, from September, 1798, to July, 1799, produced their political effect mainly through homesickness; they made Coleridge, as a shorter visit made Wordsworth, happier in his own country and inclined to separate the loveliness of its land and the goodness of its people more sharply from the abomination of Pitt's ministry. His rejection of France's actions in 1798 did not yet imply full approval of Britain's. A kind of fulcrum came in 1799 with his homesick patriotism in Germany, but he did not amplify in poems, as he did in prose, the acceptance of the war implied in *The British Stripling's War-Song*, imitated from Stolberg for journalistic use. (CPW, 317; also SPJ for 1799, p. 251) Return to England revived his partisanship, now strengthened by an accusation in *The Beauties of the Anti-Jacobin* that he had abandoned his family Jacobin-style. Jesting passages in his letters on Napoleon and on French victories in the autumn of 1799 would be called ambivalent by any psychologist who uses the word; containing more than their share of the confusion of their time, they reflect unmistakably only his continued contempt for Britain's Continental allies. He asked Wordsworth to write a great poem in blank verse that would jar disillusioned reformers out of the "almost epicurean selfishness" of domestic retirement. (CL, 527)

He arose with the dawn of 1800 in "a grand passion of political journalism." [9] With the dawn of 1801 he arose to a study of metaphysics that quickened his discovery of the immense inferiority of Locke to the German Transcendentalists, and thus provided a new philosophical grounding for his rapidly increased conservatism. "Grounding" must be taken in a limited sense. Coleridge used his brilliant mind far more rarely as a thinker than as a collecting magpie and an enthusiast. His best ideas and keenest discriminations became marginalia in borrowed books.

When Pitt resigned in 1801 because he had promised Irish Catholics what George III would go insane rather than grant, the *Morning Post* remained loyal at first to the "Old Opposition" as men of principle having no common ground with Addington's insipid new ministry. Coleridge, with an access of knotty, nauseous rheumatic pain, then with revulsion from an experiment "too often repeated," relief in laudanum; with an intensification also of pity for the working poor, worn to dull misery in the shortage of wheat and the oppression of Property (which, he felt, "stupifies the heads & hardens the hearts of our Counsellors & Chief Men"); with no hero or good man to lead distressed England—Coleridge yearned again for a quiet farm near Priestley, or even for a season's lodging in the Azores. (CL, 721, 731) As late as 22 March 1802, in an editorial recently identified, Coleridge belittled whatever in Addington might seem personally capable or publicly decent.[10]

A shaky peace came just when he began to think the war should be pressed, "the very first period, at which a war had become indisputably just and necessary," because nobody could longer doubt "the atrocious ambition of the First Consul." (EOT, 564, 566) In the columns of the *Morning Post*, when Fox honored Bonaparte with words and attendance in 1802, Coleridge urged English patriots of independent views to join solidly for reopening the war. That Fox conveyed to Parliament Bonaparte's regret at the hostility of the British press, which thwarted his peaceful intentions, Coleridge interpreted as deliberate intimidation of the press; by vainglorious distortion, he took it as a personal attack on S. T. C.[11] Here, if anywhere, is the great turn in the orientation of Coleridge's political thought, the last hurried recovery from political disappointments, the final emancipation from Locke and Priestley as well as from Fox and Bonaparte, the relief of deciding that he would never again involve his hopes in promises made by revolutionaries, liberals, or Whigs.

The main personal event of the period 1799–1802, Coleridge's sudden discovery of his love for Sara Hutchinson (he at once stripped the *h* from this second Sarah as he had from the first), gave storm-birth in 1802 to *Dejection: An Ode* and to several lesser poems, but has no direct significance for the politics in his poetry. Indeed, few bubbles remained in his poetic fount. No event after 1802, not even his turn as "diplomatic under-strapper" to the Governor of Malta in 1804–5—nor his return through Italy, of which his own version amounts to something like a theory that Napoleon persecuted him for the same journalistic insults that had earlier driven the emperor to end the Peace of Amiens—no further event has prime importance for a study of politics in poetry by Coleridge read today. He is hereafter the talker, argumentative reader, lecturer, critic, essayist and journalist, writer on current events and pontificator on society, for a time a playwright; humanitarian, laudanum-addict, theologian, sage, father (from a respectful distance), and friend; occasionally a versifier; a poet by nostalgia, seldom by practice; a liar, but a great man, intrepidly struggling for self-awareness to his very end at the age of sixty-three.

From 1804 off and on until 1817 he wrote for the *Courier,* of which Stuart was occasionally the owner, but of verse only driblets appeared there. Arthur Aspinall, the chief authority on the press of the time, concludes that Stuart did not know the *Courier* to be in the pay of the Treasury through Thomas George Street, who was frequently its conductor and co-proprietor; but Coleridge, although now a Tory himself, felt the guiding hand of the Government too heavily upon it.[12] He could not commit himself enthusiastically to the reopened war after all. As he began to say, thinking specifically of Napoleon as "a Caesar" but sensing it in all human history, political contests "begin in *principles,* and end in *men.*" (EOT, 483) It was a melancholy discovery for one who divided much of his time between the too human practices of flattery and backbiting. Fortunately he was roused to nobler thought and more philosophic or prophetic utterance by each of the grosser public acts of Napoleon. From intensive reading in history he absorbed little historical relativism but an overwhelming respect for tradition. While metaphysical burrowings strengthened his antagonism toward everything utilitarian, historical studies increased his reliance upon arguments of expediency, through appeals to what had worked in the self-conserving past. To escape expediency, he wriggled toward a transcendental organicism, to be explained as creative Idea realizing itself temporally by the interworking of nature and man's imagination, with human history as a major result. Meanwhile, there was Napoleon. Perhaps, after all, a nation had a right, a duty, of expedient self-preservation. First with the intimidated royal family of Spain against Portugal and then, in the name of Napoleon's brother Joseph, against the surprisingly independent and nationalistic Spanish *juntas*, French militarism in the Peninsula refocused the libertarian fervor of Coleridge, as of Wordsworth, from the individual to the nation.

The *Friend*, laboriously produced for twenty-seven numbers from June, 1809, to March, 1810, gave Coleridge the opportunity to record his accumulated views on the responsibilities of man in society. With the successful run of his tragedy, rebuilt as *Remorse*, for twenty nights at Drury Lane in 1813, and with further charitable encouragement from Byron, he kept hoping until 1817 to supplement the income from lectures and journalism by a more poetic activity as playwright, but obstacles—especially opium—intervened. Despite his incubus, from just before April, 1816, when he put himself under the care of James Gillman at Highgate, through March, 1819, when he completed his final series of lectures, he accomplished an immense amount of writing and publishing, which included what is possibly the most confused and probably the most influential work of all English criticism, the *Biographia Literaria*, along with the play *Zapolya*, the Lay Sermons, the *Treatise on Method*, a third edition of *The Friend*, in three volumes, and two pamphlets supporting Peel's bill to reduce the strain on children in the cotton mills (children aged six to sixteen) to less than the customary thirteen to fifteen working hours a day.

From the time of Waterloo, Coleridge had been awake to the distresses, dissensions, and discontents of the post-war Age of Bronze, as Byron called it, where landlords voted their "cent per cent" for the "grand agrarian alchymy, high *rent*." (BP, V, 570:581) Like Byron, Coleridge actively fought the Corn Law of 1815, although the philosophy of his conservatism required his championship of the landed gentry, if he pretended to any consistency at all, against the commercial classes. In *A Lay Sermon Addressed to the Higher and Middle Classes*, 1817, he objected to the utilitarian Poor Laws, the subjection of working children to "ill-fed, ill-clothed, and unfuelled winters," and in general to the capitalistic economy of boom and bust. (LS, 92–97, 101–10, 124) It has been noted that he was "generally representative of the Tory humanitarian school," especially active in the years after Waterloo.[13] Like others in the school, he thought the ancient social fabric well worth repair. Like such others as Cobbett, Wilberforce, Peel, Carlyle, and Disraeli, he resisted Utilitarian reforms. But his economic heresies, like his suggestion (not a proposal) for a graduated income tax, set him as usual apart from the rest.

His dislike for the Radical journalists whom the Liverpool Cabinet repeatedly tried to silence by imprisonment, William Cobbett, William Hone, Richard Carlile, and Leigh Hunt, he explained on two counts: they harangued the people instead of persuading the people's governors, and their excesses would necessarily "end in the suspension of Freedom of all kind." (CL, IV, 714) As an additional irritant, Hone and Carlile were professional blasphemers. Like the Church and the Government, Coleridge regarded the deism of Thomas Paine, which they advocated, an invitation to atheism.

His verse reflects new concern with distresses in a few original items but especially in minor additions to republished poems. In prose he insists very loudly that, unlike Cobbett, he writes critically of King and State solely for the learned. Similarly, for his early work, he employs Southey's defense of the resuscitated *Wat Tyler:* "It was written when republicanism was confined to a very small number of the educated classes . . . ." [14]

He employed contradictory defenses also, of course. He tried not looking back. He had never loved "Goose and Goody" surrounding and succeeding Pitt; Spencer Perceval, assassinated in 1812, seemed to Coleridge in his forties the only honorable statesman of the century, for the Foxites appeared in the new light even more contemptible than the crew of Pitt: by inflammatory appeals to the ignorant poor they had forced the Tories into acts against Liberty. Under Liverpool's administration, there were new deplorable acts designed to suppress new despicable demagogues—including one old Tory, Cobbett, turned Radical agitator. Once flaming with hope for mankind, Coleridge now spoke of the Radicals' malignant flattery of "the envy and cupidity, the vindictive restlessness and self-conceit of the half-witted vulgar." (BL, I, 144) Although he urged that landowners—who after all held their

estates in trust from God and society—educate as well as instruct
their "natural clients and dependents," to improve tomorrow, he
now distinguished man from other beasts by man's "Lying, Treachery, Ingratitude, Massacre, Thirst of Blood," and sensualities beyond the bestial. (LS, 66n, 134) From the scarcity of later verse
of any kind, this insistence on human depravity does not appear
clearly among his collected poems except in *Cholera Cured Beforehand,* written when the Reform Bill had made every Englishman
take one passionate stand or the other. Coleridge's moral complacency in these years, with some hauteur of class, is clear enough
in *The Delinquent Travellers,* 1824, to show how we are to interpret the lighthearted identification of himself as flower-thief
with poachers oppressed by the Game Laws in *The Reproof and
the Reply.* (CPW, 443:57)

Given a standpoint inevitably religious, the later Coleridge was
not required to see in the Church of England the "best and only
sure bulwark" of toleration, or a national "counter-charm to the
sorcery of wealth," or other virtuous political roles he attributed
to her. (BL, I, 131; LS, 92) Yet his allegiance to the Church, without initiating his movement from Whig to Tory as it had Swift's,
greatly fortified his Toryism. His marginal notes to Richard Hooker,
Of the Lawes of Ecclesiastical Politie, 1682, show very little
concern with Hooker's political theories, but he bristles at thought
of the annulment of diocesan Convocation, which, he says, "I
have long regarded as one of 3 or 4 Whig-patriotisms, that have
succeeded in de-anglicizing the mind of England." (B.M. Ashley
5175, p. 91) The orientation of his later thought is theocratic.

Gentleness and pity distinguished Coleridge among political
writers from his earliest effusions to his final prose. Piety entered
his work not later than 1795. These personal characteristics af-
fected his response to two broad changes occurring around him:
first, the literary transition from Romantic concern with political
principles to Victorian concern with social conditions, and sec-
ondly, the expansion of sexual modesty and linguistic prudery from
the middle classes upward and downward through the whole
society. This combination produced in Coleridge's poems of the
nineteenth century a rather mawkish chivalry, by which tyrants
were depicted and judged in accordance with their attitude toward maids and matrons. Indignation over tyrannic caddishness

first appears in the second part of *Christabel,* written in 1800. Incensed when he hears how five warriors "ruthlessly seized" the literally bewitching Geraldine, to him a maid forlorn, Sir Leoline swears to proclaim far and wide that the "recreant traitors" and "reptile souls" were "base as spotted infamy." (CPW, 229:437–45) Sir Leoline pointed the direction his author would take. In *Zapolya,* 1817, when Sarolta learns that among her servants are lewd followers of the tyrant Emerick, she dismisses them:

> Those rioters are no longer of my household!
> If we but shake a dewdrop from a rose
> In vain would we replace it, and as vainly
> Restore the tear of wounded modesty
> To a maiden's eye familiarized to licence.—
> (CPW, 905:149–53; cf. 904:113–23)

Already in the Epilogue to *Remorse* Coleridge had spoken through "Miss Smith in the character of Teresa" to denounce novels that excused their viciousness by a claim to be "founded on facts," which, "decently immoral, have the art To spare the blush, and undersap the heart!" (CPW, 818:29–31) Ridicule should be suspended until one has noticed such concrete applications of Coleridge's chivalry as his editorial denunciation of the outrage to conscience occasioned by the public whipping of female convicts. (EOT, 762) Such writings link the chivalry of his plays to humane legislation.

Besides defending maidenhood, the gentle sage of Highgate, 1817–34, who influenced the opposite religious movements of Oxford and Broad Church, was the author, according to a reviewer of 1865, of "most of that by which Coleridge is now known to men, and by which, if at all, he has benefited his kind." (*North British Review,* XLIII, 281) But the sage who ceased to write plays and poems belongs to other studies.

CHAPTER III

The Language
of Politics

> For who in the Devil's name ever
> thought of reading Poetry for any po-
> litical or practical purposes till these
> Devil's Times that *we* live in?
> —Coleridge to Street, 1817

Despite the prejudice and passion of his outbursts, politics may be described as an intellectual rather than an imaginative interest of Coleridge the poet. Politics did not permeate his poetry like sea-water; it agitated the body of his verse with severe but local storms. What has been transcribed from a manuscript as "Fragment of an Ode on Napoleon" is probably not Coleridge's at all. (CPW, 1003) It should be noted—seriously—that Coleridge did not conceive his strictly political poems too magnificently to complete them. They did not, like *Christabel, Kubla Khan,* and various polymathic projects in prose, thwart him. Political passion was one major impulse through all his life and work, but when Dr. Erdman reasons that Coleridge was "objectifying the dereliction and dismay of the times in an imaginatively controlled nightmare *The Ancient Mariner,*" he goes beyond what we can demonstrate to the skeptical. (*Blake,* p. 268) If poems by Coleridge that can be classed as political vary greatly among themselves, most of them can be isolated with relative ease from his non-political poems. His metrical experiments, containing the "nonsense" of "free" association, often suggest political and social preoccupations, but the body of his poetry lacks the political and sociological homogeneity that admirers of Milton and Wordsworth call uniformity and some other readers call monotony.

Examination of figurative language throughout Coleridge's poems suggests at least that his deepest being was not absorbed in politics. He sought, nevertheless, with great earnestness, figures that would ornament the poetic dress of political effusions. When he found such a figure, he stored it. The magpie contents of a notebook largely of 1795–98, usually called the Gutch Memorandum Book, led J. L. Lowes onto *The Road to Xanadu*, but its general character is much more political than exotic. Some of the metaphors preserved there went into Coleridge's political prose, some into his political verse: "Equality—Pity & Envy her handmaids"; "Outmalic'd Calumny's imposthum'd Tongue"; "O the supererogative virtues of our minister"; "Mars rising over a gibbet"; "Leader of a Kingdom of Angels"; "Foul stream—House of Commons' Consciences." [1] Metaphors that might otherwise be taken as commonplaces of vaguest connotation gained a place among these jottings only because Coleridge noted their origin in political activity: "Tame the Rebellion of tumultuous thought" (taken, with others, from a favorite divine, Jeremy Taylor); "Slaughter—stern Nurse of Vultures"; "The guilty pomp consuming while it flares"; and, having concrete embodiment in Georgian times, a "belly of most majestic periphery!" [2]

Several lines that he inserted in Southey's *Joan of Arc*, on the Tree manured by the blood of patriots who had died after transportation by Lord Braxfield, refer quite clearly and dangerously to the Tree of Liberty, which in this context meant something like a gallows for tyrants. (CPW, 1029:73–82) We read in the lines of *Osorio* published separately as *The Dungeon:* "Then we call in our pamper'd mountebanks— And this is their best cure!" (CPW, 185:11–12) We might suppose the lines to attack politicians in general or utilitarians in particular, but the attack seems more partisan when we place it against Book II, chapter xi, of Godwin's *Caleb Williams*, published three years earlier. There the virtuous Caleb, after counting over "the doors, the locks, the bolts, the chains, the massy walls, and grated windows" of his prison, concludes that these are "the engines that tyranny sits down in cold and serious meditation to invent." To Godwin all government was tyranny, but Coleridge made exceptions.

Perhaps he actually visualized the political image hidden in such seemingly trite phrases as "womanish fears, traitors to love and duty." (CPW, 867:114) Political alertness seems more probable when he calls upon the "imperious branches" of the woods in *France: An Ode*. He is there asserting explicitly that only among the elements of nature can claims to sovereignty be respected. For the most part, however, his metaphors present politics, as one of the subjects of a given poem, in terms of something else, and not other human interests in terms of live political realities or political terminology.

Unlike Wordsworth's, Coleridge's greatest poems are not subtly infused with political impulse. Were most of his second-best poems not palpably and avowedly political in inspiration, his essential genius might in fact seem like Keats's to be allergic to politics, for his three most famous poems avoid almost altogether the contemporary actualities of *France: An Ode* and *Fears in Solitude*. Almost, but not quite. Even when *The Ancient Mariner, Christabel*, and *Kubla Khan* are set aside, there remain hymnal musings on the dawn in France, impassioned odes on Britain's foreign affairs, poems of opinion and prophecy on current events (what their author called "Poems Occasioned by Political Events or Feelings Connected with Them"), concrete illustrations of political theory, sonnets to political heroes, versified attempts to make the Government either more responsible or more obviously evil and ridiculous in its irresponsibility, party-minded *jeux d'esprit,* epigrams both Whig and Tory, systems of imagery colored—sometimes controlled —by political beliefs, and poems that would have been different if the poet's political postulates had currently been different. In sum, most of his verse is political. Of the formal and metrical experiments less innocent of political influence than they look, an example may be in order. Desiring a Biblical passage to translate into parallelisms of the original, he chose Judges 5. The fame of the Song of Deborah might have guided him to it (and more directly, perhaps, a German predecessor), but guidance came more easily because Deborah had delivered her people from a tyrant; because her song begins, "Ye Monarchs, hear!"; because "close to their gates came War"; and because Coleridge could translate a crucial line as "Suspended were the assemblies of Israel." [3] Some of the experiments probably came into being partly because of the partisan bias revealed in them. The present study began in the further postulate, and continued in the increasingly firm conviction, that Coleridge's greatest poems can be better understood and more fittingly enjoyed—enjoyed, that is, with surer empathy—through awareness of the principal impulses and themes in the bulk of his verse.

Analysts of Coleridge's political thought, Hort, Dowden, Hancock, Cestre, Muirhead, Cobban, Brinton, Feiling, Wünsche, Hearnshaw, Beeley, R. J. White, Terrett, Colmer, Werkmeister, and others, including Coleridge himself, have generally drawn on his poems only for decoration. They have worked basically from the prose. In illustration of the advantages of their method, we know from one of Coleridge's addresses of 1795 that he then accepted the superiority of "mixed" government, which he called, to distinguish it from governments by and over the people, "government *with* the people." The prose shows us that he inherited along with belief in mixed government the doctrine of separated powers. The union of executive with legislative powers, he informed the citizens of Bristol, "is one distinguishing feature of tyranny." (EOT, 82, 84, 93) The most rational of the poems provides no such clarity. Theory and its language provide a very small proportion even of the explicit politics in his verse. Political axioms may often be inferred from Coleridge's poems; he seldom states them therein. Misleadingly, a quatrain published in the *Morning Post* for 27 September 1802, as "A Hint to Premiers and First Consuls: from an Old Tragedy, viz. Agatha to King Archelaus," reminds that "thy power is from the laws"—an axiom of unbroken descent from the Middle Ages. (CPW, 966) Coleridge presumably translated the quatrain from Voss (who probably took it from Stobaeus),[4] but he is not responsible for its incorporation in his collected poems and would not have thought of it as poetically admirable. It can be asserted flatly that his conception of great poetry did not include the statement of political axioms.

His verse avoids generally such venerable and medicinal terms as "social contract," but the rejection of that particular cure-all by Hume and then by Bentham may have influenced Coleridge's avoidance of it. Although a manuscript of *The Plot Discovered* tells us that "Burleigh lived before the contract of [the] Bill of Rights was entered into by the People & their Governors," even such a contract as that of 1689 appears seldom in his prose. (Harvard MS. Eng 947.7, f. 5) He rejected the idea of an original contract for a sense of the ever-originating bonds that create social union. (F, I, 229; IS, 315) More surprisingly, he had no rimes for "natural rights." His early political poems certainly imply intelligibly enough that government without consent of the governed is oppressive and somehow invalid, but the natural rights of the subject never quite appear by name. Later changes could not remove the original anti-monarchic intention from the invocation, in *The Destiny of Nations,* of "the Great Father, only Rightful King"; yet Coleridge is entitled ultimately to his marginal note on an autograph copy in the British Museum: "i.e. jure suo, by any inherent Right." (B.M. MS. Add. 34225, f. 6; CPW, 131:3) In a private letter to John Thelwall, who believed more in rights than in God, he tried to make Christianity attractive in 1796: "It certainly teaches in the most explicit terms the rights of Man, his right to Wisdom, his right to an equal share in all the blessings of Nature . . . ." (CL, 282) For himself Coleridge was moving very rapidly toward emphasis upon duties and a distinction between rights and claims.[5] By distinguishing between claims and rights he went slightly further than Burke.

No such explicit language can be found in his poems. The fact is, Coleridge at twenty-one had so far absorbed the essence of the revolutionary spirit of his day, despite certain explicit rejections, that he did not need to parade its language in his early verse. His political poems of 1793–1802 are much closer in sentiments and semantics to the flowers of French rhetoric quoted in the speeches of Pitt than to the declaratory speeches in which Pitt quotes them. Later, evidence is scant. A duty hinging upon contract, rather than a natural right, is implied in Raab Kiuprili's claim, in *Zapolya,* to "a right common to all loyal subjects." (CPW, 891:240) The word *rightful* appears eight times in that play with reference to legitimacy enthroned. Unlike most of those parodied in the *Anti-Jacobin,* Coleridge's poems do not provide handbook or dictionary of the political catchwords then common to verse and prose. No social contract, no general will, no natural goodness, no rights of man—at least not in their ordinary dress. Their absence is more noteworthy than comparison with the other major Romantic poets might suggest. Except for Byron with tongue in cheek, none of the major English Romantics employed the phraseology common to the pamphlets of the day. But Coleridge's early journalism in verse is otherwise similar, in language and in kind, to the political verse of Richard Payne Knight, Robert Merry, and others Jacobinically inclined. It is a pleasant surprise that he went less far than Southey toward the language of *The Vision of Columbus*, by Joel Barlow, "Where civil rights and social virtues blend," to take one of its lines; where powers of state "Rise from consent to shield the rights of man"; where the sermons of enlightened preachers "For social compact harmonize mankind." [6]

In the shadow of the Revolution, certain political words passed from denotation to detonation. One of these, *patriot,* will concern us in the chapter on sonnets to patriot heroes. For another, Dykes Campbell cited the case of a Bristol shipowner who pacified the friends of "constitution" by changing to *Freedom* the name of a vessel he had first christened *Liberty.*[7] *Liberty* had become explosively French. Although we can learn from the history of such words in the poetry, Coleridge did not always remain poetically faithful to political distinctions, and the exigencies of rime and meter often combined with the urgency of earning bread and cheese to determine his choice of nouns.

Words politically more neutral, like *social, state, government, nation,* and *people,* do enter Coleridge's poetry, and are usually given emotional content. During the 1790's the word *social* in his poems pertains to individuals and families gathered into a society within the region implied by the context, and connotes whatever is good for these families: "social Quiet," "social peace," "social Liberty," "social Poverty." [8] Social poverty as a virtue contrasts with antisocial, or at best asocial, wealth. The "Social Sense" seems to be sympathy, a kind of benevolent gregariousness, as in Samuel Jackson Pratt's poem of 1781, *Sympathy; Or, A Sketch of the Social Passion.* (CPW, 405:27)

In ugly contrast with "Blessed Society," the word *state* in the early poems, whenever it refers to a political entity and not to a condition wholly non-political, connotes the purple panoply of high rank and great power: "mitred State," "plumy State." (CPW,

118:266, 81:9, 336:37) The two denotations of body politic and condition combine in the connotation of unblessed power to expose a republican view of monarchy. Thrice in the first act of *The Fall of Robespierre* the word *state* denotes neutrally the body politic; on its fourth appearance, in Adelaide's song, "the pomp of scepter'd state," like "the rebel's noisy hate," is denounced as an enemy to the "domestic peace" of families. (CPW, 497:71, 498:108, 500:159, 501:217) From the poems, coming early politically and being poems, no intelligible beginning could be made toward the Coleridge of 1830, when his book *On the Constitution of the Church and State* defined a state as an organic whole. And yet his later political theories, expressed in prose, should be read as coming from a man who associated "state," in youth, with pomp and oppression. Although his later rimes lack the humane emphasis of his earliest poems, humanitarianism partly accounts for his repetition, from the *Watchman* through the Lay Sermons and all editions of the *Friend*, of a detailed argument that the state has positive obligations to develop in every citizen the faculties essential to his rational and moral being and a just hope of improving the lot of himself or his children. (W, 262; LS, 115–16; F, II, 68–70) The definition of government in a footnote of 1817 as "all the directors of political power, that is, the great estates of the Realm, temporal and spiritual, and not only the Parliament, but all the elements of Parliament," might serve equally as a footnote to his poetic rejection in 1798 of the excessive optimism of reformers, "As if a government were but a robe." (LS, 45n; CPW, 261n)

The political meanings of the word *sovereign* in Coleridge's poetry are neither complex nor subtle, but he seems to have felt emotional power in the word, and one oddity has an interest related to political content. He seems to have preferred Milton's spelling, *sovran,* to denote figurative use of the adjective, and the modern spelling for directly political meanings.[9] The many changes to the refrains of the *Hymn before Sunrise,* not all recorded in the standard edition by E. H. Coleridge, increasingly expressed the sovereignty of "sovran" Mont Blanc. In the most-changed line, the twenty-ninth, the "silent Mountain, sole and bare" became and remained "first and chief"; from an "unchanging silent Form" in October, 1809, it became "stern Monarch of the Vale" in November; in "the only correct copy in existence" provided for Mrs. Brabant in 1815, Coleridge gave it its final and proper eminence, as "sole Sovran of the Vale." [10]

Coleridge's poetry makes close kin of the words *nation* and *people*. Belief in the self-determination of nations, although not necessarily self-determination of common peoples as sovereign over themselves, is implied in poems like the sonnet on Kosciusko. In keeping with this belief, *nation* usually designates the whole people occupying a given territory, and thus in the 1790's bears anti-monarchic implications. But the *nation* might well contain responsible orders above the common *people*. The plural with definite article, "the nations," seems in neither of its appearances to have strongly nationalistic content, but rather to be a conventional poetic term for the world, the peoples of the earth collectively. (CPW, 167:139, 246:62) There is little or no connection between this usage and Coleridge's philosophic hope for a time when "a different Government will no longer be supposed to constitute or imply a different Nation or Country—but Laws, Manners, Religion and Language"—although he was to versify the hope as a way of declaring the national identity of England and the United States. (IS, 343; CPW, 483) A third plural, "a shout of nations" in the *Hymn before Sunrise,* simply offers ample measurement for the noise of torrents. (CPW, 379:58) During the previous century, the educated classes had subtly subverted the theory of the ultimate sovereignty of the populace by using the word *people* often in such a national way as to include not only all commoners but also Parliament and the king's ministers. Burke was out of the ordinary in excluding that large portion of the populace which lacked the education and the leisure for political discussion. Nor were aristocrats always excluded. Consequently, *people* in Coleridge's verse never has the connotation of mob, although he certainly never gives the Duke of Norfolk's toast to "The Majesty of the People." Usually *people* refers to the basic nation, even later, as in *Zapolya* where Kiuprili mocks, for Coleridge, the "shallow sophisms of a popular choice." (CPW, 895:354) The whole people, though not convened to declare the general will, exist as a nation whose will commands respect. Even in the somewhat Jacobinical poems, as certainly in the later prose, a people is Burke's organized society, with a history and institutions; it may or may not contain

authorities who have grown into place above the commons. Probably Coleridge's character Robespierre, evoking in 1794 the "almighty people," was recognizing the new claim of the poor to
that impressive designation. But Coleridge is at least this once
justified in his later claims that the Jacobinical language in early
poems was dramatic, not subjective, in intention. Usage in the
poems shows that he formed very early a view of nation and people
as aspects of an ordered society. He had the general ideas, even
if he achieved only later the organic theory that could produce a
marginal explosion against a weak thinker's weak rejection of
arguments for the sovereignty of the people. No, no, scribbled
Coleridge, both theory and phrase are nonsense, "because a People *derives* it's unity from the Government (or the State) & that
unity is *real* only where each individual of the 3 or the 30 million
yielding the same obedience to the State, all are capable of being
contemplated as *one*, as *a* people, *this* or *that* People!" [11]

His early uses of the words *nation* and *people* foreshadow also
the nationalism clearly based on a populace and its land in 1809;
the marginal note just quoted seems to return nationalism to the
verge of the dynastic. That it should not be interpreted so is suggested by the last nationalistic passage in his poems, the tribute to
Florence in *The Garden of Boccaccio,* which begins:

> The brightness of the world, O thou once free,
> And always fair, rare land of courtesy!
> O Florence! with the Tuscan fields and hills
> And famous Arno, fed with all their rills;
> Thou brightest star of star-bright Italy!
> Rich, ornate, populous,—all treasures thine,
> The golden corn, the olive, and the vine.
>
> (CPW, 479–80:73–79) [12]

As in this passage, so in nearly all his poetry, political impulses
dissolve in other impulses. But political emotions of themselves
could transform the common usages of prose. No surer evidence
of Coleridge's early republicanism exists than his treatment, as
more or less synonymous, of the words *despot, tyrant, monarch,
king,* and occasionally *usurper.* He avoids, in early poems, the distinction stressed by Polybius, noted by James I, Locke, and Burke,
and restated by Major Cartwright and then Thelwall, as the distinction between a king who holds his office in trust for the people

and a monarch who acts as if he had an individual right to sovereign power.[13] Coleridge himself allowed that Pye as Laureate might legitimately refer to George III in verse by the dissyllabic word *monarch,* whereas such usage in prose would defame "our *kingly,* not *monarchical* government." (EOT, 366) How can we tell when the defamation is significant in verse? Among the verbal changes when *France: An Ode* reappeared in the *Post* for 14 October 1802, the champion of man was decried, not as in earlier and later versions for mixing "with Kings in the low lust of sway," but for mixing—semantically worse—with "monarchs in the lust of sway." (CPW, 246:81)

In a notebook recipe for ginger beer Coleridge wrote jestingly of "the Scum—viz—the Monarchical part"; with too much intensity for humor he wrote of kings in his poems as Nimrods, mighty hunters. (CN, 162, 280; CPW, 246:80–82) He had no time for the kind of psychological analysis of Nimrods that Hugo would make in *Le Fin de Satan;* he was too busy with the crying fact: there were tyrants who hunted men and kings who egged on the Pitts and Grenvilles. More bluntly and more often his poems called kings murderers. War was "Insipid Royalty's keen condiment!" (CPW, 145:405) Miscellaneous evils were "king-bred"; various dead wretches were "monarch-murdered." (CPW, 81n, 499:149) And when we find it eight lines from a "monarch-murder'd Soldier's tomb," how are we to remove the implication of republicanism from Coleridge's description of a sublime rock, which "like some giant king, o'er-glooms the hill"? (CPW, 103:20, 28) He would have saved himself trouble later if he had always just called kings tyrants. What he could not later properly say of all kings, he could have left as a description of unspecified but un-English tyrants. It must have been Charles Lamb's abrupt command to "alter that" which caused "The tumult of some SCOUNDREL Monarch's breast," retained from 1794 in the volume of 1796, to be mollified in *Poems,* 1797, into "The aching of pale Fashion's vacant breast"; but Coleridge had other changes to make of his own later volition. (CPW, 76:36; LL, I, 96) In a line originally describing a crew of evil motives as "Rebels from God, and Monarchs o'er Mankind," Coleridge later substituted "Tyrants" for "Monarchs"; similarly, "the thron'd Murderers of Mankind" later became "Tyrants, Murderers of Mankind." [14] These changes betray totally Coleridge's original intentions. Aside from the amelioration of his views, the later specification of the tyrant as a separate class of monarch shows that the poet was not concerned until later to exclude George III from the category damned, and suggests strongly that he interpreted himself as including George III originally among the murderers. Changes of this sort, often first provided in a page of *errata,* gave legal protection to author and publisher, but actually emphasized the intent.

If Coleridge wrote, as seems likely, the two editorials on George Washington recovered by David Erdman from the files of the *Morning Post,* he praised that commanding patriot early in 1800 for "the majesty of his views," in a way that opposed the concept of majesty to feelings "wild and ferocious." [15] He could do so because majesty had been lent to the crown by the people. Originally, before Tiberius, Coleridge informed those men in Bristol most ready to believe him, "Majesty meant the unity of the people; the one point in which ten million rays concentered." (EOT, 69) As a consequence of this theory of popular sovereignty, Southey in the anti-monarchic *Joan of Arc* could make figurative use of Milton's literal phrase, "naked majesty," and Wordsworth even at fifty could salute "simple democratic majesty." (WPW, III, 200:52) But the Romantic could blame tyrants as self-engendering boils on the body politic only as long as he ignored the organic unity of life. Before Coleridge could be described as a royalist, his poetry began to show an indifference about the terms for kingliness. His metaphors of sovereignty became generally commonplace or indifferently confused as early as 1798.

He had never abandoned all caution in his vituperative eruptions. That scoundrel monarch whose aching breast was soothed by warbled airs, in *To a Young Ass,* could be any one of those notorious Continental despots, but a version sent to Southey on 17 December 1794 had dangerously identified him as the sovereign of an island inhabited by readers of the *Morning Chronicle,* for in the letter it was *"Banti's* warbled airs, that sooth to rest." (CL, 143; CPW, 76n) Banti had recently diminished Foxite enthusiasm for her voice by "aristocratic" warbling before George III and Queen Charlotte. By September, 1795, the *Morning Chronicle,* which in May and early June of the previous year had declared her "incomparable," "inimitable," and all of that, consoled itself

with stanzas on Banti's "ill use," socially, of Polonius-like Salis-
bury, the Lord Chamberlain.[16] Thus Banti's presence in the poem
said too much.

Feelings and political events aided the imagination in banishing
unmetaphorical statements of political theory from Coleridge's
poems. Before examining his varied use of particular genres, we
need to attend to feelings and images, rather than to terms of
theory, as we observe in slower motion his years when humanitarian pity led into political protest, passionate revolt, and partisan
accusation.

CHAPTER IV

Ideas and Feelings:
Pity versus Power

> For pitee renneth soone in gentil herte.
>
> —Chaucer, *passim*

I

In verses on the death of a friend, 1794, Coleridge summarized the ingredients of his own being as Reason, Truth-seeking, Patriotism, and Pity:

> To me hath Heaven with bounteous hand assign'd
> Energic Reason and a shaping mind,
> The daring ken of Truth, the Patriot's part,
> And Pity's sigh, that breathes the gentle heart—
> Sloth-jaundic'd all!
>
> (CPW, 77:39–43)

The final phrase may be safely identified with the backward glance to the innocence of childhood made in half the poems of this "thought-bewilder'd man" from the time of his fragmented sojourn as a student at Cambridge until January, 1795, when his sonnet to Godwin glanced with grateful optimism down on the period of evil from which he had looked back to innocence. Backward glances filled the melancholy air, as in Southey's poem *The Retrospect*, on days "ere yet I knew Or grief and care, or happiness and you"; but Coleridge found no place for "happiness and you" until he met the eudemonic ethic in Godwin's version of the greatest-happiness principle.[1]

Significant words in his early poetry are *gentle, calm, mild.* Next after nostalgia the motif most recurring is pity, sometimes as compassion, sympathy, or benevolence. The great subversive marriage of ideas in the second half of the eighteenth century was that of liberty with pity, for charity thereby claimed a superiority to law and established justice. Moral fervor like Coleridge's increased the subversion. He had "the sympathetic glow" for "Poverty's meek woe," what Byron called the "soft idea" of William Lisle Bowles, "first, great oracle of tender souls." (CPW, 77:21–22; BP, I, 323:327, 332) The initial move in Coleridge's Romantic rebellion against complacent faith in geometry was to give emotion its proper place in the European scene. Characteristic phrases, crowding in, almost defy selection: "Sweet is the tear . . . ," "Pity's dew divine," and opposite to these the "morsel tossed by law-forced charity." (CPW, 99:81, 107:49, 119:228) Sentiment is being raised into benevolence, a deistic expansion of Christian brotherhood:

> And he that works me good with unmov'd face,
> Does it but half: he chills me while he aids,
> My benefactor, not my brother man!
>
> (CPW, 107:51–53)

Anticipating *The Cultural Presupposition* of Auden in a later blizzard of political poetry, Coleridge's sonnet to William Linley (brother-in-law to Sheridan) chides soothing music for seducing his attention from the distresses of "miserable brethren." (CPW, 236:6; CL, 352n) None of the many strident verses with pity as principal theme have for later readers the literary importance of calmer passages. It is not the passage that has value, but its service to the whole poem, when Coleridge weaves into the close and subtle texture of *Frost at Midnight* a memory of church-bells, "the poor man's only music." (CPW, 241:29)

And yet Coleridge not only strengthened his powers as a poet in the versifying of pity, but soon led himself to recognize that inoperative sentiment molders. As one way of making sentiment poetically operative, he toyed with Wordsworth's manner of equating humble objects of nature with the outcast and downtrodden among men and nations. A blighted blossom (apparently the insufficiently cautious primrose of a related poem) is likened first to a girl nipped by consumption, then to Chatterton, and then to "poor Poland's hope." (CPW, 148–49) Chatterton, in turn, was an amaranth "Blooming mid Poverty's drear wintry waste." (CPW, 149n) Coleridge specifically renounced sentimentality. In an essay *On the Slave Trade,* based on one of his Bristol lectures, he distinguished benevolence from mere sensibility: "Benevolence impels to action, and is accompanied by self-denial." He had distinguished at twenty between "well wishers" and "well doers." At twenty-four, in a letter to Thelwall, he applied the distinction politically: "Most of our patriots are tavern & parlour Patriots, that will not avow their principles by any decisive action...." (W, 108; CL, 50, 305; cf. IS, 393) In lines chiefly dedicated to driving his pupil Charles Lloyd from "an Indolent and Causeless Melancholy," he prescribed an observation of poverty, hunger, and the burial of war widows. The reader suspects that the prescription was designed partly to satisfy a thirst for sensation, but it was also political: the awakening was designed to bring Lloyd into action heroic enough to prevent "Life's commonweal" from remaining "prey to Tyrants, Murderers of Mankind." (CPW, 158:15–16) The tear should be medicinal both for the man weeping and for the man wept over. Even he that works me good with unmoved face is better than "sluggard Pity's vision-weaving tribe!" (CPW, 107:56) Coleridge's poems of compassionate brotherhood are seldom so sicklied o'er that political action dies in them. Concern with unwed mothers was part of the cult of pity; concern with hungry orphans and "childless widows," when publicly expressed, brings pity into political action against Pitt's war. Fairly late, in *Fears in Solitude,* the poet declares that he "would full fain" ignore politics, but he "perforce must feel For all his human brethren." (CPW, 257:30–32) The patriot is not required to feel pity for Pitt.

The poet who believes strongly in benevolence and brotherhood asks his readers to think on the unfortunate and wretched. If he calls them repeatedly the "numberless," "the wretched Many," he is on the political way to calling them, as Coleridge frequently did in 1794–96, "the oppressed," the victims of "foul Oppression's ruffian gluttony." (CPW, 118:262, 119:277) He recognizes in "pageant Power," if the poor do not, "Their cots' transmuted plunder!" (CPW, 118:263–64; cf. 161:16) Marx was to call it expropriation, and Coleridge attributed the injustices of advancing capitalism to all the ruling classes. The poor are threatened as by lion, serpent, hyena, vulture, behemoth, simoom. (CPW, 118:267–95) Readers conditioned by such language soon identify automatically the unspecified oppressor in poems of mere pity, for example any tearful poem about a deserted young mother. A government that employs press gangs to snatch up recruits clearly deserves the blame for all misfortunes of the poor in time of war. In 1794 an English poem about a deserted mother was anti-war, and therefore anti-Ministerial. It is not from the doctrine of Necessity that Coleridge in *Religious Musings* pardons the prostitute and the murderer, but from resentment at malignant oppression. (CPW, 119:279–91) A sonnet written jointly with Southey, "the 6 last lines by Coleridge," similarly excuses the prostitute by condemning those who "force from Famine the caress of Love." [2]

Overwarm melancholy and tearful sympathy in the verse of Southey, Coleridge, Lamb, and Lloyd, banded in soulful company, borrows a great deal from the fashion of sentimentality, but humanitarianism was not altogether tearfully unpractical. In the 1790's the immediate aim was not to convert the oppressor, but to defeat him. Even the brotherly tactic of jackass-kissing kept the political enemy in sight. Coleridge observes the swain leading "weary oxen to their nightly shed," the "plough-man following sad his meagre team." (CPW, 90:15, 143:345) "Weary" and "meagre" here are doubled epithets: they refer not only to the poor beasts but also to the poor masters. Coleridge's most notorious lines commiserate a young ass as the symbol of "an oppressèd race" living under the rule of another oppressed race, in what should be the "fellowship of Woe." The ass's apparent sympathy with its meanly tethered mother shames, by comparison, self-considering and pitiless man. The guilt of the half-famished master in not finding a source of sympathy with the ass's woe in his own is made less culpable by the greater guilt of the master's master, represented in the poem by the word "Luxury." (CPW, 75:20, 22) If justice be happiness, as Coleridge has Joan of Arc darkly proclaim, then unhappiness must be intimately related to injustice. (CPW, 144:378–80)

Coleridge increased the shrillness of his tocsins—Oppression! Usurpation! Tyranny! Despotism!—through 1796; after that year his peal softened gradually. Tyrants include persecutors, all who enslave body or soul. Although Southey was right in finding blessings among the evils Mohammed scattered hugely, the soul-binding empire-waster was a tyrant. (CPW, 329:1–5; cf. 1016) Tyranny exists not only where the dictator is severe, but wherever the master is willful. Tyranny is present or imminent wherever there is pomp or luxury. Milton's "sumptuous Dalila" becomes, as a phrase in one of Coleridge's metrical experiments, "Sumptuous Tyranny." (CPW, 1014) Luxury and pomp are fortuitous traits of the tyrant; his essence is ravenous ambition, which gorges itself in war. Slaughter, the "boastful bloody son of pride," is the royal heir presumptive.[3] Contempt and rage coalesce in the lava Coleridge pours on "beggarly potentates" subsidized by Pitt, the egregious despots of Russia, Austria, and Prussia, and "Each petty German princeling, nursed in gore!" (W, 181; CPW, 116:179) An alteration later than 1803 in the *Ode on the Departing Year* designated George III's allies by the verse-clogging substantive, "Tyrant-Murderers." (CPW, 163:61)

Above all other tyrants he detested Catherine, "that foul Woman of the North," ravisher of Poland, "insatiate Hag," "exterminating Fiend," and "lustful murderess of her wedded lord." [4] In domestic politics revilement of Catherine meant opposition to tax-garnered loans for faithless allies, but Coleridge felt genuine moral abhorrence. In righteous indignation and in detail, coming the month after her death, his *Ode on the Departing Year* resembled a public print by Isaac Cruikshank that depicted the dying empress' visions of chained patriots, the sack of Warsaw, her murdered consort, and swirls of bodies variously poisoned, stabbed, gibbeted, and beheaded. (George, VII, 280) Coleridge adds the now more famous accomplishments of Suvorov in the massacre at Izmail. (CPW, 162:48–51 and note)

His distaste for the luxury and ambition of princes may help to explain *Kubla Khan.* He has clearly erected in that poem an antithesis between the measured and the measureless, the sunny and the sunless, the pleasure-dome and the deep romantic chasm, the pleasurable and the sacred, the decree of Kubla Khan and the prophecy amid tumult. Kubla said, Let there be a dome, and there was a dome. "But oh!" he heard from far "Ancestral voices prophesying war!" (CPW, 297:12, 298:30) Setting aside the poles of drunken and sober Freudianism, critical analyses of the poem divide basically over attitudes toward the eastern potentate. Is the poem for Kubla or against him? Or, as possible but unlikely, does it lean neither for nor against? We need to resolve this point before we can declare Kubla the symbol of a poet decreeing the thing of beauty in his imagination, instead of a temporal lord creating in a mode less durable than the poet's mode opposed to it. Coleridge certainly in 1796, and almost certainly in 1798 or 1799, would have been against Kubla's presumption. If he associated the dome of his poem with wealth and pleasure, as well as with a potentate, he would condemn the dome rather than the supernatural forces that threaten it. Purchas, his most immediate source, called it "a sumptuous house of pleasure." By the term "a Pleasure house," in a letter of May, 1799, to Thomas Poole, Coleridge refers to some kind of love-nest where a German subaltern killed his mistress and then himself. To arrive at this nest, the officer "made a pleasure party in a Sledge with a woman with whom he lived in criminal connection." (CL, 491) The German account that Coleridge seems to be summarizing contains no direct suggestion of either a "pleasure party" or a "Pleasure house." (CN, 398) It is an odd coincidence, if it is nothing more, that Leigh Hunt thought he remembered a variation of the opening lines of the poem in which Kubla Khan did "A stately *pleasure-house ordain.*" [5]

Catherine herself may hover malignly near. Kubla's "sunny pleasure-dome with caves of ice" may possibly not be constructed even partly of ice; its glamor may be enhanced merely by proximity to natural "caves of ice." (CPW, 298:36) But the "bubble of ice" in Cashmere, noted by Coleridge for use in his proposed hymn to the moon and considered by J. L. Lowes a direct source for *Kubla Khan,*[6] is no nearer to the dome and its setting in the poem than a pleasure-dome, itself of ice, decreed in a despotic whim by Empress Anna, a notable predecessor of Catherine, shortly before her death in 1740. Her ice-palace, "stately" in its perverse way, may have had a strong influence on the poem. It was "the work of man," admired, unnatural, and unworthy, as William Cowper described and condemned it for his contemporaries—and Cole-

ridge's—in Book V of *The Task* (ll. 101–76). Cannons of ice had
fired metal balls when the Empress forced a courtier in disfavor
to marry and to display himself with his ugly bride naked on a
bed of ice in the mock-palace. English interest in these cold games
began about 1770, when Hume edited a translation of General
Manstein's *Memoirs of Russia*. In 1778 John Glen King published
*A Letter to . . . the Lord Bishop of Durham . . . With a View of
the Flying Mountains of Zarsko Sello near St. Petersbourg*, including a fold-out illustration of the pleasurable device of "flying
mountains": over artificial mounds of snow, each hollowed for
a grotto, the Empress Elizabeth and her guests (and later Catherine and hers) rode in elaborate toboggans, which a machine worked
by horses then drew to the pleasure-hut on the highest mound, in
preparation for the next gay adventure.[7] Naturally the almost
iceless English were impressed.

Coleridge could not have failed to know of the Empress' ice-
palace, however incorrectly he may have remembered for the
Biographia Literaria that he had made a contumelious reference
to it in an essay of 1793: "During my first Cambridge vacation, I
assisted a friend in a contribution for a literary society in Devonshire: and in this I remember to have compared Darwin's work
to the Russian palace of ice, glittering, cold and transitory."[8] In
the agony of his love for Sara Hutchinson, perhaps in 1805, he
asked if true love were not of more worth than beauty, wealth,
or family. His words are these, in the third stanza of *Separation:*

> Is not true Love of higher price
>   Than outward Form, though fair to see,
> Wealth's glittering fairy-dome of ice,
>   Or echo of proud ancestry?—
>
> (CPW, 398:9–12)

He had tried "Stores of Gold, the Pomp of Wealth" and other
variants before he rested upon the "fairy-dome of ice" as the essence of vain glitter. Palaces of ice, originating as they did with
the foul woman of the North, displeased him over a span of years.
Nor is the limitless supernatural threatening Kubla's vainglory altogether evil. That the "deep romantic chasm" leads not only
negatively to a "sunless sea," but positively to a realm more holy
than an emperor's pleasure-grounds, may be supposed from other

associations of the image. Interpreting Southey's selfishness in 1795, Coleridge as a necessitarian optimist had written that however foul Southey's stream might run, "it will filtrate & become pure in it's subterraneous Passage to the Ocean of Universal Redemption." Elsewhere he noted "a river run under ground" as a ready symbol for abiding Truth. (CL, 168; CN, 177)

The dome of *Kubla Khan*, then, can be likened to Pitt's palace of deceitful language, as described by Coleridge in the *Morning Post* of 6 February 1800. This palace, according to Coleridge, was destroyed in Parliament by Fox: "Like some good genius, he approached in indignation to the spell-built palace of the state-magician, and at the first touch of his wand, it sunk into a ruinous and sordid hovel, tumbling in upon the head of the wizard that had *reared* it." (EOT, 371)

Such a transfer of images from Russia to Tory politics would have come easily. In the years of Coleridge's fiercest passion against ambition and tyranny, Catherine had a rival for his vituperation in the ministry of Pitt. Pitt, Dundas, and Grenville were ambitious, tyrannous, and corrupt. Coleridge cheered Horne Tooke in one of his encounters with "foul Corruption's wolfish throng." (CPW, 151:19) He observed that Pitt's power, within Parliament as outside, was bought. By comparison, in an epigram on another subject, he held the vilest and most venomous of all to be "The greedy creeping Things in Place." (CPW, 959, corrected)

The Foxite Opposition charged Pitt's administration with bullying revolutionary France into a war which they then prolonged blindly and cruelly. Coleridge, an admirer of Bowles's "mild and manliest melancholy," came readily to the crusade of words against war. (CPW, 85:8) The struttings of "ruthless War" as an abstraction in his earliest verse through 1792, with such members of its family as "Ambition, Sire of War" and Glory with "blood-stain'd palm," may sound imitatively automatic and unserious. (CPW, 33:12, 36:24, 32) By their literary stiffness they seem to deny any awareness by the versifier that actual war was imminent; but Coleridge had inherited the mode of personification from models recent and living. The chilliness of his technique does not prove absence of passion in the young objector, whose partisanship may have been intensified by his aberrant months as a dragoon. In the *Conciones* he exclaimed ironically against the poor:

"Fools! to commit ROBBERIES, and get hung, when they might MURDER with impunity—yea, and have Sixpence a day into the bargain!" By a standard method of self-protection, he placed the key to his exclamation in the table of errata: "Page 61, for murder read Fight for his King and Country." (His daughter Sara quietly incorporated the change in the text of *Essays on His Own Times* and corrected the discrepancy between "they" and "his.") The fury, increasing through 1796, of Coleridge's opposition to "the present unjust, unnecessary, and calamitous war" betrays the increasing excitement of the partisan journalist, but it parallels also a general increase of passion in poetry. (EOT, 50, 58) He began with a strong, imaginative, uninformed hatred of war. Opposition to Pitt concentrated and inflamed the hatred while it gave outlet to the creative passion building in him as a Romantic poet.

With religious conviction deepening, Coleridge really felt profound shock, and not a mere partisan superiority, at Ministerial and ecclesiastical declarations that the war against France was being continued "for the preservation of the Christian religion." This shock is central to *Religious Musings*, strengthens *Fears in Solitude*, and deepens the satire of *The Devil's Thoughts*. He plays unfairly, rejecting the conventional association of pantomimic Christmas with St. George for England, in *A Christmas Carol*, published in the *Morning Post* 25 December 1799: He has the Virgin repudiate all pretended intimacy between the Prince of Peace and a second hero hailed by monarchs, War, a "murderous fiend, by fiends adored." (CPW, 339:37)

The political trials of 1794 and the acts against treasonable utterance, seditious assembly, and combinations of labor gave Opposition journalists like Coleridge adequate opportunity to attack the Ministers as enemies to freedom at home as well as across channel and ocean. In prose Coleridge took opportunity often to condemn specific Ministerial acts of suppression and persecution; avoiding the local if not always the negative, his poems usually met the topic of freedom in an atmosphere high above the "sea of blood bestrewed with wrecks" where he kept Ministerial appointments. (CPW, 113:124) The reader breathes freer air than politics provide—although the poem means politics, morally conceived—in the self-dedication at the close of *Reflections on Having Left a Place of Retirement:* he will fight bloodlessly for

Science, Freedom, and the Truth in Christ. (CPW, 108:61–62) Similarly, in lines first published in Southey's *Joan of Arc* Coleridge asked with Romantic expansiveness, "For what is Freedom, but the unfettered use Of all the powers which God for use had given?" (CPW, 132:13–14)

Among his many metaphors involving freedom and restraint, some conventional and dead when he found them, a number actively political and topical and therefore perishable, those best use political emotion which dissolve the poet's fury against throned despots in a non-political solvent, as in the lines on a view of Saddleback: "The winds are tyrannous and strong." (CPW, 347:2) Coleridge was strengthening verses by Isaac Ritson, who called the winds "loud and strong." (Lowes, p. 604k) Here and elsewhere in Coleridge and Wordsworth the phrase "tyrannous and strong" represents a conversion of libertarian, political energy into poetic force. (CPW, 188:42; WPW, II, 129:15; CL, 638) In Coleridge's strongest tropes of confinement, political restraint usually narrows to a prison cell, as in "Th'imprison'd secret struggling in the face," or "This lime-tree bower my prison!" (CPW, 178:2, 496:21) Prisons stank for Coleridge with a political stench, associated with the tyrannous confinements of La Fayette, Kosciusko, Joseph Gerrald and the West-Indian Margarot, the "unfortunate" Despard, James Montgomery, John Binns, and with the various trials of men he knew, William Frend, John Thelwall, John Horne Tooke, Thomas Holcroft, Gilbert Wakefield, James Perry, and Benjamin Flower. As an anti-Pittite journalist he lived in sufficient danger to make his visions graphic. In the copy of *Conciones* given to the Morgans, Coleridge crossed out the passage on Muir, Palmer, Margarot, and especially Gerrald—"I saw him in the foul and naked room of a jail," and so on—and annotated vigorously: "Written by Southey. I never saw these men." (p. 22; see EOT, 18) He may have had this good reason for omitting the passage from the *Friend,* but the better poet had once shared the spirit of the passage, and probably wrote it. From Christ's Hospital days to Highgate, Coleridge knew a number of men who became bishops; he knew more who were distinguished as "acquitted felons."

That the emotions going into vivid images of imprisonment owed much of their strength to the poet's experience of political suasion does not explain why some of the images remain strong for the reader while others do not. Striking effects within the poems may sometimes come from a chance ordering of conventional elements, as in the declaration that rationalists like Newton "Chain down the wingèd thought," or in the retold myth of the evil undersea spirit who hastens to her prison-home "Ere by the frost foreclosed." (CPW, 132:29, 135:118) Somewhat more positively we can say that Coleridge's emotional attachment to the idea of freedom enabled him to give additional force to a variety of exclamations over freedom deprived.

The figurative uses of enslavement in his poetry can be clustered separately around two moral poles: (1) condemnation of the enslaver as tyrant, in a historical situation where the royal family he did not love supported the Continental despots and the trade in African slaves; and (2) condemnation of the enslaved, as a corollary implied in the maxim that only the virtuous can be free. The poet often draws the two vices paradoxically together. In *Religious Musings* the German princes who have conveyed mercenary soldiers to British wars are "Death's prime slave-merchants." Hard upon them come an unworthy people, apparently the Hanoverian subjects of George III, given in 1795 into the hands of Prussia: "Apt for the yoke, the race degenerate, Whom Britain erst had blushed to call her sons!" (CPW, 116:181–84) Where a moral view of the political state and generalizations about race thus meet, a movement has begun from emphasis on the liberties of individuals to emphasis on the freedom of nations. How broad and ethereal the cope of Liberty, and how amorphous the poet's love of it, can be seen in a change to a later poem, *Youth and Age,* where the "joys" of the poet's youth were first written down as ideals, "Beauty, Truth, and Liberty," and then more concretely as blessings, "Friendship, Love, and Liberty." [9] Ideal or blessing, Liberty remains. When focus on national freedom diffused into inclusive "moral freedom," Liberty remained, however upliftingly vague.

By his word for a third ideal, *Science,* Coleridge seems to have intended the least general of the definitions in Dr. Johnson's dictionary: "Certainty grounded on demonstration." Taken with his strong empirical strain, his choice of men to honor suggests that he regarded them as scientific not because of their exactness

in the communication of general wisdom but more narrowly, because of their experiment and invention in the natural sciences.
Freedom, religious Truth, and Science make a strong axis in
Coleridge's poetry of 1794–96. Science in union with Benevolence
begets Progress. Encouragement should be given to midwives
like Franklin, Priestley, Stanhope, and Rumford, but the process
is larger than individual efforts. Mandeville's epigrammatic
theories holding private vices responsible for public happiness
had been thoroughly purged of cynicism by optimists like Helvétius, to provide a background for Coleridge's definition of Benevolence in the *Watchman* as "Natural Sympathy made permanent by enlightened Selfishness." (W, 101; EOT, 139)
Admiration for Science is crucial to the argument, as illustrated
in John Thelwall's *Ode to Science*, 1791, and neatly by a necessitarian couplet in *Religious Musings*: "From Avarice thus, from
Luxury and War Sprang heavenly Science; and from Science
Freedom." (CPW, 117:224–25) Thelwall had noted that "social
joys, and Reason's calm controul" both rose from Science, but he
left for Coleridge the discovery that Freedom herself so sprang.
(*Ode to Science* II.1)

Extensive attention to freedom, truth, and progress through
science inevitably carried with it considerable impatience with
the *status in quo*. In his later conservative years, and heavily in
the *Biographia Literaria*, Coleridge heaped coals of irony on the
head of his erring youth, but protested noisily that he had never
been a Jacobin or a republican. (BL, I, 115–21, 142) He could
prove easily that he never believed men equal in ability, in education or aptness for power or responsibility, or in good will. He
had always feared and detested the violence of mobs. He had
always disliked dirty and ignorant persons like many around him
at Bristol and Stowey. In a letter of March, 1798, to his fatherly
brother George, he consented to be deemed a democrat, solely
because of his guilty past, but protested that he was now "no
Whig, no Reformist, no Republican." Had he not earlier, however, in protesting that he was no democrat, admitted that he
was a melioristic reformer? Had his first known letter to Southey
not hailed the new comrade in the names of "Health & Republicanism"? Had he not, moreover, then smiled upon the "golden
Hinges" of the "Gate of Democracy"? (CL, 83, 126, 397) But

here we must turn from questioning to partial admission of his own claims, for the second letter to Southey dripped with contempt for a "Welsh Democrat," and from this contempt Coleridge did not waver by the thickness of a cockade. (CL, 89; cf. 48, 91, 219, 653)

In the *Watchman* he declared that the utopian proposals of "Roebeuf" (meaning the communist Babeuf), until the happy period "when the majority of men are perfectly wise and virtuous," could presage only anarchistic rapine. (W, 246) He struck again at Babeuf and other "absolute Equalizers" in 1800. (EOT, 238, 367) In fact, he was making a common English error, for Revolutionists in France who wished absolute political equality opposed Babeuf and agrarian extremists who proposed to socialize private property. Coleridge essentially agreed with Babeuf on property but opposed instantaneous social, political, or landed equality. He was at times during 1794–96 a republican without being an egalitarian, and at times an egalitarian in ultimate aim but no republican; he was partly both, but uneasily, with shifting reservations.

II

Pleasure in pity, need for freedom, a yearning for peace and calm, and sympathy with the democratic idea had joined with events to bring Coleridge into radical politics. Not only did he detest tyrants and war; for a time he rejected wholesale all kings, "king-polluted Lords," and lords spiritual, the "mitred" atheists. (CPW, 57:2, 121:334, 123:373) He explained the Babylon of the Apocalypse as "the union of Religion with Power and Wealth, wherever it is found." (CPW, 121:315n) The language of Voltaire and Holbach penetrated far into what Basil Willey, following the reconverted Coleridge, has called English illumination by "Socinian moonlight." [10] In the prose of his Unitarian period, Coleridge attacked specifically those clergymen closest to the person and policies of Pitt, Bishops Horsley and Pretyman. (EOT, 46n; W, 48) As religion penetrated the soul, and government should thrust no deeper than to prickle the skin, he resented collaboration between them, especially in time of war; he shrank from the shrill *"Church and Constitution* scream" that shrieked in his schooldays and again after Waterloo. (CPW, 212:35) He may

not have made it clear to all readers of his poems that he was
directly challenging the church establishment as such, although
the first version of the *Allegoric Vision*, August, 1795, a prose
work usually included with his poems, supports the modern reader's suspicion that Superstition in Coleridge's early poems stalked
fiendishly in the ceremonial cloth of the Church of England,
searching for tithes and fields of slaughter. The alert editor of
Coleridge's notebooks has caught in an early entry, "The Devil
drest in black everlasting—ergo—not a sans culotte," its implication that the Devil wears the black of class distinction. (CN,
69n) More specifically, the Devil wears the sable of the "aristocratic," that is Pittite, clergy. In the *Conciones* Coleridge blamed
the rioting against Priestley and other Unitarians of Birmingham
primarily on "sable-vested Instigators." (EOT, 14) He published
in the *Watchman* a sonnet from a congenial contributor in Liverpool that closed with the vision of an approaching scene when
"Despots, Priests and Peers, in one proud ruin lie." (W, 164)

French excesses, and all that pertained thereto, and even more
perhaps his sense that he lived as a parasite, drove Coleridge
toward affection for bishop, baron, and king, but his distrust of
commercial wealth long outlived his expression in verse of fellow-
feeling with brothers shriveled by ignorance and "parching Poverty." (CPW, 185:7) His own poverty, parching enough, kept
him tenderly sympathetic for twenty years after he had ceased
to consider the commercially wealthy as part of a conspiracy of
power united under Pitt. At a satanically proud eminence, those
through whose veins ran the genuinely polluted blood of gentility
had been joined by the war's "aristocrats," the wealthy, the pow-
dered and groomed, the voluntary subscribers to war loans, up-
holders of Pitt, followers of the least erected Spirit that fell from
heaven. It is not merely conventional sermonizing against the
mammonite when the poet imagines in *Reflections on Having Left
a Place of Retirement* that the wealthy son of Bristol commerce
slaked somewhat his "thirst of idle gold" merely by looking on
Coleridge's idyllic cottage. (CPW, 106:13) He had a religious,
political, and reasoned abhorrence of the effects of trade on British
life. Enumerating the national sins in *Fears in Solitude*, he came
to a bad one: "We have drunk up, demure as at a grace, Pollutions

from the brimming cup of wealth." (CPW, 258:59–60) The war itself, he often said, was a "panic of property."

From his college months on, he counted among the evidences of commercial excess in England the enormity of the slave trade. According to the very first article in frolicking *Blackwood's*, Porson offered to show 134 examples of bad Greek in Coleridge's Sapphic ode of 1792 on the slave trade, but the poet stuck by its sentiments. He hated slavery before he read Thomas Clarkson; he needed a treatise of Clarkson's only one day before lecturing on the slave trade in Bristol; [11] and he praised Clarkson more than once before their friendship began. Between 1794 and 1799 he wrote lines against "Afric's wrongs" into at least one poem every year. (CPW, 165:88) He linked slavery with impressment for war as murder done continuously under national guidance and responsibility. It is useless to speculate on the details of a lost stanza concerning Ministerial complicity in the compelling of black men into slavery, the stanza that Stuart did not print when *France: An Ode* first appeared in the *Morning Post;* fortunately it led by figurative contrast in the succeeding stanza to one of Coleridge's finest denunciations of the French, as "Slaves by their own compulsion!" (CPW, 247:86) Later he was to express in expansive ways his sense of slavery as any "perversion of a Person into a Thing"; his early poems condemn a known abomination.

He did not regard commerce as the worst of evils, or even an evil at all if controlled for the public good. He charged against Pitt's war in 1795 that it had produced a "distressful stagnation of trade and commerce" and thrown thousands out of employ. (EOT, 38, 47) Yet neither disinterested benevolence nor personal envy accounts substantially for Coleridge's repulsion from "Bristowa's citizen." (CPW, 106:12) As fundamental as his sympathy with the oppressed, his distrust of commercial enterprise and disbelief in absolute property bound the effusions of his earliest creative years to the essays of his maturity in defense of Church and gentry. A much-reprinted work by the conservative Adam Ferguson of Edinburgh, *An Essay on the History of Civil Society*, had deplored the increasing glorification of commerce "as the great object of nations, and the principal study of mankind." (6th ed., 1793, p. 93) Excessive attention to commerce results in the preferring of individual claims, and not in subordination of the individual to the public good, as accepted and practiced by the ancients. Coleridge built one wall of his social philosophy upon this stone. A sense of the demoralizing power of commerce did not merely survive as a relic of his republican enthusiasms; it rested deeper than those enthusiasms, and probably antedated them, as a material of his humane faith in the sacredness of the human soul. Property could never be sacred, although the trust in which it was held might be. The intricate analysis in his second Lay Sermon finds a chief source of the current distress of the poor, and one source of the decline and distress of intellectuals like himself, in the overbalance of the commercial spirit. *On the Constitution of the Church and State* notably continues his effort to influence the structure of society by placing counterweights against commercial power. Various marginalia written late in life show that to the end he regarded not merely real estate but all private property as a trust. Ever since F. W. Maitland fired on the doctrines of *Church and State* in 1875, they have leaked like a sieve; [12] but Maitland objected to Coleridge's attitude toward property only on the grounds that the trend of history was totally against him. It was exactly the commercial trend that Coleridge set himself morally against. Its growth does not prove him wrong.

In *The Friend* Coleridge declared: "From my earliest manhood, it was an axiom in politics with me, that in every country where property prevailed, property must be the grand basis of the government; and that that government was the best, in which the power or political influence of the individual was in proportion to his property, provided that the free circulation of property was not impeded by any positive laws or customs, nor the tendency of wealth to accumulate in abiding masses unduly encouraged." (F, II, 27) The growth of this famous definition makes a story too complex to be told here, but in earliest manhood Coleridge made several reservations, some explicit and some secret. He felt justified in his reservations because property under George III and Pitt could neither circulate nor remain secure, and because his definition does not concern the ideal but merely the actual governments among "the present race of men." (EOT, 331, 551; CL, 214, 721, 765)

In 1794–96 he believed that those people would be happier who lived where property did not prevail. Pantisocracy provided one of the classic solutions to the problem of private property: abolition. What was desirable, as Godwin had shown, was equalization. But the second of Coleridge's theological lectures of 1795 argued the necessity of equal distribution of property even if the abolition of private estates were necessary to obtain it. (CN, 81n) Although no democrat, he was a communist, because property could be equalized much more easily than people. He was no Jacobin, for he based his communism not on equal rights but on the sympathy of the enlightened. The Pantisocratic scheme involved much more than communal ownership of property, however, and must be viewed in a wider context of political and personal feelings.

CHAPTER V

Pantisocracy

and the Dawn in France

> In expectation of emigrating on the
> Pantisocratic Plan I payed my ad-
> dresses to a young Lady . . . .
> —Coleridge in February, 1795

> Southey! Pantisocracy is not the Ques-
> tion—it's realization is distant—per-
> haps a miraculous Millenium—[*sic*]
> —Coleridge in August, 1795

The generative forces in Pantisocracy included personal elements
of reaction and withdrawal. Among Coleridge's poems as in his
life there are discrete clusters of surge and recoil. Some of his
blank verse retreats with sighs of contentment; several of his odes
take the field and assault. The separation occurred biographically.
Journalistic activity and political anger aggravated his emotional
turbulence until he recoiled. The recoils left a poetic record in
the clustered dreams of peace and calm. The need to withdraw
from the immediate confusions of his personal life in 1794 helped
to form the utopian calm of the Pantisocratic dream. Watering the
tender seeds of Southey's and George Burnett's plan for a communistic community in the new world, Coleridge lodged his previously rather diffuse dreams in the vale of Pantisocracy. Lines
To a Young Lady with a Poem on the French Revolution, variously
applied at various times but appropriately offered to Miss Brunton

with a copy of *The Fall of Robespierre*, trace the rousing of the poet's pensive, pitying soul when Freedom "With giant Fury burst her triple chain." Rising to the exultation with which he once gave his soul to the Revolution, the lines progress to the heartache of the poet at the fall of the Oppressor, "though Mercy struck the blow." Spent by the excitement, he seeks utopian calm: "With wearied thought once more I seek the shade . . . ." (CPW, 65:18, 28–29) The S-curve begun in pensiveness, and continued in exultation and weariness, turns for fulfillment toward the shaded calm of Pantisocracy.

Although he visualized the ultimate reformation of Europe, Coleridge's direct aims were more reasonable, limited, and negative than most critics apparently believe. Pantisocracy has been often described, with only seven-tenths truth, as absent-mindedly erected on sentimental faith in the positive powers of Nature and the natural goodness of man. Its negative elements have not been sufficiently stressed. The immediate values expected of the experiment were not contingent upon its ultimate success or failure in reforming society. It aimed first to reduce the temptation of greed, among a few choice but fallible Englishmen, to the lowest minimum practicable. As an experiment for some twelve couples, the plan envisioned by Coleridge additionally combined the several aims of domestic repose, fraternal love, knowledge, equality not merely of rights but of condition, agricultural industriousness in a rural valley, and health. Health was only possible—and therefore treated as inevitable—where knowledge and industry could combine and neither poverty nor riches would intrude. Although fearful of selfishness like Southey's, Coleridge unfortunately did not allow at all for "unmotivated" egoistic weakness like his own.

The initial means much resembled the ultimate aim: bucolic bliss. The emotional and theoretical materials lay at hand. First, let there be no debate about Coleridge's temporary acceptance of a theory where means and aim united: common ownership of land. Southey defined Coleridge's aspheterism as "the generalization of individual property." [1] The Gutch Memorandum Book, which notes that the present organization of society violates the principle that property should "secure to every man the produce of his Toil," lists among projected works: "Pantisocracy, or a practical Essay on the abolition of indiv[id]ual Property." [2]

In all editions of *Political Justice,* Godwin recommended that accumulations of wealth be equalized, but he warned sternly against any expropriation whatsoever. For self-preservation one may justly delay the payment of debts, but only in the emergencies of bare existence would one be justified in taking by force what another has earned, accumulated, or inherited. Like Coleridge, Godwin regarded landed property as a trust, but to Godwin each of us must regard the other man's trust as sacred. How then could the equalization of property come about? Godwin, who distrusted the state and deplored all associations as subversive of independent reason, had one answer for all questions: the slow education of individual judgments. We must educate until the rich man sees the unreasonableness of excessive riches. Pantisocracy accepted the more feasible solution of common ownership. Coleridge, then, was not following Godwin.

In studying the influence of Pantisocracy on his poems, a distinction can be maintained between the microcosm of the practical experiment and the universe of the utopian dream. Pantisocracy as an experiment has a smaller place in Coleridge's poems than the utopian dream that was to have "aspheterized the Bounties of Nature." (CL, 84) And yet the project of 1794 arose among ideas concerning sympathy, benevolence, natural goodness, Necessity, and fraternity by then common among second-rate minds and popularized by fourth-rate writers. Once contemplate a belief such as Locke's that the minimum of government is best, accept conversion to a necessitarian faith like Priestley's that social improvement is inevitably consequent upon the individual's cultivation of benevolence (a faith that came to final English flower in George Eliot), and you are ready to accept two other shared beliefs of Coleridge's youth, first that "vice is the effect of error and the offspring of surrounding circumstances," and second that a practical if distant goal for Europeans is the perfect society. (EOT, 28) You hardly notice that you have described the source of vice in the terms of a believer in natural goodness. You postpone a conclusion on whether or not man is naturally good, certainty seems not to be needed on this point, because you believe that institutions as constituted are bad, that the Londoners you have seen could be improved, and that sympathy is basic in human psychology, as Hume, Hutcheson, Hartley, and Priestley agree. So

Coleridge. Without his gentleness and the hunger of his affections for an answering affection, the doctrine of sympathy would none-theless have taught him to call all men, as in lyric and reflective poems of 1795–98, his "brethren." All are fraternal sons of one God. He could avoid the personal embrace of individuals. With his passionate determination to find the will of a benevolent God at work in all things, he kept very busy arguing optimistically, as in *Religious Musings*, that all apparent evils serve in a chain of causation for ultimate good; and even if all men were naturally evil, their wickedness would be used by God for the ultimate good of man. Such was the necessitarian modification of Mandeville's praise of private vices.

While absorbing much of the current revolutionary spirit, Cole-ridge rejected or qualified nearly all its elements when he re-garded them individually. He considered progress inevitable only when he thought about it abstractly. He considered men natu-rally good until he thought about them. Allowing for three years of gradual retraction, and for his desire to placate his guardian brother, the cautious George, the following passage of March, 1798, probably represents something not far from Coleridge's considered view at the noontide of Pantisocracy: "Of GUILT I say nothing; but I believe most stedfastly in original Sin; that from our mothers' wombs our understandings are darkened; and even where our understandings are in the Light, that our organiza-tion is depraved, & our volitions imperfect; and we sometimes see the good without *wishing* to attain it, and oftener *wish* it without the energy that wills & performs—" (CL, 396)

If Coleridge never believed whole-mindedly in a general theory of Progress, as he did for a time aggressively believe in the more rigid doctrine of Necessity, he retained a hope and faith in the improvement of society throughout his life, as do most men who continue to publish concerning society's problems. In 1795 he spoke hopefully of political progress under the Constitution. (EOT, 68) Thereafter he hoped for Constitutional progress de-creasingly, but not steadily so, rather with flare-ups whenever a sharpening of antagonism between classes accompanied unusually obvious signs of poverty, as in 1816–17. When he read Malthus' sizable essay on "Population as it affects the Future Improvement of Society," in 1798, and examined the problems Malthus had raised, Coleridge conjectured that "the march of the Human Race" might be cyclic rather than linear. (CL, 518) The Pantisocrats of a few years earlier had planned a contribution to linear advance.

All-benevolent Nature under various guises exacted the tribute of worshipful praise from most articulate Englishmen of the day, not totally exempting even Bentham. The movement back to Nature produced simple, progressive Unitarian meeting-houses and, a little later, atavistic, encrusted Gothic churches. On his way to adopting one of the extremer primitivistic theories, the common eighteenth-century reader first saw the value of withdrawing from the noisy, threatening city in order to think. Man, observed Goldsmith sadly, made the city; Nature stayed in the country. However diverse, all primitivists wanted London unmade. Pantisocracy, looking like a temple to Nature, rose partly from the need to exorcise the diabolical forces of the city. Convinced by Hartleian psychology that the mental associations of the child determine the moral character and nearly all else of the adult (as his monolithic friend was soon to put it, "The child is father of the man"), Coleridge wished to gather a few enlightened, benevolent fathers together in a rural setting so that their children would develop as far removed as possible from men in their civilized, fallen state. Even after meeting Wordsworth, Coleridge seems to have been more intent on staying away from the city than on living in the country for its own sake. Four versions of the poem On Revisiting the Sea-Shore, of 1801, ask what Nature cares if "Fashion's pining Sons and Daughters" drown, since they "love the city's gilded Sty." [3]

Pantisocracy gave Coleridge a practical interest in the cost and arability of land near the Susquehanna, and in the degree of immunity from attack by Indians. Professor MacGillivray once stressed the practicality of Coleridge's attention to Brissot, Priestley, Thomas Cooper, and others who had recently planned settlements along the Susquehanna. Other scholars have emphasized the idyllic elements in works on the New World by Brissot and other Girondists, where geographic and political idyls combined, and their similarity to the idyllic "American" ideals of equality, peace, and hope in the Quaker journal of John Woolman. [4] Coleridge saw and considered the practical problems, but lived the idyl, which had more poetry in it.

Yet Coleridge renounced geographic primitivism in one of its extreme but common forms, belief in the noble savage. He had read with attention too many exotic books of travel not to notice that even in the most ecstatic primitivistic accounts the savage usually lived unaware in stench and disease and that the neighbor or visitor, whether pale-faced or native-hued, could get scalped. Even Hoxie N. Fairchild's *The Noble Savage* exonerated Coleridge from belief in the perfection of primitive life. Fairchild cited an unsentimental observation in a letter from Coleridge to Southey, 21 October 1794, concerning Pantisocracy: "Wherever Men *can* be vicious, some *will* be." (CL, 114; Fairchild, p. 197) More to the immediate point, in lines on the wheel of Fortune whose first known appearance is the volume of 1796, Coleridge says that fit retribution for "the sanguinary Despot" would be "to wander in some savage isle." (CPW, 90:20) One of his masters, Priestley, had pointed out that much more progress could be gained by art than by the "idleness, treachery, and cruelty" of uncivilized states.[5] In the spirit of Priestley's observation, Coleridge depicted tired savages living in the ferocity of primitive nature and rousing themselves only when invited by European villains to banquet on the blood of civilized settlers.[6]

The Foster-Mother's Tale, from the play *Osorio*, may possibly contain unconscious autobiography, or, slightly more likely, it may embody a self-examination consciously ironical. The narrator tells how an old woodman raised at his master's cost a foundling, who grew up a "pretty boy, but most unteachable." (CPW, 183:29) And yet he learned the names and ways of birds and flowers; later, under tutelage from a friar, he became so learned that at twenty he had "heretical and lawless" thoughts. When he communicated unholy ideas to the young Lord Velez, the earth heaved under them, and Velez was seized with fever. In consequence, the foundling was thrown into the dungeon of the Velez castle. When he sang there a doleful song about the enviably sweet life of a naked man at liberty "on lake or wild savannah," a servant made possible his escape on a voyage to discover "golden lands." A companion told how the youth,

In spite of his dissuasion, seiz'd a boat,
And all alone, set sail by silent moonlight
Up a great river, great as any sea,
And ne'er was heard of more: but 'tis suppos'd,
He liv'd and died among the savage men.

(184:77–81)

The tale certainly does not represent simple primitivism. In context within the play it contrasts two uses of the heart, for injustice and for justice. Its inner point, I believe, is that the simple child of physical nature, taken suddenly from his naturalism and thrust into the entanglements of religious and metaphysical speculation, uttered impieties out of his consequent insanity. He "read, and read, and read, Till his brain turn'd." Unjust imprisonment by the piously superstitious Lord Velez helped turn the unfortunate's disordered thoughts toward liberty, which was obviously not to be found in civilized Spain but according to his reading was available among noble savages in the New World. When permitted to escape by an act of benevolence, the "poor mad youth," it is supposed, "liv'd and died among the savage men." Insane, he would not perceive the inconveniences of untutored life.

In the ode addressed to the Duchess of Devonshire, Coleridge called her what he believed himself and all true lovers of Liberty to be, "free Nature's uncorrupted child." (CPW, 336:19) As his letters show, he believed his genius to be a natural gift and his heart to have been preserved, through vigilance, from urban taint. But his poems emphasize the opposite view. Repeatedly they contrast his own unnatural childhood at Christ's Hospital, pent in the dark city, with the rural light and freedom vouchsafed to the Wordsworths and Hutchinsons, and guaranteed, despite all satanic efforts from publishers to lure the father into the flames of London, to the son Hartley. The father has become again a child of Nature, but not from rearing. Justly famous lines addressed to Charles Lamb, *This Lime-Tree Bower My Prison*, doubly invert the normal contrast. Lamb, a former Bluecoat boy still pent in the city, daily chained to a clerical stool in the India House, on this one day walks abroad storing beauties and feelings from Nature for future strength, while emancipated Coleridge today sits imprisoned. Yet the poet has learned from the confinement, otherwise vexatious, how Nature has earlier taught his heart to contemplate the beauties his unconfined friends are now enjoying, and to notice the details of leaf and stem that can give joy within the narrowest plot, "be but Nature there." (CPW, 180:50, 61) The city will be a prison only so long as Nature is excluded.

Under Pantisocratic conditions, knowledge and industry would beget what Coleridge in 1794 already lacked, health. For health he would accept a limited, imperfect settlement in Wales. When the plan for a community dissolved in a Welsh cloud, he retained for about five years the ideal of living near the western border of England and raising food out of the ground, with a minimum of animal flesh, to preserve the health and innocence of his own family. The wealthy son of commerce from Bristol could see that Coleridge's cottage at Clevedon, in the "Valley of Seclusion," was "a Blessèd Place." (CPW, 106:17) Blessedness in a valley links this passage to the larger utopian dream. In contrast, although the impulses to find a fairer climate in 1801 made him recall to Southey "the blessed Dreams, we dreamt some 6 years ago," I think the impulses had then become almost totally negative urges to escape bodily pains, nausea, opium, wife, and self. (CL, 728)

Within the poetic cluster of Nature, peace, and calm, Pantisocracy appeared in five of Coleridge's poems as a quiet vale, enclosing toil, health, love, peace, and "mild Equality."[7] A sixth poem included among Coleridge's works in 1907 and 1912 with a query, *On the Prospect of Establishing a Pantisocracy in America,* contains no vale, and there are other internal signs that Coleridge is not its author. (CPW, 69)

The most noteworthy and notorious poem inspired by Pantisocratic fraternity is *To a Young Ass.* The most remarkable fact about his acknowledging the poem as his own is not that it appears in all collections published by Coleridge except *Sibylline Leaves* —which is notable—but that he continued to publish a sober version although the earliest known manuscript ends in burlesque. This manuscript I have not seen, but the apparent errors of E. H. Coleridge can be checked against the transcription by J. D. Campbell and the earlier description of the manuscript that appeared in *Chanticleer,* the magazine of Jesus College, for Easter, 1891. (pp. 22–24; JDC, 477) Coleridge gave it to William Smyth, poet and Whig, a Fellow of Peterhouse, who was later to rise under the patronage of Lord Henry Petty to popularity as university

Professor of Modern History. One might speculate that Coleridge first wrote a version now lost, in serious, sentimentally humanitarian fraternity with the ass, and then responded to ridicule by making burlesque alterations. Possibly; but subsequent years of public ridicule as acknowledged brother to an ass did not make him withdraw or alter it. Lamb, whose suggestions for revision Coleridge frequently accepted and whose criticism seems to have led (as noted earlier) to the suppression of "scoundrel Monarch" from the last line, had no larger effect, unless he brought about a change in the order of poems, when he asked in February, 1797, if the ass were not "too trivial a companion for the Religious Musings." (LL, I, 96)

The version with elements of burlesque bore as its heading: "Monologue to a Young Jack Ass in Jesus Piece. Its mother near it chained to a log." The poem fitted the heading. Later versions described the Dell, to which the ass would be invited, as containing Peace, Toil, Health, "mild Equality," Laughter, and Plenty, but no longer explicitly named it Pantisocracy, a coinage Coleridge would have thought forgotten. Instead of the final family of personifications, the October version described in burlesque the Dell

> Where high-soul'd Pantisocracy shall dwell!
> Where Mirth shall tickle Plenty's ribless side,
> And smiles from Beauty's Lip on sun-beams glide,
> Where Toil shall wed young Health that charming Lass!
> And use his sleek cows for a looking-glass—
> Where Rats shall mess with Terriers hand-in-glove
> And Mice with Pussy's Whiskers sport in Love!
>
> (CPW, 75n; JDC, 478)

To the line about smiles gliding on sunbeams (and not to the preceding line, as indicated by E. H. Coleridge), the author appended a note in the same spirit: "This is a truly poetical line, of which the Author has assured us, that he did not *mean* it to have any *meaning.*—Ed." The mood of this version is reproduced at the close of a letter to Francis Wrangham, written the same day:

If there be any whom I deem worthy of remembrance—I am their Brother. I call even my Cat Sister in the Fraternity of universal Nature. Owls I respect & Jack Asses I love: for Aldermen & Hogs, Bishops & Royston Crows

I have not particular partiality—; they are my Cousins however, at least by Courtesy. But Kings, Wolves, Tygers, Generals, Ministers, and Hyaenas, I renounce them all—or if they *must* be my kinsmen, it shall be in the 50th Remove—May the Almighty Pantisocratizer of Souls pantisocratize the Earth, and bless you and

S. T. Coleridge!—

(CL, 121)

E. K. Chambers, who deserves the special gratitude of all who despise Coleridge, said specifically of lines quoted from the version of October: "There is no evidence that he wrote in irony." (EKC, 32) The evidence of the manuscript in fact suggests that the two chief ironies of the poem were designed by Coleridge as at least partially comic. The poem presents to the reader the irony, comic or not, that the extreme sadness of the ass may come not from its own miserable lot or anticipation of the worsening lot that awaits it, but from pity for its more strictly chained mother, and the related irony that the master of the pair has not learned from his own very similar state of oppression, "Half famish'd in a land of Luxury," to pity his fellow beasts of burden. (CPW, 75:22) Even when reduced to the inhuman level of a jackass, the man has less pity than the jackass has. The core of the poem is serious, I think, even in the October version; it prefigures "the one Life within us and abroad." (CPW, 101:26) In no version, however, are its exaggerations of humanitarian sympathy to be taken solemnly. As 1795 began, Coleridge promised Southey to come from London to his fiancée in a wagon: "There are four or five Calves Inside—Passengers like myself—I shall fraternize with them! The folly & vanity of young men who go in Stage Coaches!" (CL, 148) If he had had cash enough, he would have ridden in a coach—if not to Bristol or Bath, then somewhere else —but he feels a genuine fraternity more with calves than with wealthy, vain young men. The poem is not distant in spirit from this letter.

Coleridge later protested that the *Young Ass* "might be called a ludicro-splenetic Copy of Verses, with the diction purposely appropriate." (CL, III, 433) For once the manuscripts support him against the common assumption that everybody saw the joke except the author of it. Cleared of the more obvious elements of burlesque, the version submitted to Cottle (preserved in the

manuscript album at Rugby School) introduced a new touch of
the ridiculous: its poet would fain take the ass "in the Dell Of
lofty-soul'd Isocracy to dwell." Euclidean equality gave way in
turn to the more tranquil "mild Equality." Daring as Coleridge's
identification of man with ass now seems, he was not alone in
making it. The author of *Lewesdon Hill*, whose political valor
Coleridge celebrated in the *Watchman*, published a dryly ironic
analogue, *Inscribed beneath the Picture of an Ass*. This author,
William Crowe, admits no surprise that the erroneous crowd
should associate folly with the "despised race" of the ass, since
the same crowd throws "impious howlings in Heaven's awful
face." [8] Implicit comparison of an ass with Heaven is as bold as
the original reference to a scoundrel monarch at the end of Coleridge's address to an ass.

At least a kind of courage belongs to Coleridge's continued reprinting of the poem, as a Biblical flaunting of the wisdom of
this world. To offer an ass a place as brother in the vale of equality,
"spite of the fool's scorn," challenges most of us to be scornful
fools, but the lines are politically intelligible: they called attention to a political proposition by exaggerating it deliberately, in
much the same way that the Ancient Mariner's killing of the albatross and blessing of the water-snakes exaggerate a related metaphysical and religious proposition. (CPW, 75:26) In the slighter
poem Coleridge is not arguing metaphysically that we are joined
in divinely plastic and organic brotherhood with ass and snake,
where an albatross may be taken as a symbol of all life; although
less profoundly, he is asserting politically that Nature so desires
human brotherhood that the ass may be taken as symbol of the
downtrodden meek to whom the more fortunate should bend in
human comradeship. Renouncing all power over our fellows, we
seek—in 1794—equality of condition. Political sentimentality
created much worse confusion when Coleridge added to his monody on Chatterton, at about this time, three stanzas of lamentation
that the downtrodden marvelous boy was not alive to join fellow
Pantisocrats in the Susquehanna dale, where, in lieu of his com-
radely presence, a cenotaph would be raised. The lines to an ass
state political and humanitarian principles, as the poet intended,
in an intelligible and fittingly exaggerated way, whereas the tribute
to Chatterton became less stable when Coleridge inserted auto-

biographical stanzas that thenceforward have had to be explained with biographical reference to a passing enthusiasm. A reader of the altered monody on Chatterton will conclude that a self-pitying poet, desiring escape, sought a solution theoretically political. The *Young Ass*, in both the burlesque and the soberer versions, has its own qualities built in, and must be taken on its own symbolically asinine terms, political and affective.

As the practical experiment in Pantisocracy vaporized, Coleridge conceived anew the macrocosm of the revolutionary utopia ordained by teleological Nature. *Religious Musings* contains his apocalypse: With the French Revolution the culminating storm has begun. The fifth seal of the book of final things will be opened; the Lamb of God will judge and cast to earth the Rich, the "Kings and the Chief Captains of the World," and will overthrow the scarlet woman of Babylon, who is the established union of religion with governmental power; in the following millennium the Coleridgian saints, "all who in past ages have endeavoured to ameliorate the state of man," will stride in joy, while "the vast family of Love Raised from the common earth by common toil Enjoy the equal produce." (CPW, 121:310, 122:341–43, 122n) Although in quieter vein, the Pantisocratic millennium became also the New Jerusalem as Coleridge concluded his praise of the low cottage at Clevedon in *Reflections on Having Left a Place of Retirement*:

> Ah!—had none greater! And that all had such!
> It might be so—but the time is not yet.
> Speed it, O Father! Let thy Kingdom come!
> (CPW, 108:69–71)

In a less utopian mood of April, 1796, in fact partly to raise three guineas, Coleridge projected an essay on Count Rumford's plan for building garden cities, "a subject of importance unconnected with Politics," in which he would adapt the plan to the specific needs of Bristol, Manchester, and Birmingham. (CL, 206) The scheme was foresighted, practical, and moderate. But the economically egalitarian spirit of Pantisocracy, which aided Nature's and Rumford's call for garden cities, remained with Coleridge all his life. It imbues those lines first published at the beginning of his monody on Chatterton in 1829, asking the fear of death to avoid the poor and attend instead upon "coward Wealth and Guilt in robes of State." (CPW, 125:9) His early desire for the abolition of private property conditioned his permanent denial that the possession of property was ever absolute or total. This early social ideal fathered the utopian concept of a custodial clerisy advanced in the prose of his maturity. The idea of a clerisy can be foreseen within the spiral of history preceding the millennium in *Religious Musings,* at the creative center of change where Philosophers and Bards, hating unseemly disproportion, "Brook not Wealth's rivalry." (CPW, 117:229)

The quiet vale is directly related to the perfect society envisioned in *Religious Musings* and in the heroic closing speech by Alhadra in the play *Osorio:*

> Knew I an hundred men
> Despairing, but not palsied by despair,
> This arm should shake the kingdoms of this world;
> The deep foundations of iniquity
> Should sink away, earth groaning from beneath them;
> The strong holds of the cruel men should fall,
> Their temples and their mountainous towers should fall;
> Till desolation seem'd a beautiful thing,
> And all that were and had the spirit of life
> Sang a new song to him who had gone forth
> Conquering and still to conquer!
>
> (CPW, 596:311–21)

Outside the Pantisocratic vale, Nature continued to labor for man's quiet, or, when Coleridge changed the metaphor, continued in labor for the birth of twins, Equality and Peace.[9] For convenience to his verse he usually made Nature present her social and political lessons through trinities. At the beginning of 1797, for example, in contrast with the cruelty of man's dungeons, Nature heals with "melodies of woods, and winds, and waters." (CPW, 587:130) In what may appear to be paradox but is not, the need to pluralize his expression of awe for Nature issued from the thirst for Romantic unity, as a famous letter to Thelwall illustrates: "My mind feels as if it ached to behold & know something *great*—something *one & indivisible*—and it is only in the faith of this that rocks or waterfalls, mountains or caverns give me the sense of sublimity or majesty!—But in this faith *all things* counterfeit infinity!—" (CL, 349) Prose here splits nature into four phenomena, but in English verse the phrasal grouping between pauses favors the tradition of mystic trinities.

The Coleridgian trinities of Nature, like the land, sea, and sky of the United States Marine Corps, confirm not only the strength but equally the metaphysical rightness of the polity involved. Nature also gave both metaphysical and metaphorical support in the equation of revolution with sunrise. For about five years this equation appeared frequently, indeed monotonously, in Coleridge's political verse. I find no factual basis for the otherwise attractive theory recently advanced by J. B. Beer, in *Coleridge the Visionary*, that the symbolism of light in the early poems derives from cabalistic and Neoplatonic writings, although Coleridge's metaphor begins metaphysically in the identity of light with perfection: God, divine Wisdom, Love, the Logos. Within the first hundred lines of *Religious Musings*, the light that enrobes the regenerate, when dark passions pass from them, prefigures the passing of dark night from the reforming earth. (CPW, 112:87–93) Further on, to know ourselves part of one wondrous whole is our "noontide Majesty." (113:127) At the close of the poem, the post-millennial blaze of God's throne comes like dawn after stormy darkness. As a budding poet, Coleridge had often recorded the attractions of sunrise and sunset. Among his earliest poetic tools, the diurnal cycle used metaphorically had given a degree of structural unity to juvenile verses. The nine "Songs of the Pixies" progress from dawn to dawn. In one early poem, the sun that sets among stormy clouds of melancholy will rise in brightness. (CPW, 90:5–8) The political poems fluctuate between versions of this slack metaphor, whereby the sun of hope reveals social progress and reform, and a tauter metaphysical identity of light and political reform.

Far from being Coleridge's by undisputed natural right, the metaphor had established itself all over Europe, in descent from one of man's most primitive symbols, as a part of the divine right of kings. Thomas Sprat, to be sure, had momentarily captured it from monarchy in his famous Cowleyan ode on the death of Cromwell: "Thou, the great Sun, gav'st light to every star." [10] Then to Europe came *le roi-soleil*, Louis XIV, and a galaxy of enlightened despots. For Coleridge's use, Freedom by more recent elevation had become one of the divine attributes. His poems sent this new sun higher. Freedom burns with divine Light as brightly as the divine sun: the reign of complete freedom among men will bring the blaze of noon. Meanwhile, with noon inevitable, revolution struggles into dawn. Coleridge represented his metaphorical norm justly by a review of his earlier apostrophes in a summarizing couplet of *France: An Ode:* "Ye storms, that round the dawning East assembled, The Sun was rising, though ye hid his light!" He had avowed in the preceding stanza: "For ne'er, O Liberty! . . . I dimmed thy light or damped thy holy flame." In the first stanza the metaphor had completed a circle; the rising sun (of Freedom) had *freed* itself for the dawn: "Yea, every thing that is and will be free!" (CPW, 244:18, 245:39–40, 47–48)

The sestet of the sonnet *Pantisocracy* intensifies the usual simile: eyes that ached with sorrow will now, at dawn in the vale, be cleansed by tears of joy, like the eyes of one who awakens suddenly at sunrise from the precipice of a terrifying dream. (CPW, 69) Soon again, staggering from the nightmares of *The Fall of Robespierre,* Coleridge encountered in his imagination a light more troubled than the arc of the sun. In the lines to accompany a copy of the play, Freedom has burst forth with the scorching Dog Star, Sirius, glowing fiercely on her forehead; her banners flow "like a midnight meteor." (CPW, 65:20) Coleridge continued to vary the milder but steadier metaphor. When the Archduke Charles Louis of Austria turned back the French at the Rhine in 1796, Pitt's ministry was mad enough to think the sun would stop rising, but the bard knew better: "One cloud, O Freedom! cross'd thy orb of Light." [11] Quite simply, his metaphor said over and over that God favored rapid reform.

A few disillusioning years later Coleridge could not let the revolutionary metaphors go unqualified. In *Thoughts Occasioned by Dr. Parr's Spital Sermon,* 1801, Godwin declared that a few men, by watching with exultation while the Revolution cleared away old abuses, had "worshiped the rising sun." On Lamb's copy, now in the British Museum, Coleridge wrote, during or just after the Peace of 1802: "No! it was the discord & contradictory ferment of old abuses & recent indulgences or connivances—the heat & light of Freedom let in on a half-cleared, rank soil, made twilight by the black fierce Reek, which this Dawn did itself draw up.—" (B.M. C.45.f.18.[3], p. 3)

Late in life it was not political progress dated from 1789, or even from Perceval, but religious enlightenment from the Reformation onward, that drew the poet back to the morning arc of the sun, at the close of *Lines Suggested by the Last Words of Berengarius:*

> The ascending day-star with a bolder eye
> Hath lit each dew-drop on our trimmer lawn!
> Yet not for this, if wise, shall we decry
> The spots and struggles of the timid Dawn;
> Lest so we tempt th' approaching Noon to scorn
> The mists and painted vapours of our Morn.
>
> (CPW, 461:30–35)

The intellect now lighted further detail, as of "our trimmer lawn"; but the glow of passion had gone with the setting of the revolutionary orb. And yet the poet's defense of "recreant Berengare" bears a nostalgic glimmer of political apology for a youth not altogether misspent in "spots and struggles." In his late forties, when he did not mind translating a Hebrew elegy upon the death of George III, Coleridge had the self-consciousness to explain dryly in a note that "the Crown, the Peerage, and the Commonalty" were represented as sun, moon, and stars, "in the spirit of Hebrew Poetry." (CPW, 436n) This has somewhat the air of meaning "in the Pickwickian sense." For it can be said of the commonplace identifications of light with wisdom and sunrise with hope, at the very least, that politics united them in Coleridge's verse when he was most hopeful of the dawn.

The importance of intellect and science to Coleridge's vision of political change, along with his poetic and private character, can be seen by contrasting his metaphors of increasing light with Byron's typical symbols for the future: a great crushing tide, as in the Appendix to *The Two Foscari;* or the sequence of aroused popular violence in *Don Juan,* too intricate to be used more than once, beginning in the unruliness of a galled jade, progressing to the flinging of pebbles at Goliath, and arriving finally at "the tug of war" without gentlemanly code or limitation of weapons. (DJ VIII:50–51)

When Coleridge turned directly to the actual Revolution in France, which accounted for the stormy weather in the almanac of perfectibility, he first regarded it as no less divine than the sun but soon found it far less steady in brilliance. In France, according to one poem, "slumbering Freedom," in company with giant Fury, "burst her triple chain." (CPW, 65:17–18) In a sonnet, Gallic Liberty is as fierce in victory as Minerva, yet it is not from the pagan head of Jove that she sprang; she "from the Almighty's bosom leapt With whirlwind arm, fierce Minister of Love!" (CPW, 90:9–10) That is, she represents the birth not so much of reason as of benevolence, conceived in patriotic passion and herself as passionate as the goddess of narrower love. Aroused by Wordsworth's recollections, Coleridge reminds himself in 1807, in the poem on *The Prelude*, that in France "Hope sprang forth like a full-born Deity!" (CPW, 405:37) Too soon she was made to travel monarchic ways.

Some of Coleridge's expressions of belief about Liberty and the French Revolution can be lifted intact out of the poems. Others might be called poetic beliefs, in the sense that they constitute experience as embodied in a poem, and cannot be removed and restated except by adulteration. Still another group of expressions can be left in place, but because of ambiguity, sometimes accidental, sometimes ingenious, could (and can) be reinterpreted to fit changing beliefs and external circumstances. Such an expression occurs in the second stanza of the *Ode on the Departing Year:* "Still echoes the dread Name that o'er the earth Let slip the storm, and woke the brood of Hell." (CPW, 161:33–34) As the poem of 1796 demonstrably meant to say, the dread name of "divinest Liberty" (line 37) awoke the monarchs of the Continent and their sinful paymaster, Britain, excoriated throughout the poem and here responsible for "the brood of Hell." A footnote of 1803, identifying the "dread Name," reproached the Revolutionists along with the monarchists: "The Name of Liberty, which at the commencement of the French Revolution was both the occasion and the pretext of unnumbered crimes and horrors." (CPW, 161n) In 1796 even this footnote, had it appeared then, would have seemed just ambiguous enough to be legally unactionable, at the same time a sympathetic reader of Coleridge would have imputed all the crimes, whether arising by pretext or by occasion, to the enemies of France. Even concerning the Terror, Coleridge's review in 1798 seems to accept the thesis that Paris actually had treason (and that not Robespierre's) to stamp out: "Domestic treason, crushed beneath her fatal stamp, Writhed like a wounded dragon in his gore." (CPW, 246:56–57) Perhaps the lines approve, as Coleridge certainly approved, the stamping down of royalist insurrections in the Vendée. In a vehement, driving ode he did not need to specify that he had blamed Pitt and the Jacobins equally (or rather alternately) for the ferocity of slaughter in the Vendée and Brittany. (EOT, 11, 37, 170)

The perplexing stanzas of *Lines Composed in a Concert-Room* combine allegiance to Nature and the natural with topical allusions that suggest Jacobinical excess. (CPW, 324) Until the date of the poem has been fixed, however, its allusions cannot be explained. (See Appendix D.) Coleridge's movement toward Jacobinism is more apparent there than the restraining doubts that grew stronger and stronger after 1796. He supported the Revolution almost solely on principles: personal and civil liberties, intellectual freedom and responsibility of the individual, justice up to the point where sympathy required charity, opposition to hereditary privilege, national self-determination, peace, the sacredness of human life. By the blasphemous Feast of Reason —without a flow of soul—the Revolutionists offended both his piety and his belief in sympathy and affection as the springs of everything good in human action. They used unnecessary force, as condemned in the Moors of *Osorio* by the faithful Maurice:

> And ye like slaves, that have destroy'd their master,
> But know not yet what freedom means; how holy
> And just a thing it is! He's a fall'n foe!
> Come, come, forgive him!
>
> (CPW, 585:76–79)

The Jacobins abused civil liberties, exercised manifold tyranny, committed murder, promoted war, began imperial expansion.

Coleridge found it especially hard to respect demagogues who fed the desire for equality. In the first act of *The Fall of Robespierre* Tallien denounces the mob-blinding, "plausible harangue" of Barrere; Adelaide and Tallien agree that the mob, "confusion's lawless sons," grow weary of the demagogue Robespierre because of his stern morality. (CPW, 496:35, 502:247) I remember only one defense of demagogues in all of Coleridge's poetry: *Religious Musings* puts the case, a classic one, of well-meaning leaders who

arouse violence beyond their power to control; fortunately, however, reflective "Philosophers and Bards," much superior to the
merely well-meaning, stand ready to create a new harmony out
of revolution's chaos:

> These on the fated day,
> When, stung to rage by Pity, eloquent men
> Have roused with pealing voice the unnumbered tribes
> That toil and groan and bleed, hungry and blind—
> These, hush'd awhile with patient eye serene,
> Still watch the mad careering of the storm;
> Then o'er the wild and wavy chaos rush
> And tame the outrageous mass, with plastic might
> Moulding Confusion to . . . perfect forms . . . .
>
> (CPW, 118:239–47)

Philosophers and sage poets must order the chaos, but the stim-
ulative, the orators who brought the chaos, had also been stung
into action, and earlier than the philosophic, by pity. Normally
Coleridge had that contempt for opportunism in politics finally
revealed in the long passage of his second lay sermon, based on
denunciations in Isaiah, Jeremiah, and Ecclesiastes, best summarized in the headlines supplied by Henry Nelson Coleridge for
the second edition: "CHARACTER / OF THE DEMAGOGUE / IN ALL
AGES / A DECEIVER, / AN INCENDIARY, / . . . / A MALIGNANT, / A
TYRANT, / A HYPOCRITE AND A SLANDERER." (1839 ed., pp. 328–36)
The ellipsis occurs because it took two pages to treat the activities
of the demagogue as incendiary.

When Coleridge tried to admire the Jacobins of England, and
the Girondists if not the Jacobins of France, demagoguery stood
in his road. Fortunately, political talent could make itself felt by
other means than demagoguery. As we are now ready to take up
poetic genres practiced by Coleridge in the order of their in-
volvement with "local and temporary" politics, we can begin appropriately enough with his sonnets on patriot heroes and their
antitypes.

CHAPTER VI

Patriot Heroes

in the Bed of Procrustes

> There are no such mighty talents necessary for
> government as some ... would make us be-
> lieve. ... Great abilities have generally, if not
> always, been employed to mislead the honest
> unwary multitude, and draw them out of the
> plain paths of public virtue and public good.
> —*Cato's Letters,* 1724

> In the first place, history, by displaying the
> sentiments and conduct of truly great men, and
> those of a contrary character, tends to inspire
> us with a taste for solid glory and real great-
> ness; and convinces us that it does not consist
> in what the generality of mankind are so eager
> in pursuit of.
> —Priestley, *Lectures on History,* 1788

> But histories incomparably more authentic
> than Mr. Hume's ... confirm by irrefragable
> evidence the aphorism of ancient wisdom, that
> nothing great was ever atchieved without en-
> thusiasm.
> —Coleridge, *The Statesman's Manual,* 1816

I

Articles and dissertations have analyzed, rather thoroughly, Romantic concepts of leadership. The Romantic poets studied lead-

ers, and it is right that we examine their views on political qualifications. Their skylarking enthusiasms for great men will justify
use of the word *hero* for the leaders they fitted into the heroic
traditions of poetry. From the true leader, the hero, they demanded the extraordinary. Although skilled himself at logistics,
Byron was not attracted to Napoleon by the Code. Nor had Wordsworth's Happy Warrior shrunk in 1806 to a sea-going administra-
tor. Romantics admired "the Great," the energetic, the "classic."
Was it merely a poetic mode colored by the straight talk of the
new science that made the Commonwealth men, students of Roman and other republics, praise their contemporaries for being
wise and heroic not specifically like Cato or Brutus but in this or
that way generally Roman or Venetian? After them Coleridge,
Wordsworth, and Byron, like the Revolutionary orators in Paris,
saw in contemporary heroes a Fairfax or a Sydney who were like
the greatest doges who were in turn veritable Romans whom the
poet can and does name.

In the transparent self-portrait, *A Tombless Epitaph,* published
in 1809, Coleridge described himself as "honouring with religious
love the Great Of elder times." (CPW, 413:7–8) Great men of the
past imbued the English air and refined the souls of worthy contemporaries. Stephen Spender's tribute to those who "left the
vivid air signed with their honour" recognizes their living presence
in the external nature they interpreted; George Eliot's "choir invisible" lived again for her in "minds made better by their presence"; for Coleridge, whose vision transcended the psychological
and ethical, the heroic dead have always inhabited a timeless
reality toward which they draw listening men of all ages. He asserts idealistically in the lines *To William Wordsworth:* "The truly
great Have all one age, and from one visible space Shed influence!" (CPW, 406:50–52)

Granted Coleridge's desire to praise, we have three pendent
questions: who his heroes were; what ideals of leadership these
heroes embodied; and what place heroes, hero-worship, and ideals
of leadership have in his poetry.

However timeless the existence of great men may be ideally,
their days as heroes to Coleridge were, with few exceptions, strictly
numbered. The gravediggers in his pantheon were busy as resur-
rectionists; the apotheosis of a newly found hero often reversed

or colored the principles on which the poet had to select a new set of tenants, usually for one or two quadrants and occasionally for his entire pantheon. Sometimes, of course, he created upheavals in the metaphysical or political or belletristic quadrants without immediately modifying the occupancy elsewhere. External forces acted, too. When Coleridge identified "a very beautiful little Woman" paying attention to him in Germany in 1798 as the daughter of "our Lord Howe's Cousin," the possessive *our* was partly political. (CL, 429) In 1794 ministerial newspapers had exalted Lord Hood, naval occupier of Toulon and Corsica— and a relative of Pitt; opposition newspapers had advanced the greater claims of Admiral Howe, inspiriting victor in the English Channel. Among many contributions to the party skirmishes that followed, Howe had awarded too little praise in his dispatches to his second in command, Lord Hood's brother.[1] Thus party politics made it easier for Coleridge to write of "our" Lord Howe. Romanticism decreed that there be heroes; international and domestic politics submitted a slate of candidates from which the Romantic could elect those who passed further scrutiny by head and heart.

With and without external pressures, Coleridge's lists of irreproachables change like those of the favorites at a race track. Allowing for differences in purpose, a few representative lists will indicate his excessive range: Milton, Priestley, Newton, and Hartley in *Religious Musings,* the last two overthrown in a note to Southey's *Joan of Arc,* probably written by Coleridge between February and August, 1795. (CPW, 122:364–71; 1112–13) La Fayette, Roland, Brissot, perhaps Vergniaud and Tallien in *The Fall of Robespierre.* (CPW, 497:56–59) Republicans Milton, Harrington, Algernon Sydney, Brutus, and Leonidas; the Cambridge hero Locke; the stubbornly independent James Burgh; Samuel Parr's rashest pupil, Joseph Gerrald, soon to die in Botany Bay; and Joan of Arc; all in 1795 when Brissot had become "a sublime visionary." (EOT, 18, 62; CPW, 132:10) Commerce-begetting Locke was making a final stand on clay feet. In the busy spring of 1796, Priestley, Franklin, Kosciusko, La Fayette, Washington, King Alfred, Sydney, Milton, Howard, Count Rumford, Hartley, apparently everybody on a list including "Brissot, Roland, Condorcet, Fayette, and Priestley," certainly George Augustus Pollen, a Cambridge man who had made good in erudition, benevolence, and Parliament, and somewhat surprisingly "that gallant officer, Sir SYDNEY SMITH." (W, 23, 87, 255, 292) Brave, theatrical Captain Smith had been captured by the French. On 1 November 1796, a day given over to Christian thinkers, Coleridge did not particularly admire Rousseau: "Bishop Taylor, Old Baxter, David Hartley & the Bishop of Cloyne [Berkeley] are *my men*." (CL, 245) And so on.

To the variability of such lists must be added, for further comprehension of the problem, Coleridge's tendency as a poet to be more faithful to a striking idea or a good phrase than to a proper name first associated with the idea or phrase. Samuel Butler, as companion to Otway and Chatterton in lines of 1790, gave way to Spenser in 1794. (CPW, 13:16–18, 126:36–38) The same lines in praise of pity and benevolence were made to describe now Chatterton and now the Man of Ross. (CPW, 57:5–7, 127:58–59; cf. 14:33–35) Part of the answer is that the lines describe Coleridge as he benevolently viewed himself, but the discrepancy remains. Before hostile witnesses in wild Wales, according to an account for Southey, Coleridge gave a toast to General Washington; at the next telling, he had given the toast to Priestley. (CL, 89, 91) His companion, Joseph Hucks, perhaps to protect Coleridge, in *A Pedestrian Tour through North Wales*, 1795, assigned the action of toasting to an unnamed Welsh democrat. (p. 25)

Any commendation of Coleridge's, short of ecstatic hero-worship as of Hartley or Wordsworth, is subject to the additional qualification, if it appears in his personal letters, that Coleridge usually adapted his sentiments to what he thought his correspondent would be pleased to have him write. On 1 November 1800 he cheerfully assured his patron, Josiah Wedgwood, that his landlord at Greta Hall could provide him with "nearly 500 volumes of our most esteemed modern Writers, such as Gibbon, Hume, Johnson, &c &c." (CL, 644) Gibbon and Johnson had seemingly risen in Coleridge's esteem since early September, when he had described the library to Godwin as containing "almost all the usual Trash of the Johnsons, Gibbons, Robertsons, &c." (CL, 619) It is noteworthy that Charles Lamb's lifelong animus against gentlemanly "*things in books' clothing*," including Gibbon, Robertson, and Hume, first appears in a letter of the previous March.

(LL, I, 177; and see Lamb's *Detached Thoughts on Books and Reading.*) An outrageous discrepancy divides Coleridge's statement to William Taylor on 25 January 1800 concerning Fox and the other leaders of his party, that "more profligate and unprincipled men never disgraced an honest cause," from his assurance to Josiah Wedgwood ten days later that "Fox possesses all the full & overflowing Eloquence of a man of clear head, clean heart, & impetuous feelings." (CL, 565, 568) But then the second passage resulted from a contrast with Pitt, and the first because Coleridge was angry with Sheridan. When aesthetic and journalistic aims are additionally injected, we approach versified praise hesitantly.

Coleridge retained through life faith in at least two heroes, Milton and the sage warrior, scholar, and demos-weighing giver of laws, Alfred the Great. Setting a pattern of strophe and antistrophe interesting for ode-writers at Oxford but scarcely usable in Cambridge, Robert Holmes had hailed in 1778 "British Alfred, patriot King." (*Alfred, an Ode, with Six Sonnets,* p. 20) It was harder to praise the "Great Father of thy people" after 1800, when Joseph Cottle diluted him in the poetically absurd epic, *Alfred.* But Coleridge had his own enthusiastic way, as when he modified lines from Samuel Daniel in order to praise "our glorious Alfred" for founding courts of equity and inventing the jury system, by which Alfred "Join'd with the King's the good man's Majesty." (CPW, 1121) Letters, political writings, and literary judgments in lectures, margins, and the crevices of books all attest Coleridge's worshipful admiration for Milton, poet, theologian, patriot. By replacing Bibliolatry with Bardolatry, Coleridge lifted Shakespeare as creator into a realm of divinity beyond the heroic. Like most pious men, he made his god uphold his own ideals. Shakespeare, said the admirer of Spencer Perceval, delighted in "those hereditary institutions which have a tendency to bind one age to another, and in that distinction of ranks, of which, although few may be in possession, all enjoy the advantages." [2] Despite this Burkian reason for praise, we may assume from evidence partly negative that the congenital admirer never apostatized from such martyrs of liberty as Algernon Sydney and William Tell. (CPW, 309, 335)

As Coleridge has been thought to praise the union of genius with judgment in Shakespeare as a form of self-adulation, and to analyze himself when he finds Hamlet a dreamer who dimly perceives the external world, a hero irresolute of will and averse to action, it might be presumed that he habitually sought heroes as mirrors of Coleridgian traits. Let us modify this presumption slightly. In his own dramas the praise of conventional virtues, adherence to truth and justice, courage and courageous action, loyalty, selflessness, and near-equanimity, was always implied and occasionally stated, even before Coleridge's political views and *Osorio* underwent revision together. Although mistaken, Velez defends Osorio for "an heroic fearlessness of danger." (CPW, 522:90) Alhadra makes a careful distinction concerning her husband: "He hath a lion's courage, But is not stern enough for fortitude." (528:242–43) A later, monarchic addition, in *Remorse*, glows with praise of Alvar's kingly visage:

> That spiritual and almost heavenly light
> In his commanding eye—his mien heroic,
> Virtue's own native heraldry!

> (CPW, 866:54–56)

As for courage, so for other virtues acceptable to Sir Walter Scott, an array of quotations from Coleridge's dramas could be mustered. This congregation of virtues belongs to a tradition larger than that of classical republicanism, through which, in part, it reached Wordsworth and Coleridge. In one of the best of the dissertations on Romantic concepts of leadership, Carl H. Edgren shows us (in confirmation of Zera S. Fink and Jane Worthington Smyser) that the Romantics believed in the classical republican virtues of frugality, modesty, simplicity, courage, love, wisdom, magnanimity, and zeal for common welfare.[3] It is equally demonstrable that Coleridge shared this heritage almost as fully with Gibbon as with Harrington.

The early poems, as well as the early prose, select for admiration less conventional virtues, all to be found in Coleridge's Cantabrigian heroic ideal, "the Patriot Sage." The first that Coleridge hailed in person was William Frend, fittingly identified in the *Dictionary of National Biography* as "reformer and scientific writer." The premium on dual activity becomes clear from Coleridge's tributes to Horne Tooke, "Patriot and Sage"; Rumford; Stanhope; Franklin; and "Priestley there, patriot, and saint, and sage." (CPW, 118:234, 123:371, 150:13) In 1799 Bonaparte had virtue as "a man of Science." (CL, 533) Coleridge took both the concept and the term "commanding genius," the dramatic yard-stick used in measuring Bonaparte, Pitt, and Washington, from Schiller's *Wallenstein;* the less commanding but twice-capable Patriot Sage is more fittingly his own. His friend William Smyth, in an *Ode to Reason: Written in 1794,* distinguished in Coleridge's manner between the "patriot hero" who goes to war for Freedom and the "patriot sage" who more locally braves the "storm of Folly's rage, and would a world have saved." (*English Lyricks* [Liverpool, 1797], p. 24) An acquaintance, S. J. Pratt, narrowed and degraded the idea of "patriot-sages" in *Bread, Or the Poor,* 1801, to designate aristocrats and men of wealth who had aided victims of enclosure by enabling them to keep a cow or a pig or to buy coal at a moderate price. (2nd ed., 1802, pp. 77–80) In the country at large, the sagacity of sages was not uniformly suspect, but the name of patriot bore an accumulation of bad meanings.

When Hume in his brief autobiography contrasts "Patriot and Courtier," he gives *patriot* its most common eighteenth-century meaning: a supporter of Parliament against the Crown. But the word acquired also the tainted connotations of cant and treason. Political cant on parade was made forever more suspicious by Dr. Johnson's rejoinder, reported by Boswell, that "Patriotism is the last refuge of a scoundrel." Already Dryden had written in *Absalom and Achitophel* that the Patriot

> Is one that would by Law supplant his Prince:
> The People's Brave, the Politician's Tool;
> Never was Patriot yet, but was a Fool.

Lines from Cowper a century later, mild and naïve in comparison with Dryden's, suggest that standard condemnation of the patriot as pretender always sprang from a live conception of the true patriot: "a band, call'd patriot for no cause But that they catch at popular applause." The tinge of insincerity found in all public patriotism had perhaps deepened from frequent association with Bolingbroke. Like Johnson, Cowper was Tory enough to find "patriotism" excessive when far short of John Wilkes's; any de-fender of the revolution in America was one for whom, as Cowper made him declare in *The Modern Patriot,* "civil broils are my delight." It is this connotation of fraud that survives in the more inclusive rejection of bustling Englishmen by the Devil in Shaw's *Man and Superman* as "not public-spirited, only patriotic."

When Coleridge's observation of politics began, one's views of articulate patriotism depended upon one's attitude toward the chief declared Patriot, Charles James Fox. When Fox entered the coalition with Lord North in 1793, a caricature depicted him selling his copies of Locke, Sydney, and other libertarians—"An Analysis of Modern Patriotism." (George, V, 693) In assessing Coleridge's role as a cooling Pantisocrat and part-time trimmer, it is worth while contemplating how often he managed to avoid explicit declaration of his views on this titular head of the Patriot party. Confining versified treatment of Fox to epigrams and *jeux d'esprit*, he stands apart from the average poetic supporter of the Opposition by celebrating Fox's birthdays with (as far as we know) not a single ode.

Until the Revolution, *patriote* in France meant generally "a man who belongs to my *pays*, my part of the country"; converting the *royaume* to a *patrie*, the Revolution confirmed for the French a national meaning for *patriote* similar to that long national in England.[4] In his weekly bulletin, from 1789 to 1791, Camille Desmoulins used the word to designate a republican, and this revolutionary meaning crossed the channel and became associated with the meaning of Foxite liberal. It is in Desmoulins' sense, as Ernest de Selincourt noted, that Wordsworth in Paris "did soon Become a Patriot." (*The Prelude*, 1805, IX, 123–24n) The Foxite Patriots shared much of the sentiment of John Thelwall: "Patriotism, or the love of our country, is after all but a narrow sectarian principle; the source very often ... of very splendid actions, but the parent at the same time of much illiberality and injustice, of contentions, massacres, and devastations. The true actuating principle of virtue, is the love of the human race; the benevolent sentiment which ... sanctifies the universal equality of rights."[5] Noting in the Preface to *Joan of Arc* in 1796 that the subject of his poem was the defeat of his country, Southey declared with an openness for which he was later very sorry: "If among my readers there be one who can wish success to injustice, because his countrymen supported it, I desire not that man's approbation." (p. vii)

To avoid the implications and consequences of Thelwall's internationalism and Southey's impetuosity, most Patriots in political life explained philosophically that true patriotism required liberty instead of Pitt at home and peace instead of war abroad. The new Patriots-of-the-World openly espoused tenets abhorrent to English lovers of the inherited past. For such espousal they were denounced as vicious in word and still more vicious in concealed intention. In *Thoughts on the English Government*, 1795, John Reeves declared it one of his purposes "to take off the mask from *Patriots* and *Reformers*." (p. 79) "Inflamed patriots" were pleading the cause of the enemy. When Coleridge declared to Thelwall in November, 1796, that "Homer is the Poet for the Warrior—Milton for the Religionist—Tasso for Women—Robert Southey for the Patriot," Southey was being recommended as internationally "inflamed." (CL, 258)

During the first excited months of their friendship, the worthiest patriot had been to Coleridge and Southey the tyrannicide, Brutus or Harmodius, for in no way more praiseworthy than to unbeard a tyrant might a man give or risk his life for his country. After saturation in French speeches, Coleridge made his Revolutionists of 1794 hurl the word *patriot* about as claim and ironic accusation. (CPW, 497:44, 498:99, 499:125, 502:237) His Robespierre denounces as "*English* patriots" those who wish freedom of debate in order "to clog the wheels of government." (499:144–49) The exemplary patriot, implicitly dominating Coleridge's act of *The Fall of Robespierre*, is Brutus. The tone of the act is perplexed. Puzzling and horrible it may be that patriotism should be soaked in blood, but so it must be shown. It is difficult to ascertain which men are truly patriotic guardians of the country's freedom; but why even the true patriot must employ violence —in France as in Rome—is a mystery probably not soluble. Robespierre's son detects the irony of the common murmur: "O the great glorious patriot, Robespierre— The *tyrant guardian* of the country's *freedom!*" (498:111–12) The irony plays upon firmer principles, evident from the whole Coleridgian canon. No patriot may employ tyranny; however sincere the tyrant, honor requires the patriot to cut him down. Manuscript pages in the British Museum show how hard Coleridge worked on the lines, finally lodged near the beginning of *The Destiny of Nations*, concerning Brutus and Leonidas and the enduring Harp of Freedom, which "gives oft A fateful Music, when with breeze-like Touch Departed Patriots thrill it's strings." Southey had worked almost as hard, for *Joan of Arc*, on the sword shrouded in myrtle by Aristogiton and Harmodius, to be virtuously plunged into the tyrant's impious breast.[6] Tempting though George III and Pitt sometimes made the local application of honor for tyrannicides, the young reformers could, and usually did, think of the tyrant-killer as a foreign hero trying to gain liberties that an Englishman could achieve by means less sudden.

Perhaps Coleridge never got around to the projected work indicated in the Gutch Memorandum Book by a reference to Berkeley's "Maxims concerning Patriotism," but Berkeley's emphasis on duty and conscience appears in Coleridge's distinction for the people of Bristol between "dough-baked patriots," either extreme or fluctuating, and those who are detached despite their "sympathetic passions," the "small but glorious band, whom we may truly distinguish by the name of thinking and disinterested patriots." (EOT, 13, 16; CN, 174[21]) A nearer realization came in the paragraphs of the *Watchman* headed "Modern Patriotism," which apply Berkeley's scrutiny of the private lives and religious beliefs of would-be patriots. (W, 73–74) Brissot, too, had taught him to distrust self-styled patriots who possessed exquisite vases in gilded homes. (EOT, 26) Hobhouse was to observe in his notes to *Childe Harold*, in 1818, that "what was once *patriotism*, has by degrees come to signify *debauch*." (BP, II, 493) Coleridge may have contributed to this descent in the *Watchman* essay, where he attacked Modern Patriotism as an aberration of rich, comfortable, atheistic logicians who had studied Godwin and liked to spout patriotism without practicing charity or justice. They "love a Tavern," whether to imbibe or whether to spout is not made clear. Lewis Patton is probably right in interpreting this as primarily an attack upon the fashionable Whigs of Carlton House.[7] Earlier and later in the *Watchman* Coleridge uses the word *patriot* favorably, once as synonymous with "the Friends of Freedom"; at its close he recommends the *Cambridge Intelligencer* to "the Patriot and the Philanthropist." (W, 58, 324) In a letter he describes the retiring Watchman himself as "*itinerant Patriot*." (CL, 212) By his full range of usage in the *Conciones* and the *Watchman*, a patriot is a man who acts with concern for the state. He was complaining in "Modern Patriotism," then, of men without belief in the family, God, or a hereafter who were bringing his kind of patriotism into disrepute.

It may have been a hungrier variety of atheistic patriot, like the unwashed democrats for whom he developed a distaste while traveling in quest of subscribers to the *Watchman,* that evoked his flat declaration to Josiah Wade, in August, 1797, that "the *Patriots* are ragged cattle—a most execrable herd—arrogant because they are ignorant, and boastful of the strength of reason, because they have never tried it enough to know its *weakness.*" (CL, 339) They were not, to use our term, Romantic.

Henceforward he was to alternate praise for the patriot as lover of Britain, especially in private utterances, with denunciation of the patriot-atheist. The fall of Napoleon allowed patriotism to become less militant; even during the loll and lull of Elba, Coleridge proclaimed pacifically, in an essay on "the noblest works of peace," entitled *On the Principles of Genial Criticism concerning the Fine Arts,* that "whatever raises our country in the eyes of the civilized world, will make that country dearer and more venerable to its inhabitants, and thence actually more powerful, and more worthy of love and veneration." (BL, II, 220) In short, the artist can be a patriot without concerning himself with public affairs. In a copy of *The Friend,* 1818, that passed from his son Derwent eventually to the Morgan Library, Coleridge changed the militant member of the "glorious band" (II, 254) into "the Christian Patriot." Although the Christian and artistic patriot remained a creative individual of moral stamina and socially oriented wisdom, he withdrew a long way from the barricades.

II

Coleridge's densest concentration of patriot-hymning and hero-worship may be felt in his "Sonnets (as it is the fashion to call them) . . . to eminent Cotemporaries," first run as a series in the *Morning Chronicle* during December, 1794, and January, 1795. (CPW, 79, corrected) The sonnet as a form, which had suffered vicissitudes throughout the eighteenth century, awaited restoration by Wordsworth. About three thousand had been written, but poorly written. Why try to carve heads, as Dr. Johnson had put the critical consensus, on a cherry stone? Coleridge himself had written some thirteen sonnets and six near-sonnets before he projected the series on eminent characters. These effusions, as often noted, were woefully indebted to Charlotte Smith and William Lisle Bowles, "maudlin prince of mournful sonneteers."[8] Mrs. Smith had published sonnets to prominent acquaintances; but it is one thing to think up reasons for praising persons you wish to write sonnets on or to, and another to choose persons who represent qualities you wish to praise. Romantic sonnets to heroes, in the latter category, took pattern from Milton's sonnets to Cromwell, Fairfax, and Vane. Perhaps the "Hydra heads" and "serpent wings" in Milton's sonnets gave excuse to the unnatural menagerie in Coleridge's; mostly, however, if the shadow of Milton lies on the sonnets of 1794, it is a shadow that braces.[9]

Although Milton inspired Coleridge directly to patriotic deeds with the pen, part of the Miltonic influence came indirectly. Coleridge contributed to the genre of the patriotic sonnet little beyond his budding genius. He employed the irregular rime-schemes and hybrid forms then in mode. He exercised, along with adept Freedom, the dotard abstractions of Religion, Justice, Wisdom, Mercy, and Hope, and the recently busy Pomp, Error, Oppression, and Corruption. Of course he was meeting the challenge of a literary genre that excited him as well as a thriving convention of political journalism that excited and paid him, but I cannot conclude that Coleridge first conceived of a verbal structure, or a striking conceit, or a passionate phrase for any of these sonnets, not even that on Kosciusko, before choosing its politically effective subject. Although the influences of Milton, Bowles, and desire for fame were real, the influence of newspapers, which has been ignored, was equally real. He must have been reading such sonnets steadily in the *Morning Chronicle* as well as the *Cambridge Intelligencer*.

Six unsigned sonnets of a numbered series in Benjamin Flower's *Intelligencer*, from September, 1793, to January, 1794, were addressed to Fox, Burke, Washington, the despots who had partitioned Poland, the slaves of the West Indies, and Greece, where "the sanguine tyrant glares."[10] Political poems signed with the initials of the industrious John Towill Rutt were appearing concurrently. His sonnet to John Gurney, 29 March 1794, on Gurney's successful defense of Daniel Eaton in a trial for libel of the King, foreran the spate of tributes to Erskine, including Coleridge's, later in the year. Bolder and more radical than our poet, although gaining some legal protection by the use of initials, Rutt addressed verses not only to counsel but to the accused and the convicted: on 11 January 1794, for example, he saluted Muir and Palmer, recently sentenced in Edinburgh.

The *Morning Chronicle* had published about thirty sonnets during the first eleven months of 1794, including patriotic sonnets by "H." (probably Thomas Holcroft), by "Miranda," and a sonnet on 19 April, not openly political, by Coleridge's friend George Dyer: *To Dr. Priestley on His Going to America.* On most ostensible subjects, whether churchyard, seashore, or shipwreck, Miranda damned the vanity of tyrants as stridently as in her *Sonnet to Liberty* (14 November). During the same months the *Chronicle* paid varied tribute, in verse and prose, to Priestley, Kosciusko, Erskine, Sheridan, La Fayette, and Stanhope, all to be further hymned by Coleridge. In addition, the paper offered for his consideration Holcroft, Tooke, Hardy, and Thelwall, among those tried for constructive treason. In normal course it hailed Fox, Admiral Howe, Rousseau (defended against Burke on 30 May and 3 June), one or two heroic Poles, and most of the leading Whigs. The current butts of the Tory press, and thus available to Coleridge as heroes, were Fox, Sheridan, Paine, Priestley, and Price, all the Frenchmen the press could name, increasingly Erskine and Stanhope, not for the moment Godwin, but of course the men brought to trial for treason and sedition. Proscribed enemies of the *Chronicle* were the chief ministers, Pitt, Dundas, Windham, Chatham (Pitt's brother), Portland and Fitzwilliam after they joined the Government, and Richmond, along with the Duke of York and the Continental despots. The *Chronicle* anticipated its new sonneteer in sorrow over Burke. Coleridge made his choices; added his politically congenial friend Southey and his idol with feet of sentiment, Bowles; and at the Salutation and Cat, with his fountain drying despite the "tobacco, Egghot, welch Rabbits, metaphysics and Poetry," borrowed from Lamb a sonnet on Mrs. Siddons. (LL, I, 60) Although he had recently declared to Southey, "I think not so highly of him as you do," he included Godwin, as the most acceptable living political philosopher. (CL, 115) Coleridge was no crackpot, no extreme radical, neither was he an aligned Whig, Foxite or otherwise. He was politically turbulent without being rash.

Of eleven sonnets in the series, nine are openly political; the sonnet to Southey, which applauds lyric aspects of a republican poet, may be more political in purpose and original effect than in characteristics that survive. The virtues described as Bowles's bear upon politics only in the sense that pity and sympathy— "not callous to a Brother's pains"—form the sap of Coleridge's radicalism as well as of his divergence from Godwin; yet Bowles, like Southey, had emitted a political glow bright enough to illumine Coleridge's tribute for readers of 1794. (CPW, 84:4) Freedom appears by name in only six of the sonnets, but impulse guided the type toward heroes of liberty, more specifically toward the poet's ideal of Patriot Sage. Of the Englishmen, no mere statesman could win admission. Yet surely the learned Porson and Parr were possible candidates for tribute. As prophet and craftsman, Coleridge felt a challenge to search among the current heroes of the Opposition for those enduring political qualities and associated virtues that would stir him to compose verses better than the average. We in turn should find, when we identify topical facts behind his phrasing, materials for the unleashing, rather than the limiting, of poetic composition. Although most of the sonnets are honestly didactic and generally inferior to his best work, their ultimate subjects are ideal political traits seen in particular men, and his uppermost aim for them was the initiation of delight through imaginative creation.

In the volume of 1796 the sonnet to Thomas Erskine was to become Effusion 6, but Erskine marched first in the *Morning Chronicle*, as the hero of the nonce. With the habit of briefly reporting his many defenses of individuals charged under wartime measures, the newspaper on 7 August had praised Erskine's "usual eloquence and ability." From late October on, it reported his informal public appearances as well as his speeches for the defense in the trials of Hardy, Horne Tooke, and Thelwall. Erskine was not only courageous; he was successful. Coleridge's sonnet to this success has little cohesion except in Erskine and the elaborately treated symbol of light as libertarian wisdom. When flame-bearing Erskine caused British Freedom to check her flight, she was departing for "an happier land." If Coleridge paused to think what that land would be, he must have decided, not that it was France, but that it was the Susquehanna of Pantisocracy.

A sage glows with wisdom; a Patriot Sage blazes with light. Thomas Erskine, who in life has been (like Coleridge) a "hireless Priest" tending the flame of Freedom, beyond the tomb will cast such a burning light as the sun dipped beyond the horizon. In other sonnets La Fayette is the lark who soared from France to call forth the dawn. Like the aurora borealis in Finland, Godwin shines "t'illume a sunless world." Priestley in Pennsylvania is a kind of Helios "Calm in his halls of brightness." The flame at the altar of freedom partakes of the sun's divinity.

Planning sixteen sonnets altogether, the poet soon called the first one "a bad Specimen." (CL, 137) Although he declined a chance offered through George Dyer to be tutor to young relatives of Erskine, his admiration of Erskine's apt eloquence increased.[11]

The second sonnet, on Burke, published on 9 December, finds a shrunken Patriot Sage in the eminent character. The sonnet takes the form of a dream-vision, suggestive of Southey, but specifically Miltonic. It begins:

> As late I lay in Slumber's shadowy vale,
>> With wetted cheek and in a mourner's guise,
>> I saw the sainted form of FREEDOM rise:
> She spake! not sadder moans the autumnal gale—
>> (CPW, 80:1–4)

Throughout this period Coleridge drew upon Milton for diction, emblems, occasional metrics, and libertarian fervor, but here he builds upon the structure of a sonnet by Milton, private rather than public, of which the first, ninth, and final lines are these:

> Methought I saw my late espoused Saint . . .
> Came vested all in white, pure as her mind . . .
> But O, as to embrace me she inclin'd,
> I wak'd, she fled, and day brought back my night.

Freedom, addressing Burke as "Great Son of Genius" and "Spirit pure," regrets the bewilderment of soul with which Burke has led "Oppression's hireling crew" in the blasting of Freedom's fame, but she asserts that "never, BURKE! thou drank'st Corruption's bowl," and laments that no purging of "Error's mist" has enabled her to clasp him again as her son. (Compare the thwarted embrace in Milton's sonnet.) Although a Patriot Sage, or, as the poem puts it, the son of Genius and Freedom, Burke has abused one parent by dishonoring the other. Soon, as we shall see, and perhaps at once, the poet read into his own words, "Son of Genius," by facile but fitted punning, an overcast Sun of Genius. The energy of the poem produces light almost incidentally. Freedom speaks to her wayward son in a storm of metaphors, whirling together "wizard spell" and "meteor fires," unclarified by syntax. The diction is certainly not Milton's, although he might have admired the pro-lepsis of "purgèd eye" for a spiritual organ as yet unpurged. Despite diction even less purged than Burke's eye, poetic order in Coleridge's sonnet has certainly been intensified by the indebt-edness. Somewhat as waking intercepts the embrace of Milton, and returns him to darkness, failure of vision in Burke thwarts Freedom's yearning to embrace her once-free son. Any reader per-ceiving the debt would gain poetic pleasure from a heightening of the political point as he set against the once-pure Burke Mil-ton's still-pure espoused saint.

It has been stated with increasing frequency that Coleridge's sonnet derives substantially from William Lisle Bowles's *Verses to the Right Honourable Edmund Burke, on his Reflections on the Revolution in France.* I find little influence, if any. Repelling the charge of Tom Paine that Burke had pitied only the plumage of the dying bird, and the thrusts of other English Jacobins at Burke's lamentation over departed chivalry, Bowles denies that Burke has mourned merely for "the wizard's Gothick fabrick rent." The "wizard spell" of Coleridge's sonnet belongs to Burke's alli-ance with "Oppression's hireling crew." Bowles's wizard is an il-lusion, an airy nothing; Coleridge's rules Britain. At most, the sonnet is offered as a correction to Bowles by asserting that Burke's virtue, which admittedly once soared, has sunk. If anything, in-fluence may have passed from Coleridge to Bowles's later modifi-cations.[12]

Coleridge was gradually to absorb much from Burke's anti-Revolutionary works. Even in the sonnet of 1794 he writes as a betrayed admirer and disciple. Nor is he gazing down without hope on a Burke gone to bottomless perdition, like the sonneteer of 1793 in the *Cambridge Intelligencer,* who cried: "Go baffled Hero ... How thou art fall'n! to rise no more." (5 Oct. 1793) As already noted, the "wizard spell" in this sonnet refers specifically to Burke's adoption of Tory friends. Yet the metaphor had been applied more generally to Burke by other writers. Porson exploited the wizardry, as well as Burke's unmagical reference to the "swinish multitude," in "A new Catechism for the use of the Natives of Hampshire":

Q. Did God make you a *Hog*?
A. No. God made me man in his own image; the *Right Hon.* SUBLIME BEAUTIFUL made me a Swine.
Q. How did he make you a Swine?
A. By muttering obscure and uncouth spells. He is a dealer in the black art.[13]

Orator, thinker, stylist, classical in eloquence, unpolitically sagacious in his *Origin of Our Ideas of the Sublime and the Beautiful* and its appended discourse on taste, polyhistoric editor of the useful *Annual Register,* Burke had been within memory Bristol's own genuinely elected Member. Yet Coleridge but paused on the edge of severer disenchantment. Toward the evil of encouraging Oppression, according to the sonnet, Burke had been drawn by his own "stormy Pity," his "proud Precipitance of soul," and less nobly by "the cherish'd lure Of Pomp," but not by a single sip from the inebriating bowl of Tory largess. A footnote to the sonnet in the volume of 1796 quoted evidence from the *Cambridge Intelligencer* of the previous November that Burke had after all stooped, and more than once, to Corruption's bowl. The ambit of the sonnet is enlarged by word-play upon it in the *Watchman:* "Alas! we fear that this Sun of Genius is well nigh extinguished: a few bright spots linger on its orb, but scarcely larger or more numerous than the dark *maculae* visible on it in the hour of its strength and effulgence." [14]

Until Burke's *Letters on a Regicide Peace* bore to Coleridge in the autumn "all his excellencies without any of his faults," exasperation with Burke increased. He called the riposte to Bedford "rampant Billingsgate." (CL, 210, 252) It must have been of a different book, perhaps the *Reflections on the Revolution in France,* not upon first reading but later when the metaphor seemed worth preserving, that Coleridge wrote in the Gutch notebook: "I shuddered while I praised it—a web wrought with admirable beauty from a black bag of Poison!" (CN, 24) The spidery metaphor may owe something to the standard depiction of Burke as Don Dismallo, Jesuitical casuist, caricatured in the garb of Ignatius Loyola, but Coleridge generally and notably avoided the iconographic images that had become journalists' commonplaces—if we except the metaphors of revolution as dawn and of patriot as sun.

Two days after the sonnet on Burke came one on the contrasting Patriot Sage without blemish, Joseph Priestley. From Priestley in especial, Coleridge had imbibed faith in the religious necessitarianism which "gives a man greater confidence of success in his own labours, since none of them can be in vain," a rationalistic pantheism whereby "the idea of *real absolute evil* wholly disappears." [15] He regarded Priestley as the head of the Unitarian party in politics and religion to which he himself belonged. Among his several tributes to Priestley in verse, the first published version of *Religious Musings* records a "childish pang of impotent regret" that he had not with his "fleshly eye" beheld the sage. (CPW, 123n) The regret was doubled in that he had hoped to meet Priestley as a fellow Pantisocrat in the valley of the Susquehanna. Like himself and Lamb "a Unitarian Christian and an Advocate for the Automatism of Man," Priestley was a sort of ideal uncle in brotherhood. (CL, 98, 147, 372) Since the political action of David Hartley's son in behalf of slaves and American Revolutionists could not be attributed to the father, Hartley was ineligible for the sonnet awarded to Priestley, but it might be asked further to what extent it was the energetic Priestley who brought impulsive Coleridge to a necessitarian landing-place, and how far the more innocuous name of Hartley stands elsewhere in Coleridge's hero-worship for admiration given a little more daringly to Priestley. Coleridge was not the sort who would name a son Wilkes, Priestley, Trotsky, or Vanzetti rather than Hartley, Berkeley, or Schweitzer. Outside Cambridge, Hartley's name would be esoteric. At Newtonian Cambridge, it was not controversial. In youth, when external pressures abated, Coleridge preferred live heroes who were active scientifically and politically. *Religious Musings* departed from paraphrase of Hartley largely in the politics that Coleridge shared with Priestley. In March, 1801, just when he had "overthrown the doctrine of Association, as taught by Hartley, and with it all the irreligious metaphysics of modern Infidels—

especially, the doctrine of Necessity," Coleridge still longed to occupy a farm in America near Priestley. (CL, 706, 710)

Whether or not we should sometimes read Priestley when the verse says Hartley, Priestley's admirer emitted fourteen lines of unqualified praise in December, 1794. The *Morning Chronicle* had prepared readers through reminiscent details about the burning of Priestley's house by the Birmingham mob in 1791, in explanation of his departure for the land that had recently mourned Franklin. On 8 August "Librarius" had verbally and verbosely knelt in Priestley's honor. Assuming this preparation, Coleridge's sonnet begins with a whiplash. Southey cited the first line in a footnote to *Joan of Arc* in 1796 as "Though roused by that dark Vizier, RIOT rude &c." (IV.294, p. 139n) Southey and after him all the commentators have taken Coleridge's "Vizir" in apposition with "Riot," but apposition is syntactically impossible:

> Though rous'd by that dark Vizir Riot rude
> Have driven our PRIESTLEY o'er the Ocean swell . . . .
>
> (CPW, 81:1–2)

The vizier roused the riot that drove Priestley across the Atlantic. The poet could not place the blame more squarely, but he placed it more clearly in *Religious Musings:*

> Him, full of years, from his loved native land
> Statesmen blood-stained and priests idolatrous
> By dark lies maddening the blind multitude
> Drove with vain hate.
>
> (CPW, 123:372–75)

Without guidance, most readers would assume the "dark Vizir," political ally of "mitred Atheism," to be no ordinary liberty-killer, like John Reeves, but Satan's fit companion, William Pitt. And so he is. But Coleridge had originally the thrill of shooting at a cow yet more sacred.

In the *Morning Chronicle,* the first line had read: "Tho' King-bred rage, with lawless uproar rude." This, as Dr. Erdman has noted, was "an indiscreet allegation of royal complicity in the Birmingham riots." However indiscreet, it joins most separable phrases in the sonnets as evidence that their language, though turgid, is explicit in reference much more often than it is the mere mouthing that rapid reading like Crane Brinton's has taken it to be. Nor did the phrase "dark Vizir" enter as an obscurer attack upon the King. When Coleridge mitigated his charge, the context of the sonnet also changed. In the volume of 1796 the sonnet on Pitt came between those on Burke and Priestley, with the result that reading them in sequence would make the "dark Scowler" Pitt put on the robes of "dark Vizir" in the new first line to the sonnet following that on himself. The Prime Minister thus absorbed the blame originally assigned to monarchic government. That the name "Grand Vizir" became one of the Opposition's standard labels for Pitt may be largely or partly Coleridge's fault. Although it conveniently alliterated with "Riot rude," the most significant change in the opening line was the introduction of "roused," by which the charge of deliberate instigation fades into a suggestion (somewhat anachronistic) that Pitt's policy of alarm had an unfortunate effect on the bigoted wretches of Birmingham. Coleridge conceivably forgot the significance of "that dark Vizir" when he made the sonnet on Priestley once more follow that on Burke, but considering that Burke had driven "Oppression's hireling crew" against Freedom by "wizard spell," and since he had actually done more than Pitt in 1791 to stir up anti-Jacobin passion, and had been far more venomous than Pitt against Unitarians in the Parliamentary debates of May, 1792, he could easily don Pitt's robes as black magician if not as evil minister of state.

Arranging the sonnet to Priestley around the idea of the "virtuous exile" (Southey's term), Coleridge specifies three heroes in one, the promoter of Justice, the anti-Babylonian who freed Religion "from the Papal spell," and the scientist for whom "Meek NATURE slowly lifts her matron veil." Priestley's "mild radiance" has, then, illumined Justice, Religion, and Nature. His future "halls of brightness," surely more durable than even fixed Philadelphia could know, I take to be Miltonic chambers in heaven. Although Coleridge did not again point to a solar under-meaning in Nature's "gazing Son," the veil of Nature lifts, and Justice wakes, in that revolutionary dawn now reflecting on earth light from the eternal halls of brightness.

The next two heroes represented general wisdom, if not science, as well as courageous action at the new dawn. The sonneteer regarded Kosciusko and La Fayette as martyrs. Earlier that year

Foxite Whigs had argued in Parliament that La Fayette was a constitutional monarchist whose release from Prussian imprisonment should be urged by Britain as vigorously as the United States was urging it. Burke in turn called him "a horrid ruffian." (*Parl. Hist.*, XXXI, 51) To radicals like Thelwall he was moderate. In the lectures of 1795 Coleridge was to compare him with Queen Elizabeth's Essex, who later inspired (at several removes and not enough) the dramatic fragment *The Triumph of Loyalty*. (EOT, 1003) During December the *Morning Chronicle* had reported rumors of La Fayette's escape and recapture. It was felt necessary, in fact, to note that Coleridge's "above beautiful sonnet" was "written antecedently to the joyful account of the Patriot's escape from the Tyrant's Dungeon." In the octave of the sonnet, with beauty now less overpowering than some may have felt it when the crisis was current, the "imprison'd Matin Bird" accompanies rejoicingly the songs of his distant fellows who are free under the same "rising radiance." By a transition implying that larks call the dawn into being, the sestet gives La Fayette, who awoke "Life's better Sun from that long wintry night," the joy of certainty because "Slavery's spectres shriek and vanish from the ray." (CPW, 82) Thelwall wrote frankly: the sonnet was spoiled "by being to Fayette & by the turgid nothingness of the 9th, 10th & 12th lines." [16] He could have included the fourth and half of each remaining line. At the periphery of the sonnet the busy spectres of tyranny, dungeons, and slavery advertise the poet's failure to make La Fayette's imprisonment the hub of such a giant wheel. In the haze the treason of the Jacobinical eleventh line, "Thus in thy Country's triumphs shalt rejoice," escaped detection.

Although the *Chronicle* had been following since spring Kosciusko's rebellion against Prussia (the same unloved ally that imprisoned La Fayette), its enthusiasm for the Polish commander had been tempered by various circumstances until autumn, when his capture was known. Coleridge had written privately in July: "Poor Poland! They go on sadly there." (CL, 86) Like slack verses signed "S" on 20 December and *Stanzas*—really couplets —written at this time by William Smyth (*English Lyricks*, p. 14), Coleridge's sonnet would have been read under the current assumption that the hero had been murdered in his cell. A little behind the news, Coleridge apparently thought Kosciusko had

died in the field, "beneath a Hireling's sword." Patching a topical
poem is tedious work. Uncertain where, how far, and in whose
sight Kosciusko fell, Coleridge altered and hedged until the hero
merely fell but Hope died.[17] Like the yell of triumph by one of
Catherine's barbarous Cossacks, a fearful shriek froze in the chill
air, amplified as if a thousand souls who viewed the fall "one
death-groan pour'd." (82:2) Complicated into grotesque originality, this metaphorical dirge for Hope has given the sonnet on
Kosciusko a fame beyond its fellows. Pale Freedom, recognizing
as she bends over the fallen hero her own "destin'd bier," has
such anguish as if she had in "mere wilfulness, and sick despair
of soul" gulped from a mystic urn all the tears ever shed by Patriots. As a visualization of how much the forces of right have lost
in one heroic fall, the exaggeration, however grotesque, has great
power for a sympathetic reader. (Unfortunately, the ambiguity
of "such anguish" permits contrary readers to see Freedom swelling into sick blubber from all those tears, since the lines do not
explicitly make Freedom weep floods into the bier.) Coleridge's
international excitement was so great that he could be exhilarated
by visualizing Freedom dead drunk with sorrow, "E'en till she
reel'd intoxicate of soul." The baroque involutions here contrast
sharply with the naked simplicity of Byron's imaginative epigram:
"That sound that crashes in the tyrant's ear—Kosciusko!" (BP,
V, 551:167) Furtively Coleridge improved Freedom's shriek from
a ridiculous ode on William III by John Dennis: "Fair Liberty
shriek'd out loud, aloud Religion groaned." [18] Politics more often
than religion stirred him into baroque Romanticism. He here sub-
limated political fervor into baroque complications. In *Kosciusko*
immaturity, imitation, and enthusiasm have not resulted in the
"coldly measured violence" of J.-L. David; with some of the ruthless exuberance of Goya, Coleridge was carried by general politics, as Goya would not have been, beyond both realism and
introspection.

William Godwin, a more recondite figure than the international
heroes of nationalism toasted at Whig dinners, had recently picked
the *Morning Chronicle* in which to publish anonymously his cursory strictures on the charge of Lord Chief Justice Eyre to the
jury in the trial of Hardy. Coleridge had been in correspondence
with the author of the strictures; before the sonnet on Godwin
was published Coleridge had talked with him at Porson's; and

Coleridge's series like the paper in which it appeared reveals a topical concern with the trials for treason. Yet immediate reference to Godwin's strictures is belied by every word in the sonnet and even by its title, *To William Godwin, Author of "Political Justice."* Like the sonnets to Bowles and Southey, and unlike those on Erskine, Priestley, and Burke, this is a personal testimonial: it tells how Godwin changed the poet's life, and its retrospective gratitude bears no trace of journalistic expedience.

In 1811 Coleridge remembered that he had written the sonnet, "at Southey's recommendation," without reading Godwin. (CL, III, 315) The sonnet makes no such admission. Its second quatrain asserts that the speaker has taken pleasure in observing while the steady eye of the illuminant has shot glances through the windings of the dark machine of Oppression. (CPW, 86) By syntax it is apparently not Godwin alone, but rather or also Coleridge on beholding Godwin's arrowy illumination, who has thus come within hailing distance of "th' All-lovely" future. The "All" here is a tribute to Godwin's doctrine of perfectibility. Its context, "bade th' All-lovely 'scenes at distance hail,'" carefully recalls a line from the stanza on hope in Collins' ode, *The Passions*, where Hope herself "bade the lovely scenes at distance hail." As Coleridge admitted to avuncular George in a letter of November, "I appear to myself to see the point of *possible* perfection at which the World may perhaps be destined to arrive." (CL, 126) At Coleridge's request, Southey wrote out eight lines to replace a "most miserably magazinish" opening; he too, without seeing the magazinish octave, portrayed Godwin as a champion against Oppression, no vengeful Samson to destroy the vile temple but a peaceful savior thrusting back Oppression's sacrificial sword. (CL, 141n)

Coleridge's sonnet, less analytic of Godwin's function than Southey's lines are, may have factual autobiographic value in the sestet. It records a moment of looking back toward his collegiate misery, which according to this record had ended when Godwin's *Political Justice* suddenly grasped the youth who was gazing sadly toward his own lost innocence and turned him toward the brighter future of mankind:

> Nor will I not thy holy guidance bless,
>   And hymn thee, GODWIN! with an ardent lay;
>   For that thy voice, in Passion's stormy day,

When wild I roam'd the bleak Heath of Distress,
Bade the bright form of Justice meet my way—
And told me that her name was HAPPINESS.

Since "Passion's stormy day" had cleared during the summer into the sunshine of Pantisocracy, either Coleridge read Godwin earlier in 1794 than scholars have thought (and earlier than he later remembered), or he depicts himself as having done so for dramatic heightening of his "hymn," or, what seems likeliest, he roamed in October the heath of distress (blackened mostly by a letter from Mary Evans), read Godwin then "with the greatest attention," and saw no reason for recording in the sonnet what he wrote to Southey, "I think not so highly of him as you do." Yet Godwin's logic must have helped Miss Evans' passionate suitor when her final rejection in December sent him back onto the black heath, for Coleridge, vowing to do his duty by marriage to Sara Fricker, assured Southey, "He cannot be long wretched who dares be actively virtuous." (CL, 115, 145) The sonnet was a week or two old then, but this sentence epitomizes its theme. Crabb Robinson recorded more simply than Coleridge's sonnet a similar reaction to *Political Justice:* "I never before felt so strongly, nor have I ever since, I fear, felt so strongly the duty of not living to one's self and that of having for one's sole object the welfare of the community." (HCR, I, 3)

Less bewitched than Robinson and most other progressives, Coleridge disliked all along Godwin's atheism and his repudiation of the duties and affections felt in personal relationships. These objects show in the double negative that begins the sestet of the sonnet: despite reservations, the poet will acknowledge his debt to Godwin, not in accordance with universal justice but on the poet's principle of personal duty and personal affection. It deserves recognition that Coleridge did not, like Wordsworth, give himself to Godwin's logic and then suffer the shock of revulsion; at best, he found such political hope in Godwin's *Enquiry* that his religious and moral revulsion was temporarily quieted. To the citizens of Bristol in 1795 he first remarked mildly that Godwin's plan for peaceful reform was impractical, but from 1795 through 1799 his revulsion emerged often from his notebooks into brief public comments. Only inertia prevented the projected expansion of his attack in the *Watchman* on Godwin's principles and his atheistic disciples. (EOT, 21–25, 135–36, 164) His charge that the principles were vicious and the book "a Pandar to Sensuality" did not seem lessened by admission that he had written a sonnet to Godwin, because "the lines and the subject were equally bad." Notations in the Gutch book suggest that Coleridge planned an adverse review of *St. Leon*, 1799, just when the preface to *St. Leon* showed how Godwin, as he later declared, had learned from a certain argumentative youth the necessary priority of "home-born" feelings over universal benevolence. (CN, 254n; EOT, 25) The poet disliked Godwin personally on first acquaintance; he found despicably shallow Godwin's "disciple" Holcroft, who disbelieved not only in God but also in His poet Bowles. (CL, 138–39) Coleridge first praised Joseph Gerrald and "that *black* gentleman, Margarot" as virtuous martyrs transported for sedition, but he came to think of their rumored atheism and immorality exactly what Wordsworth demonstrated concerning the Godwinian perverting of Marmaduke in *The Borderers:* first a passive reading of Godwin, then denial of God, then murder and rape. (CL, 214, 221) After setting in motion an avalanche against Godwin's reputation, just at this wrong moment, Coleridge commenced a long half-friendship with the anti-emotional and atheistic philosopher at the end of 1799.[19]

Finding Coleridge basically honorable but inconsistent so long as he sympathized both with the reform societies and with Godwinism, John Colmer also scolds him for collecting anecdotes unfavorable to the character of Godwin and his disciples.[20] Coleridge was always ready to repeat gossip that confirmed his prejudices, especially the prejudice that he was superior to all men of mere talent; but the intellectual point against the Godwinians was the moral effect of their doctrines: in each anecdote, discipline of the mind rather than of the heart has proved itself inadequate in obvious failures of benevolence.

Like Godwin (and Bowles), Robert Southey had to be fully identified for the original readers. For whatever reason, he is made into a sort of Bowles with a second register, emitting "joyance" as well as "sadder strains"; his fervent service to politics as the poet "for the Patriot" is suppressed, surely not by chance. Did Southey desire not to be labeled publicly as a patriot poet? The *Anti-Jacobin* was to demonstrate in 1797–98 what he could imperfectly predict: a man praised by the Opposition would be hunted down by the Ministerial press. Spies threatened even more than lampoons. What damage lampoons could not do, spies might. And Southey had relatives to placate. For inclusion in the series, Coleridge had selected Southey over several lesser Bristol friends to whom he was likely to be more indebted financially than intellectually: for example his publisher Joseph Cottle, whose verse in *War, A Fragment* then seemed less lumpy to a Foxite taste than his *Alfred* would seem when Bristol had politically cooled. Apparently Coleridge did not fall under the scientific, reformist, and philosophically Germanizing influence of Dr. Thomas Beddoes, an exile from Oxford, until later in 1795. Meanwhile Southey stood for mind in Bristol and Bath.

On its surface, the sonnet *To the Rev. W. L. Bowles* would seem even emptier of politics than that to Southey. "What Coleridge admired in Bowles was the tenderness," wrote Garland Greever, ". . . the simplicity in thought and expression, the connection of human emotions and moral principles with external scenes, and the soothing, indefinite sentimentality." [21] Except for the indefinite sentimentality, Coleridge left explicit testimony on each point, and his early poems confirm the whole list. But the original version of his sonnet to Bowles may have identified two further assets when it attributed to Bowles the speaker's awakening to "Fancy, Love, and Sympathy!" (CPW, 84) When these three sisters of the post-Augustan spring, with Bowles's techniques for conveying emotion inexplicitly, are set over against the utilitarian clarity and the rational, Jacobinical ideals of a competing senior poet, Erasmus Darwin, it becomes clearer why Bowles would excite rather than soothe a burgeoning Romantic. By the inclusion of "Sympathy," partly for poetic force but partly as autobiography, Coleridge attributed to Bowles the awakening of his busiest political emotion. The "thought-bewilder'd" speaker in this poem could be called Coleridge by the strictest avoiders of the intentional fallacy; persona or not, he wears the mask of Coleridge as fully as self-consciousness could dress him, and as pertinently as the ghost in *Le Tombeau de Charles Baudelaire* wears the mask of the Baudelaire who was meaningful to Mallarmé.

The original version of Coleridge's sonnet attributed to Bowles "Romantic" imagination and the essential brotherhood of man. In the volume of 1796, the three abstractions, "Fancy, Love, and Sympathy," gave way to the sadness that soothed like the murmuring of wild bees, at least partly for greater concreteness, but incidentally as a sign that Southey had been abandoned as a renegade from virtue, because "the murmuring Of wild-bees in the sunny showers of spring" moved over word for word from descriptive praise of Southey to perform the same service for Bowles.[22] But when the abstractions gave way to honeyed murmuring, the assertion of early sensitivity to the brotherhood of man also disappeared. The cause of tender feelings, which in the first version was "a Brother's pains," became less political, if perhaps also more euphonious, as "the mourner's pains." (84:4, 85:4) The original version, before Coleridge had corresponded with his idol, associated Bowles's sympathy and pity with the doctrine of universal brotherhood and its revolutionary implications. In March, 1797, he wrote smoothingly: "The base of our politics is, I doubt not, the same. We both feel strongly for whomever our imaginations present to us in the attitude of suffering." (CL, 318) Bowles had lamented slavery, ambition, war, and lazarettos made infamous by John Howard.

If anyone ever thought of Richard Brinsley Sheridan as a *savant*, it was not Coleridge. But Sheridan had earned his place among the besonneted sages partly by specific acts. He had addressed a crowd in praise of Erskine. His evidence in favor of Horne Tooke had the Opposition just then gleefully contrasting Sheridan's frank testimony with Pitt's "loss of memory." He had earned his sonnet more generally through progressive activity described by the *Morning Chronicle* on 26 November as "manly, clear, and consistent," and still more broadly by exerting "such wildly-various power" as befits a patriot sage. (CPW, 87) The octave contains praise, later spilled also into a footnote, for Sheridan's honeyed classical attainments and the bittersweet sadness of his verse. This aspect of the portrait may be regarded as having nearly as much mawkish Romantic distortion as Keats's early sonnet to the "sweetly sad" Byron. One would never guess that Sheridan had made his fame by the bombardment of sentimental comedy with volleys of facile laughter. Of his early love poems, however, still passed in manuscript, the sizable number that had been recently published had filled poetic corners, especially in the *European Magazine*, with the dropping and drying of tears and the hushing of sighs where willows dripped and wilted with dew. Coleridge's emphasis on sweet sadness has mild political import in that pity had for him a liberating, reforming virtue that comedy could not approach. No sage could be without compassion. It was of course by literary activity that Sheridan gained the sonnet which might as well have gone politically to Fox or the Duke of Bedford. The imaginative point of the exercise was to bepraise Sheridan "by enumerating the beauties of his *Polygraph*." (CL, 141)

Turning squarely to the active patriot, the sestet portrays a Sheridan better known to journalism, the Whig M.P. whose tones now swell with "patriot Rage and Indignation high," and whose eyes now send dancing beams toward the apostate Pitt with scorn and "Wit's quaint revelry." The Sheridan of the sestet is the oratorical opponent of Warren Hastings, of Pitt's war, Pitt's taxation, and Pitt's ministry. Coleridge sent a trial version to Southey on 17 December. (CL, 141) By a few sensible verbal changes, the published version allowed Sheridan himself to rage and rally in Parliament while Pitt writhed like "that elder Fiend beneath great Michael's sword." Through the transposition of two lines, Coleridge created a final couplet after three irregular quatrains—as in most of the sonnets—here in order to delay and concentrate the thrust at Pitt.

Three years later Sheridan fell over the narrow precipice of Coleridge's esteem, and failed in several casual efforts to climb to the top again. Having nothing to do with politics, despite his finding Sheridan guilty in 1800 of emitting "the most foul & sanguinary Aristocracy," Coleridge's disrespect stemmed from his belief that Sheridan solicited a tragedy from him in 1797, kept it overlong, rejected it without reading it through, and laughed in company at a "dripping" passage in it.[23] The irresponsible Sherry had become an easy man not to love, and Coleridge grasped the first chance tenaciously.

The sonnet to Sheridan ended the series on 29 January 1795. Two days later appeared a sonnet *To Lord Stanhope on Reading His Late Protest in the House of Lords*, which may be by Coleridge. If so, he deliberately concealed his authorship not merely by separating it from his numbered series, but also by choosing an unlikely signature, "One of the People." Contrary to his otherwise steady practice, the title refers topically to Stanhope's most recent formal protest against interference in the internal affairs of France, printed in the *Morning Chronicle* on 12 January. The poem lacks the metaphorical gaudiness and anti-ministerial sting of Coleridge's other political sonnets.[24]

Stanhope loomed before Coleridge at this time with pronounced, even excessive, claims as a patriot sage. He was courageous and aggressive, in the Lords and in the mob-filled streets. Brother-in-law to Pitt and once of Pitt's party, he seemed the only relative who had refused lucrative office. Called by his own consent "Citizen" Stanhope, "the minority of one," he had maintained correspondence with Barère and for a year had introduced motions against interference with the French republic. He had invented printing equipment, steam vessels, and fire-resistive stucco; even more to the poet's awe, he had published daring theories on electricity and other new mysteries of science. His sanity was generally doubted. Coleridge had brothers and friends who would think it insanely Jacobinical to praise Stanhope publicly, but he unquestionably wrote at least one sonnet to Stanhope at about this time. Often cautious, usually vacillating, he nearly always responded to restraint by sudden foolhardiness.

His own account, at a later date when he regretted incaution, has Cottle sending a copy of the poems of 1796 to Stanhope with a letter, contrary to the poet's wish. He claimed to have written the sonnet "in ridicule and mockery of the bloated style" of the French Jacobins; contradictorily, in attempting to dissociate his reformed self still further from "the glorious Minority of one," he protested that the sonnet itself had been inserted by Cottle against his will.[25] Accepted facts bear him up just this far: he certainly wished to reject the poem by October, 1796; dropping the whole political series solved the problem in 1797; and it was his illness and inertia that allowed Stanhope to re-enter, in the volume of 1803, merely because all the "effusions" of 1796 were restored. (CL, 242) Lacking omniscience and some of the original documents as well, we have to remember that Cottle himself had something to hide, did to our knowledge hide much, and may have countered Coleridge's disingenuousness with some of his own.

But the album of manuscripts in the Temple Reading Room of Rugby School, all in Coleridge's handwriting and all pertaining to the publication of his poems by Cottle in 1796 and 1797, includes the draft of a dedication, on the verso of the Preface for the first edition and on paper watermarked 1795. Except for slashes inserted here to indicate Coleridge's divisions for centering it, the dedication reads: "To Earl Stanhope / A man beloved of Science and of Freedom, / these Poems are / respectfully inscribed / by the Author." (cf. CPW, 1137) Somebody, probably Cottle, has canceled this evidence of Coleridge's intention by a single vertical line. Perhaps the dedication went as far as page proof; the published volume contains no dedication, but has a half-title before the title page, unusual if not unique among volumes published by Cottle. When Stanhope consented to the marriage of his daughter with the son of an apothecary, the Watchman crying the state of the nation wrote, or rather published, on 1 March 1796: "Earl Stanhope does not *talk* only: he feels, and acts in contempt of aristocratic prejudices." (W, 28) Did Stanhope snub Coleridge, perhaps unintentionally, soon after this date? *Poems on Various Subjects* appeared on 11 April. Coleridge's account of Cottle's sending the volume with a dedicatory letter ends in a bitter memory that Stanhope, "to prove that he is not *mad* in all things," in 1796 treated both the poem and the dedicating letter "with silent contempt."

As its fiery blasts burn for themselves, I print it in full, with the footnote and the pattern of capitalized words as they leaped out in 1796:

> NOT, STANHOPE! with the Patriot's doubtful name
> I mock thy worth—FRIEND OF THE HUMAN RACE!
> Since scorning Faction's low and partial aim
> Aloof thou wendest in thy stately pace,
> Thyself redeeming from that leprous stain,
> NOBILITY: and aye unterrify'd
> Pourest thine Abdiel warnings on the train
> That sit complotting with rebellious pride
> 'Gainst * her, who from the Almighty's bosom leapt
> With whirlwind arm, fierce Minister of Love!
> Wherefore, ere Virtue o'er thy tomb hath wept,
> Angels shall lead thee to the Throne above:
> And thou from forth it's clouds shall hear the voice,
> Champion of FREEDOM and her God! rejoice!
>
> * Gallic Liberty

The hesitancy about calling Stanhope a patriot acknowledges his position as benevolent citizen of the world. The reference to "Faction" does not compliment Fox or Sheridan. Concerning Abdiel, as a dissenter from Satan's Tories, readers needed to remember the line in *Paradise Lost:* "Among the faithless, faithful only hee." The various tombs and monuments in this and other sonnets in the series, visualized with personifications leaning over them, recall the monuments to military heroes deposited during those years in the aisles of Westminster Abbey; the kinship may be half-conscious and imitative, in a tradition that encompassed several arts, or it may result from a fully conscious irony of rejection: the replacement of monarchic fodder with true patriots.

If the sonnet to Godwin came to seem poetically the worst, that to Stanhope the most rash, and that to Sheridan equally wasted, the poet also regretted occasionally the sonnet on his anti-hero, William Pitt. This is the poem—and not, as Coleridge's editor has it, the innocuous *Pity*—condemned in a letter to Thelwall, November, 1796: "I was glad to hear from Colson that you abhor the morality of my Sonnet to Mercy—it is indeed detestable & the poetry is not above mediocrity." (CL, 254) Coleridge had reprinted the mediocrity twice that year under the title *To Mercy,* first with the collected poems and then in the *Watchman.* The other three sonnets that do not by plain apostrophe hail the eulogized by name, those on Priestley, Kosciusko, and Burke, face the reader directly: only this one, for the purpose of restraining its own passion instead of outfacing Pitt heatedly, addresses an abstract quality. To Coleridge, indeed, Pitt was always something between an abstraction and a mythical monster. In time he would be the model for mechanical failure and short measure, a Lockian "Little-ist" of no genius, no imagination, no creative reason. He "was cast, rather than grew." (EOT, 320) In 1794, when Coleridge's Romanticism had not yet found its terminology, Pitt represented Argus-eyed "secret influence" and blind suppression of liberties.

Leading from the *suppressio veri* of the title—for who would connect Mercy with Pitt?—the opening lines of the sonnet feign a sentimental softness. Soon a seven-verse synopsis of Pitt's career leads to the warning that softness is not always apt. Mercy should avoid Pitt even as he has avoided her. Identified among Satan's fallen generals and even as Satan himself in other sonnets, Pitt as Judas in this poem seems more slandered than usual only because the metaphor tracing his political career is here more prolonged and detailed. As Mercy would obviously have had no previous acquaintance with the Prime Minister, the synopsis tells her how he came (in 1784) with "proud words of dear-lov'd Freedom," but at once "kiss'd his country with Iscariot mouth," then "fix'd her on the Cross of deep distress" (1793), and from a safe distance watched the lance pierce her pregnant side. Treacherous assassin of his mother, Pitt is even a kind of Judas Christ, by a parenthesis that read in the first two printings, "Staining most foul a Godlike Father's name," and later with altered but hardly lessened profanity, "Ah! foul apostate from his Father's fame!" Segments of the American press have tried to achieve Coleridge's ends with milder references to dog-owning, piano-playing, and golfing Presidents. For a more rugged public, Coleridge was trying to project for Pitt, partly out of Milton, a Satanic iconography. As study of the odes will confirm, much of the best political poetry of Coleridge, as the best of Byron in quite different ways, is negative. Despite his disclaimer, he had some wish to qualify for the office of "Historiographer to the King of Hell." (CPW, 163n)

Jesus said, according to Luke, woe unto him through whom offenses come, and this was license enough for a necessitarian optimist of 1794. It would be an honest Unitarian act to take Jesus at his word and hang a millstone around Pitt's neck. The sonnet reaches its conclusion: If Mercy's stern sister, Justice, should be strangely blind to what must be done to the dark scowler, then Mercy herself must seize "more terrible th'avenging brand" and like Jehovah-Jupiter "hurl her thunderbolts with fiercer hand." Mercy cannot risk mere justice; her hand must be still fiercer than her sister's, her brand more terrible, for this Judas is chief of the fiends who repeatedly ignore the Abdiel warnings of Stanhope.

If Wordsworth never brought himself to forgive Wellington for Cintra, Coleridge never considered forgiving Pitt for 1793–1806. After quoting perfidious Pitt in one of the printed lectures of 1795, he cried out: "O calumniated Judas Iscariot!" (EOT, 44; cf. 14) To make a distinction in October, 1803, between resentment and envy, Coleridge recalled as resentment the pain he felt at the beginning of 1801, "at Mr. Pitt's being the Author of the Irish Union, deemed by me a great & wise measure / & introducing a subversion of my *Theory* of Pitt's Contemptibility." (CN, 1606, f. 70) Twenty-four years after the minister's death, the author of *The Statesman's Manual* wrote in James Gillman's copy of the work: "Mere Experience (I mean a Statesman so endowed) unenlightened by Philosophy is Cyclops with one eye, and that on the back of his head. Such a Statesman was MR PITT—hinc naturae Lacrymae!—" [26] The anti-hero of political theory, for Coleridge as for Shelley, was Malthus, but Coleridge rebutted him mostly in marginalia. Pitt was the anti-hero supreme, hated with joy in prose and verse for thirty years. (CPW, 212, 957, 323:54–61; EOT, 1003)

Pitt's opposite in Coleridge's Plutarchan portrait for the *Morning Post* in March, 1800, was to some extent Bonaparte, as advertised, but to an even greater extent the "philosophical historian," Charles James Fox. (EOT, 319) Too much can hardly be made of Coleridge's failure to celebrate Fox openly in verse. Benign, innocently daring George Dyer could have failed of appearance among the eminent characters because Coleridge lacked the courage to endorse publicly a fosterer and friend even more transparently befuddled than himself, or for any of several equally simple reasons. Fox's absence goes deeper. Probably related to Coleridge's concept of his own role as anti-partisan seer, it suggests that circumstances made hatred in a partisan spirit easier than admiration. Cottle insisted that Coleridge once idolized Fox, but the poet and journalist usually saved his praise for antitheses with Pitt, wherein Fox became typically (in 1800) "a man of clear head, clean heart, & impetuous feelings." [27]

At the moment of writing the phrase "clean heart," at least, he forgave the libertarian statesman for gambling, adultery, and speechifying in taverns. Catherine of Russia's ostentatious regard for Fox would not have increased esteem for either sinner. Later, to Coleridge as to De Quincey, Fox was flatly unpatriotic. Coleridge may have written the two epigrams on Fox's death sometimes attributed to him; nothing makes his authorship less likely than the unqualified praise of Pitt in both. (CPW, 970–71) From 1794 on, Pitt stood in Manichaean contrast with sages like Priestley, but the head of the Opposition failed to appear poetically among the "eminent Cotemporaries." Coleridge began as he ended, a passionate partisan of personal heroes but independent of party, even when swayed by a journalist's wages.

CHAPTER VII

Eminent Characters
in the Bed of Ware

> John Thelwall had something very
> good about him. We were once sitting
> in a beautiful recess in the Quantocks,
> when I said to him, "Citizen John, this
> is a fine place to talk treason in!"—
> "Nay! Citizen Samuel," replied he, "it
> is rather a place to make a man forget
> that there is any necessity for treason!"
> —Coleridge, *Table Talk*,
> 27 July 1830

Just ten sonnets by Coleridge in the political series, counting the Bowles but excluding Lamb's Mrs. Siddons, have been positively identified. Besides charging him with the *Morning Post* Stanhope, David Erdman believes that Coleridge came tardily through with the sonnet to Mrs. Siddons printed immediately below his Sheridan in the *Post* for 29 January 1795.[1] Between December and March the number of additionally promised sonnets on undesignated characters declined from six to five. We have few materials for speculating on Coleridge's intentions. He may have tried to fit his verses to Thelwall into the sonnet's narrow bed, but probably not before May, 1796. It now appears that Wakefield was to have been somehow celebrated in the *Poems* of that year, but no verses concerning him have been identified. (CL, 137, 156; see Appendix A)

Gilbert Wakefield, patriot and classicist, would seem a strong contender for eulogy among anti-Pittite sages. Coleridge's letters, as well as the Gutch notebook itself, contain evidence of attention to pamphlets published by Wakefield in 1794 (and later) and reveal an interest in the man, from "one who remembers him respectfully." (CL, 153) Coleridge had boasted to Southey that Wakefield, along with Parr, Bowles, two prominent Unitarians, two bishops, and four lords, had subscribed to the first of his never-finished projects, the imitations from modern Latin poets. (CL, 101) To Wakefield went one of the bouquets of sonnets gathered by Coleridge for private printing in 1796. A highly industrious, independent classical scholar and equally independent Unitarian, neither of which would alienate Coleridge in 1794–95, Wakefield was said by Porson, when they tangled over the utility of accentual marks in Greek, to be as violent against accents as he was against the Trinity. With regard to Greek accents as in other matters, Coleridge's practice followed at an irregular distance Wakefield's theory.

The *Conciones* of 1795 and other early works by Coleridge parallel rather closely the expressed thought of Wakefield. A pacifist who opposed public fasts and all claims of a Christian basis for the war with France, Wakefield cried out against the bills and acts to restrict freedom; argued that a continuance of the war was likely to result in the abolition of private property; tempered praise for Godwin's *Political Justice* with insistence on the primacy of personal affections; lamented La Fayette's languishment "in the dungeon of a ruffian tyrant, our beloved and immaculate ally"; derided Pitt's "forgetfulness"; and attacked those mitred bugaboos, Horsley and Pretyman. In *The Spirit of Christianity Compared with the Spirit of the Times in Great Britain*, 1794, he decried the same remark by the Duke of Portland, on the Christian purpose of the war, castigated by Coleridge in a note to *Religious Musings*. (*Spirit*, p. 14; CPW, 115n) Either Wakefield influenced Coleridge, or they shared the same mind in some other way.

After the series in the *Morning Chronicle*, patriot heroes were awarded ampler room than the sonnet: John Thelwall was allowed only two extra verses, but fifty-two lines went to Horne Tooke and one hundred twelve to Wordsworth. Coleridge's public attentions to prominent women, to be noticed in the second half of the present chapter, broke not only the narrow walls of the sonnet but also the newspaper conventions of direct tribute. In the sonnet on Kosciusko or the tribute to Thelwall, the fanciful indirections may have found directions out; in the poems to prominent women, indirections found out further indirections.

A bolder Coleridge might have saluted Thelwall in the *Morning Chronicle*. Public lecturer and chief orator of the Corresponding Society, one of those for whom the term "radical" was coined, Thelwall had qualified as an eminent character by his trial and acquittal along with Hardy and Tooke. Delicate as it was, the friendship with Thelwall was warm, honest, and mutually enlarging. It elicited letters the most interesting intellectually, the most secure emotionally, and yet morally the most admirable, of any Coleridge wrote before the age of thirty.

When their friendship began, Coleridge reported himself on the point of defending Thelwall in the columns of the *Morning Chronicle* against the "base, & anonymous attack" in Godwin's *Considerations on Lord Grenville's and Mr. Pitt's Bills,* 1795, but he subsided into convincing Dr. Beddoes that Godwin, who had signed himself "a Lover of Order," was a vicious calumniator. (CL, 214)

In the *Tribune* (III, 259) Thelwall cited Coleridge's argument against the gagging bills in *The Plot Discovered.* When Thelwall declared in *An Appeal to Popular Opinion,* 1796, that the bills had as their purpose "that John Thelwall shall open his mouth in public no more," his new friend wrote with concern: "the 'no more' jarred me." (*Appeal,* p. 11; CL, 307) Pleased with a visit in 1797 from "perhaps the only *acting* Democrat, that *is* honest," Coleridge nevertheless seemed uneager to have Thelwall move into the neighborhood. (CL, 339) As one consequence of the visit, Wordsworth's neighbors and landlord thought he should move out, and there were other repercussions in the gossiping Quantock Hills and the rifling Home Office. "Taken up as a spy & clapped into Fort Augustus" on 5 September 1803, Coleridge emerged to have breakfast with the governor the next morning; but no official invited him to breakfast when the Home Office sent a spy to Alfoxden to look into his, Wordsworth's, and Poole's doings with Thelwall, however ridiculous it all seemed later.[2]

It was probably near the beginning of their friendship that

Coleridge wrote the verses "To John Thelwall," for the presence of two imperfect versions among the Cottle papers at Rugby School suggests that the poet and his publisher considered issuing the tribute in *Poems,* 1797. The first eight lines (in structure a Petrarchan octave) oppose Thelwall to the self-styled patriots who rage in the closet, "sketching mimic war." In contrast, Thelwall "mid thickest fire Leap'st on the Wall." (MS. Rugby; see CPW, 1090) In consequence, Freedom chooses simple, ungaudy flowers to "weave for thy young locks her *Mural* Wreath," a crown, that is, as for the Roman soldier who first scaled a fortified wall. The contrasted patriot "without or rent or scar" represents in some sense, generally or specifically, Godwin.

The last eight lines of the poem rewrite the sestet of the sonnet addressed to the author of *Political Justice,* to the extent that they recount more intimately how in "ill-adventur'd Youth" at Cambridge the poet "Pin'd for a woman's Love in slothful woe," until taught first by Thelwall's "fair example . . . to glow With patriot zeal." Godwin he had thanked for turning him from black distress to just pursuit of happiness. Thelwall, the very model of a seditious lecturer, turned him more dramatically from erotic languor to political action. The verses image the change in a transition from Coleridgian use of Roman symbols to Miltonic and Wordsworthian austerity:

> from Passion's feverish dream
> Starting I tore disdainful from my brows
> The Myrtle crown inwove with cypress boughs—
> Blest if to me in manhood's years belong
> Thy stern simplicity & vigorous song.

In the first version he had written less lucidly of what he there called "ill-adventur'd Passion's feverish dream," but the contrast of before with after was already clear enough. Although both versions stress his funereal woe rather than erotic longings before Thelwall made a patriot of him, the general sense supports the standard Oxford readings of "slothful ease" and "Cyprian bough." But the manuscript actually reads "slothful woe" and "cypress boughs." Coleridge has achieved in the revised ending, especially in the crisp Tudor finality of the closing couplet, the dignity he senses in Thelwall.

John Horne Tooke, as learned as Wakefield and in his capacity as deacon technically more religious than the atheist Thelwall, had won Coleridge's respect philologically with the first part of Ἔπεα πτερόεντα, *Or the Diversions of Purley,* and politically as an old-fashioned lover of liberty who had rather start such associations as his Constitution Society (1771–80) than maintain party alliances. He had seceded from John Wilkes in 1771, and later had refused to join the party of Fox. Like Thelwall, he was a newly acquitted felon; in fact, he had been fined and imprisoned in 1778 for his support of the American colonies. Tooke had contested Westminster against Fox in 1790, and Perry might not have encouraged a sonnet to him in the *Morning Chronicle,* especially when none came forth for Fox. When he was defeated by Fox a little less overwhelmingly in 1796, Coleridge wrote out fifty-odd lines in the atavistic form of heroic couplets—"You must read the lines, two abreast," he explained to Estlin. (CL, 224) After six couplets on the "Matin-bird" and the reformers' sun much risen since 1790 (but not much changed since the sonnet to La Fayette), he hails the "Patriot and Sage" whose attempted imprisonment in 1794 was so vile that "Science and Freedom" will not allow Tooke to falter out of weariness and distaste but will insist that he relate in full "How dark and deadly is a Coward's Hate." (CPW, 151:42) Even Estlin was not expected to fathom the government's deep vileness from the shambling verses alone, for references to "the unnatural Villain" and "Two lovely Mourners" were explained in a footnote: "Dundas left thief-takers in Horne Tooke's House for three days—with his two Daughters *alone* . . . ." (CL, 225) It was such outrage as this, the poem concluded, that made Lucius Junius Brutus, "Rome's *first Consul,*" swear ruin "Not to the *Tyrants* but the *Tyranny!!*"

Leaving these lines in Perry's office, along with the poem *On a Late Connubial Rupture,* Lamb expected to find them in the *Morning Chronicle* for 30 June. (LL, I, 33) There they are not to be found, but recently Mrs. Lucyle Werkmeister has discovered a version in the London *Telegraph* for 9 July 1796. In this version, with less respect for persons, the dagger is raised "To strike the tyrants and the tyranny." Thus either Coleridge or the *Telegraph* lapsed from scrupulosity about the means suggested for Reform. Coleridge grew friendly with the sexagenarian for a while in 1800, somewhat along the pattern of his relations with Godwin.

In contrast with his salutes to active contemporaries, Coleridge twice honored William Tell, probably in 1797, as a hero of liberty from the legendary past. *Tell's Birth-Place* translates the original from Stolberg rather closely, but Coleridge began his rendering of one concrete passage, "*Er gab dem Knaben warmes Blut, . . . Im Felsennacken freien Sinn,*" with political generalization: "God gave him reverence of Laws, Yet stirring blood in Freedom's cause—." (CPW, 309:13–14, 1126:13, 15) The association of Tell's apple-splitting with political liberty can be felt in Coleridge's use of the archetypal myth of kin-grazing in *Zapolya*. Emerick, a demagogue and tyrant, in addressing a base steward, excuses the disloyal Casimir, thought to have connived at his father's death:

> Lord Casimir did, as thou and all men.
> He loved himself, loved honours, wealth, dominion.
> All these were set upon a father's head:
> Good truth! a most unlucky accident!
> For he but wished to hit the prize; not graze
> The head that bore it: so with steady eye
> Off flew the parricidal arrow.
>
> (CPW, 927:43–49)

The second opportunity to celebrate Tell's defiance of an Austrian despot had been afforded by the Duchess of Devonshire. In campaigning for Fox in 1784, the Duchess had encouraged notoriety by approximating the caricatures that showed her kissing butchers at the hustings. Notoriety was already hers, for *An Interesting Letter to the Duchess of Devonshire*, 1777, the anonymous work of William Combe, was not unusually scurrilous when it warned her against continuing her residence at gaming tables and complained that the large plumes on her hats set a bad example even to prostitutes. The first of her three legitimate children, a daughter, had been born eight years after her marriage —another convenience for political lampoonists. The Whig leader Charles Grey was rumored (with seeming accuracy) to be the father of one of her other children. She had been "exiled" for two years, and was supplanted at home by a friend, who later succeeded her as duchess. The Foxite press, of course, used ink in her defense.

On 19 December 1799 a poem in thirty stanzas by the Duchess, entitled *The Passage of the Mountain of Saint Gothard,* was pub-

lished in the evening *Courier,* and on the 20th in two other Opposition papers, the morning *Post* and *Chronicle.* The poem had been
written a few years earlier and dedicated "To my Children." Mount
St. Gothard came into the newspapers at this time, Pittite as well
as Foxite, because of its timeliness in the war. The French and
Austrians had been driving each other from entrenchments there
since May. Suvorov had come to relieve the Austrians in August,
and had dispossessed the French of St. Gothard near the end of
September, but had been himself repelled by Masséna early in
October. Foreseeing the secession of Austria from the war, the
Post warned on 17 December: "The march of a strong army from
Mount St. Gothard to Milan would compel the Austrians to evac-
uate the whole of Piedmont . . . ." These facts lie behind the title,
in the *Post* on Christmas Eve, of Coleridge's "Ode to Georgiana,
Duchess of Devonshire, on the 24th stanza in her Poem, entitled
'The Passage of the Mountain of St. Gothard.'" Beneath the title
he quoted as an epigraph the pertinent stanza, which hails "the
Platform wild" where the archer preserved his child and felled
the tyrant. Neither stung into poetry nor quite tickled into it,
Coleridge had produced in a short time an irregular rhetorical ode,
as descended from Cowley, in four numbered stanzas, the last two
each exceeding twenty-five lines. Highly exclamatory, it somehow
flows. Although his editors have omitted the evidence, Coleridge
had justice in his complaint that it was "horribly misprinted." [3]

The first short stanza sets the theme. Recurring with incremental
changes, it acts as a refrain. Here it is in the final version:

> Splendour's fondly-fostered child!
> And did you hail the platform wild,
>   Where once the Austrian fell
>   Beneath the shaft of Tell!
> O Lady, nursed in pomp and pleasure!
> Whence learn'd you that heroic measure?

>   (CPW, 335)

The longer second stanza enlarges the point: Among "Rich viands,
and the pleasurable wine," unearned by toil, you, O Lady, were
reared far from "all that teaches brotherhood to Man"—"And yet,
free Nature's uncorrupted child, You hailed the Chapel and the
Platform wild . . . ." The third stanza begins to solve the paradox.
Genius kissed you in your cradle; therefore, though from your

training you might have written, like other fine ladies, of "Laurelled War and plumy State," to steel the rich into mockery of the poor, instead, as free Nature's uncorrupted child, you hailed the Platform wild. Only a child of Nature would admire a "shrine of social Liberty." Although it is now well established that the Duchess was a child of Nature, the stanza ends with the original question: Whence learned you?

The last stanza begins with, and expatiates upon, the answer that satisfied the poet and consummated his poem: "You were a mother! at your bosom fed The babes that loved you." Thus, shaping the souls of your infants, you gave birth in effect a second time, "Without the mother's bitter groans." Rousseauistic nursing of her own children was a frequently noised fact about the Duchess. Coleridge could have learned it from Charles Pigott's anonymous work, *The Female Jockey Club*, 1794; from any of several other Foxite sources; easily enough in conversation; or in the ordinary way from Fox's political opponents. A new letter from Combe in 1784, described on the title page as a new edition of the original letter, reminded Her Grace that she was a mother, although she as yet had no heir for the Duke, and admitted that "the tenderest office of Nature, which modern Mothers inhumanly disregard, was by *you* most religiously performed!" [4] The Tory caricaturists made what they could of her motherhood. In one print of 1784 Georgiana canvasses while the Duke changes the diaper of his infant. In a caricature by Rowlandson, titled "Political Affection," Georgiana nurses a fox at her breast as her own baby screams on the ground neglected. There were others. (George, VI, 106–7, 153–54)

External and political considerations such as these are usable for an understanding and appreciation of Coleridge's poem. Seized with a glowing idea about Nature, he took Foxite clichés and fused the resulting political argument with the imaginative idea, which in itself required a scheme of unfolding question and answer. The topical significance of St. Gothard gave an additional turn to the immediate delight. His pride in the poem can be seen even in his excuse to Southey: "Had I done all I had planned, that Ode to the Dutchess would have been a better thing than it is— it being somewhat dullish." He thought it would do for Southey's *Annual Anthology,* and Southey agreed. (CL, 552, 554) Near the end of the poem a small daring myth tells the Duchess how, when the Angel of the Earth turned his gaze for a moment from God toward her, "New influences in your being rose." (337:73) Coleridge canceled the passage in one copy of the *Annual Anthology* after Lamb asked, "By-the-by, where did you pick up that scandalous piece of private history about the angel and the Duchess of Devonshire?" But he seems to have decided afterward that most minds would be less profane than Lamb's. (LL, I, 203) God, who made the Duchess a mother, agreed with Rousseau from there on. The unifying theme, of the gain for Liberty when a peeress returns to the Nature that nourishes us all, asked for free experiment in technique. Georgiana herself, valorous child of Nature, also called for what George N. Shuster designates as the "trochaic interludes" (presumably including the trochaic opening line) and for other experiments in asymmetry.[5] Theme and duchess called in fact for further and more Romantic innovations than the poet achieved. However much the metapolitical theme and the active electioneeress prompted spontaneity and experimentation, the successes as well as the failures of the poem lie in the execution rather than the ideological content, or at least in the complexity of adjustment between idea and execution, the more especially if facile sentiment be regarded as a matter of style. Yet we misconstrue the place of poetry in civilized life unless we see the importance both of the political cry, "Return to Nature," and of the revolutionary feminism of a physically attractive Whig; they have importance for the environment and inspiration of the poet, for the poem itself, and for us as readers.

External influences probably inspired the poem even more than has been so far indicated. Coleridge apparently had entered a period of mellowing toward Fox and other Devonshire House Whigs, including Sheridan, who may still again have offered promise of producing *Osorio*. Dr. Erdman points to good internal evidence for assigning to Coleridge an editorial in the *Morning Post* on the same day as the ode addressed to the Duchess. Here, less than a month before Coleridge protested against Stuart's tolerance for Sheridan's lies, Sheridan is praised as "eminently qualified to feel with reason, and to reason with feeling." Stuart, and probably Coleridge, would have seen the ode as an aid to Sheridan and Fox. One year later the Duchess of Devonshire, like Fox, would receive a copy of *Lyrical Ballads,* Second Edition, with an escorting letter dictated by Coleridge. (CL, 665)

Discounting the first of his Saras, contemporary women celebrated in Coleridge's verse needed to be in some specific way talented. Usually there were also political qualifications. Innocent as it looks nestling in a forgotten corner of his collected works, the unfinished poem *To the Snow Drop,* beginning "Fear no more, thou timid Flower!" bore political overtones beyond its fundamental of pity for the weak, which in itself implied opposition to pitiless Pitt and resentment at aristocratic exclusiveness. A poem by "Perdita" Robinson, *Ode to the Snow-Drop,* evoked Coleridge's lines. An actress, a poetess in the Della Cruscan group squashed by the *Anti-Jacobin,* and a beauty, Mary Robinson, née Darby, had become mistress to the Prince of Wales in 1778, "Perdita" to his "Florizel." Publicly abandoned by George, she was awarded a pension by Fox in 1783: rumor from Brighton joined her next to Fox. As if to nationalize her troubles with Mr. Robinson, a petty and private sponger, she was for twenty years journalist, embarrassment, and charge of the Whig party. She is the Laura who tends the sensitive snowdrop in the "freezing night" of Coleridge's poem. He would have known that General Banastre Tarleton, Whig M.P. for Liverpool, had recently deserted her, for she had proclaimed in newspaper verses the full course of their liaison.

Ill, indeed paralyzed, Perdita had linked herself by simile with the winter-chilled flower at the close of her own *Ode,* available to Coleridge both in the *Morning Post* and in her novel, *Walsingham:* "For I have known the cheerless hour . . . And WEPT, and SHRUNK LIKE THEE." Coleridge, then, is commending a fellow poet of the Opposition, exuding pity for the downtrodden, and quizzing once more the Prince, as in his versified sigh over the connubial rupture of 1796. Literally, he says that the snowdrop need tremble no more before the killing wind, because Laura (from one of Mrs. Robinson's pseudonyms, "Laura Maria") has made its chilled being immortal in her verses. The last two stanzas push very intimately into Laura's dreams: "Remember'd LOVES illume her cheek With Youth's returning gleams." [6] For "illume" Coleridge originally wrote "relume," which brought the Prince slightly closer.

Although dated 1800 by all editors, Coleridge's snowdrop burst into ink in January, 1798. For its intended audience, readers of the

Morning Post, he introduced the poem with a letter to the editor
signed "Zagri," in hidden allusion to *Osorio.* Coleridge later told
his companions in Germany, Clement Carlyon and George Bellas
Greenough, that he first abused Mrs. Robinson's poetry, then
agreed with his friends on atonement by eulogizing her in a newspaper sonnet, and in response to the sonnet received a highly com-
plimentary letter from her and a splendidly bound edition of her
works.[7] This story, long treated skeptically, is now in most points
confirmed. We owe to R. S. Woof and David Erdman recognition
of its partial confirmation in a letter of 20 January from Stuart,
which accompanied a presentation copy of *Walsingham,* and further confirmation in a note added by Tom Poole to a copy of
Stuart's letter. (B.M. MS. Add. 35343, ff. 168–69) In this note,
about 22 January, Poole informed Coleridge: "Mrs R.'s letter to
Francini is benevolent and flattering .... I wish the compliment
had been as sincere as she thinks it." His words are explained by
one of Stuart's many passionate advertisements of Perdita and her
novel, in the *Morning Post* of 4 January: "Mrs. ROBINSON's WAL-
SINGHAM has never received a more gratifying tribute of praise
than the *beautiful poem,* by FRANCINI, in our paper of yesterday:
such commendation is honourable, as flowing from the pen of classical elegance, and true poetic inspiration." Here then is Coleridge's compliment—or was, for the *Morning Post* of 3 January
1798 is missing from all known files and no stray copy has yet
been found. Fortunately, however, Mrs. Werkmeister has found
a reprinting of the poem (without any equivalent to the letter
signed "Zagri" but with an additional stanza) under the title of
The Apotheosis, Or the Snow-Drop, in Stuart's *Express and Evening Chronicle* for 6–9 January.[8]

The pseudonym Francini, which appears in the *Express* version,
may support 1797 as the date of *Kubla Khan.* From 1623 until
Coleridge's schooldays members of the Francine family, beginning with Tommaso Francini of Florence, held the office and title
of Intendant-General of the Waters and Fountains of France, or
more fully "l'intendant des eaux et fontaines, grottes, mouvements,
aqueducs, artifices et conduits d'eau des maisons royales, châteaux,
palais et jardins." [9] When it is remembered that Mrs. Robinson
knew a version of *Kubla Khan* not later than October, 1800, and
perhaps earlier, and when the analogy of such other pseudonyms

as Albert, Zagri, and Mortimer is applied to this one, with its reference to grottoes and fountains, "Francini" suggests the existence of *Kubla Khan,* and aspirations for it, in January, 1798. (On the pseudonyms see Appendix B.)

Coleridge met Mrs. Robinson within London circles of the Opposition at the end of 1799. When they both withdrew from London in 1800, she wrote in October the verse tribute to him, signed "Sappho," in which she quoted with rapture from *Kubla Khan*—either a little inaccurately or in a version not now known. She also filled a whole column of the *Morning Post* for 17 October with an "Ode, Inscribed to the Infant Son of S. T. Coleridge, Esq. Born Sept. 14, at Keswick, in Cumberland," dated at the close five days earlier than its appearance in public. Borrowing perhaps from the poet's promises to an older son in *Frost at Midnight,* the ode assures Derwent that possession of his father's genius will enable him to hear "the soft voice of wood-wild harmony." In praising the Nature that will be open to him, she invokes the name of Skiddaw three times, and surrounds it with the proper names of kindred mountains, lakes, and cataracts. As a further stimulus to Coleridge's verse reply, or in reference to it, she wrote from her sickbed (as Coleridge quoted her to Poole): "O! Skiddaw!—I think, if I could but once contemplate thy Summit, I should never quit the Prospect . . . ." (CL, 669)

His answering poem, which came to be titled *A Stranger Minstrel,* was a kind of coy irregular ode that outgrew its original heroic couplets. (CPW, 350) It reports a wretchedly bathetic colloquy between Skiddaw and himself as he lay supine midway up the mountain's side. Since "A lady of sweet song is she," and "Her soft blue eye was made for thee," the poet wished she were present. Proud Skiddaw, in "sullen majesty replying," assumed that the lady dwelt in scenes less bleak. When at this the poet's tears fell faster, old Skiddaw softened: "(His voice was like a monarch wooing)." Having revived her "remembered loves" in the poem encouraging the snowdrop, could Coleridge have callously forgotten her history when he contrasted sullen majesty with a monarch wooing? He assured Poole that Perdita would have been a "noble Being" had she only married the right man. Apparently he likened her failings to his own. We now know that *Alcaeus to Sappho,* sent by Coleridge for the *Morning Post* of 24

November 1800 and included in modern editions of his poems, was written by Wordsworth, but the introduction of the name Sappho was probably Coleridge's compliment to Perdita. Coleridge asks us to believe that he wrote before the age of fifteen the quatrain he applied to her a month after her death, wherein "Ev'n in the cold Grave swells the Cherub Hope." (CL, 669; see CPW, 443n, 996) Aside from the bonds of literary and political journalism, the whole relationship suggests that Coleridge felt an incestuous kinship between his own talents, weaknesses, and plight, and Mrs. Robinson's. They borrowed from each other to the detriment of both, as in her dilution of *The Ancient Mariner* in *The Haunted Beach,* a ballad that Coleridge promoted excitedly.[10] Psychological speculation could have it that he identified himself with her in their likenesses and projected himself into her lavish career even while he tried to recall her from its vestiges and its cruel end.

Perdita Robinson and the Duchess of Devonshire were luminous counterparts to the patriot sages. With the salute to a third woman, the last we need attend, Coleridge's decline can be traced from political declamation in the stanzas to the Duchess, downward to the partisan aura of his public chats with Perdita, and finally to the bowdlerized chivalry of his later years, visible in the blank verse lines *To Matilda Betham from a Stranger,* dated 9 September 1802. The "Rose-buds, and fruit-blossoms, and pretty weeds" of "a sweet instrument—thy Poesie" were instantly for me, says the stranger, a coronal to "twine around the brows of patriot Hope." (CPW, 374–75) As perpetual stranger he gives public advice to a representative woman: By patient study and watchful eye Matilda can become the maiden glory of "our own Britain, our dear mother Isle," just as the less holy—that is, less virtuous—Sappho is forever the maiden glory of Greece. He can urge her to be wisely bold so long as she is essentially meek. (The poem contains seven superior lines on self-limited poetic emotions: a poet's feelings toss in strong gales like boughs with fluttering leaves, but stay fixed to the solid trunk of Truth and Nature.) Miss Betham was already at work on her biographical dictionary of celebrated women, as Coleridge had probably learned from her friends Sir Charles and Lady Boughton. Since his lines stress only buds and tendrils in the English landscape, at least by metaphor, it is not completely clear that he had read her several narratives in *Elegies and Other Small Poems,* 1797, romanticizing Britain's Arthurian and Saxon past. Except for deprecating men's wars, a deprecation allowable in a feminine "patriot Hope," she seems to have eschewed politics. Abandoning political panacea, Coleridge was turning, several years ahead of the nation, to a potion of moral and social curatives, infused with a disarmed chivalry. His point is not that Miss Betham need be explicitly patriotic, but that virtue, by which alone a nation can be free, requires a nation's women to be pure, honored, and honored for their purity.

CHAPTER VIII

Poems for Pay and Party

A cursory reading . . . will in each case
assign the palm to the most literary
efforts— But a more careful study
will reveal in the less adorned words
. . . some of that debating superiority
which renders an argument irresistible
for one moment of time and unread-
able for the rest of eternity.
—Harold Temperley, *The Victorian
Age in Politics, War and Diplomacy*

I

For pay and for party, Coleridge wrote verses more similar to political broadsides than to *Christabel* or *Kubla Khan*. The stanzas addressed to the Duchess of Devonshire have clear political themes,
and may have been written partly to regain the favor of Sheridan
or other Whigs who gathered at Holland House, but they have
a poetic kinship with Coleridge's other odes. Some of his newspaper verses are more closely kin to penny ballads sold on the
street. Later he gave this metrical journalism an acknowledged
place among his collected poems. He did so partly in rivalry of
Wordsworth's grouping of sonnets "dedicated to Liberty." He did
so even more obviously to eke out his otherwise lean body of poems
both superior and completed. Therefore he collected the journalistic pieces not more than partly because he recognized genuine
poetic value in them. Yet there is value to recognize. That their
author had incidental reasons for reprinting pieces first published
in newspapers makes the handful of major political poems among

them no less powerful and the bundle of topical pieces no less intellectually vigorous or verbally ingenious. By a half-title in *Sibylline Leaves,* "Poems Occasioned by Political Events or Feelings Connected with Them," Coleridge grouped five items: the odes on the Departing Year and France, *Fears in Solitude,* and two works less sober, *Recantation* and *Parliamentary Oscillators.* Next, segregated with its own apologetic preface, came *Fire, Famine, and Slaughter.* The first piece of medium length in the volume was *The Raven,* with no half-title to classify it. The dates of these last four pieces have not yet been fixed with certainty, but they come between 1796 and 1798, early among the group of *jeux d'esprit politiques,* or political pop-ups, to which their partisan risibility assigns them. They were the carnival fireworks that crackled and hissed among the dragon-fires of more solemn prophecy. Although only two of them were so signed, these were the voluminous works of "Laberius." (See Appendix B.) They vary from "Strong spirit-bidding sounds" to what he called "Expectoration, or Splenetic Extempore." (CPW, 399:1, 477n)

The fiercest pop-up, *Fire, Famine, and Slaughter: A War Eclogue,* is possibly the earliest. (CPW, 237) The three hags of the title gather on a depopulated tract in La Vendée, whence Fire has been called (by Pitt) from Ireland. Although Coleridge grieved publicly over these two places of desolation in 1795 and 1796, at Bristol and in the *Watchman,* he might well have blamed Pitt similarly for desolating them at any time up to 8 January 1798, when his hags jangled in the *Morning Post.*[1] Fear of prosecution would adequately explain any delay in publication. At the urging of Burke, the ministers attempted during 1796 to add troops to their subsidies for the Royalists in La Vendée; intimidation by terror in Ireland, equally by ministers and rebels, intensified in the spring of 1797. The burning of huts and cottages in Ulster by the drunken soldiery of General Lake, in March, was so memorable that Arthur Bryant pauses in his brilliant account of the mutinies and glorious victories of the Navy to describe the nauseous ravage.[2] It is tempting in retrospect to regard this holocaust as the earliest possible date for Coleridge's eclogue. A little more than a week after the poem appeared, an article that may have been written by Coleridge himself, "Ireland and La Vendee," in the *Post* of 17 January, treated the devastation in La Vendée as comparatively remote and comparatively just. The writer of this article would have preferred to set *Fire, Famine, and Slaughter* in Ireland, with La Vendée as a reminiscence for the hags. The rebellion of 1798 came too late. For "eight years" or "ninety moons," according to Fire, Pitt had catered to Famine and Slaughter. To end in 1796, this period would begin fittingly in Pitt's alliance with Holland and Prussia; adjusted for publication in 1798, it would begin at the fall of the Bastille and the "emigration" of virulent French noblemen, both hard to blame on Pitt. If the assault on the Bastille and the original emigration be Pitt's works, the poem was certainly apt in saying he "came by stealth" to unlock the door of Slaughter. In the ritual magic of *Fire, Famine, and Slaughter*, of course, a numinous number like ninety might not wait on history, and thus may be valueless for any exact dating of the poem.

Too cerebral to climb the volcanic heights of the more compulsive odes, this "eclogue" dances at their base. So dancing, it achieves the incantation the odes sought but missed. It is called an "eclogue," with a bow toward *The Shepherd's Calendar* of Spenser, because it presents a rural scene showing how Colin Clout and his fellow rustics fare under Pitt. Coleridge probably recognized a metrical debt to Spenser, perhaps especially to the eclogue for February, which, as we shall see, he studied also for its union of poetic and political methods. Metrics were here an important force for persuasion. The dramatic incantation of the hags has a tetrameter jog, with very few reversed feet but frequent anapests, often stamping from one headless iambic line to the next, and yet able to gallop unchecked through a line like the forty-first, with its eight unaccented syllables: "I had starved the one and was starving the other." The author of *Christabel* trained here. The variation in unaccented syllables from line to line reduces monotony, and the shortened lines lend additional dread to the total unholiness.

This eclogue is a witches' round, violently comic. Slaughter is about to answer Famine's question about who sent her and Fire to La Vendée, when Fire hushes them, "No! no! no!," because "Spirits hear what spirits tell" and once when she named *that man* within the hearing of souls in Hell, the mere naming set off a gleeful anarchy, a holiday of demonic anticipation. But Slaughter satisfies her sister's curiosity by whispering, so that the spirits in hell cannot be sure what she says and thus start celebrating carnage to come. "Letters four do form his name." This formula thwarted actual censors, as well as censors imagined among the spirits of hell. In hallooing choruses we learn that the same four-letter wizard has freed Slaughter to drink the blood of "thrice three hundred thousand men." He has freed Famine to surrender the battle dead, out of delicacy, to her rivals the dog, wolf, and carrion crow, but then to make up the loss by feasting on baby and widow. He has freed Fire to prolong daylight in Ireland by burning cottage roofs down on discontented "old bed-rid nurses," so that naked Rebels trying to escape may be shot down in the unnatural light. To pay their four-lettered patron due honor, Famine proposes to gnaw the multitude until they "seize him and his brood"; Slaughter, always brief, adds, "They shall tear him limb from limb"; but Fire denounces the ingratitude of such short shrift. His ninety-months' service would be repaid by sisters Famine and Slaughter in an hour, but faithful Fire will "Cling to him everlastingly."

A similar ghoulishness elongates the epigrams in the Opposition newspapers, modified from an ancient tradition, that rejoiced almost daily to discover Pitt on the gallows, in hell, in liquor (an easy home-thrust), on the mountebank's stage, in mire, and at the evacuating end of John Bull. Let one epigram on the Grand Vizier serve for many:

> They say the GRAND VIZIR will soon tax our heads,
> If the People don't take it amiss:
> Unwillingly, then, I must pay for my own,
> But would gladly pay double for his.
>
> (MP, 7 Nov. 1798)

A typical caricature had Sheridan and Fox comment on Pitt at the gallows: "May our heaven born minister be *Supported* from *Above*." (George, VII, 342) More cryptically, Jacobins struck even higher than Pitt. A popular domestic design arranged smiling portraits of contemporary monarchs at its edges under plump portraits of George III and the Prince of Wales; a scene at the bottom depicted the cruel machine by which the unfortunate Louis XVI lost his head; in the center, beneath a large portrait of benign Tom Paine, was inscribed "The Rights of Man." The Tree of Liberty often meant a gibbet for tyrants; in turn, Ministerial caricatures placed Fox's head atop such trees. (George, VII, 335; cf. 164, 267, 272, 283, 449) Coleridge's later shame was probably not so much at creating the socially forbidden as at joining a low crowd. He shuddered, also, to recall that he had toyed with dogma, like Hamlet declining to send the soul of Claudius straight to Heaven. An intense religiosity distinguishes Coleridge's damnation of Pitt from passages by Byron similar in intellectual point. In the sunny distinction John Drinkwater made between the accusation that attempts to recall the accused to nobler qualities and the malediction that has only a bitter delight in denunciation,[3] this eclogue has swung all the way toward malediction.

Southey reprinted *Fire, Famine, and Slaughter* in the *Annual Anthology,* 1800, whence it reappeared, unsigned, in the *Cambridge Intelligencer* for 22 November. It became widely known, and its authorship known more widely than Coleridge guessed. His lengthy Apology, published in *Sibylline Leaves,* became as well known as the eclogue. Without revealing names and without perceiving that a ruse had been played on him, he furbished for the Apology an actual incident. He told how Sir Walter Scott had recited the verses with obvious pleasure in their poetic quality; how the amiable host, William Sotheby, had denounced the malignity of heart that the verses exposed; and how he, before confessing authorship, had defended and explained their motivation. Citing an analogous execration by Jeremy Taylor, he asked if the gentle Bishop could be thought malignant: "Or do we not rather feel and understand, that these violent words were mere bubbles, flashes and electrical apparitions, from the magic cauldron of a fervid and ebullient fancy, constantly fuelled by an unexampled opulence of language?" If he were to meet for the first time the images and strong feelings of this unknown poet's war eclogue, he would "judge that they were the product of his own seething imagination, and therefore impregnated with that pleasurable exultation which is experienced in all energetic exertion of intellectual power; that in the same mood he had generalized the causes of the war, and then personified the abstract and christened it by the name which he had been accustomed to hear most often associated with its management and measures." Far from encouraging readers to hope Pitt would burn in hell, the eclogue meant that "good men will be rewarded, and the impenitent wicked punished . . . ." (CPW, 1100, 1104)

Nothing in sociology or psychology is more demonstrable than Coleridge's correctness about the excitement of poetic creation, the moral certitude of the poet serving a party, the self-generation of half his passion, and the abstractness of the political opponent. And yet many a man who commits a crime for his party can make a defense similar to Coleridge's, often equally valid. Coleridge is no doubt percipient when he argues that the man who shouts with such public ferocity lacks the dangerous malevolence of the Shylock who nurses his grudge softly and tenderly; but the kind of incantation he produced is a rite for destroying one's enemy. Shooting him would lack the fascination of magic. Coleridge omitted to say, what he at least suspected, that his kind of anger was the offspring of fear. (EOT, 642) Sartre has said, in explaining human emotion, that one runs from a tiger because one cannot instantly accomplish a dead faint, which would abolish the tiger altogether. An incantation like *Fire, Famine, and Slaughter* kills the enemy with enough danger to give one moral satisfaction, and yet leaves him there stunned, as one thinks, to be killed again.

Turning from the *"stupid insipid* Charlatan" Pitt, we encounter in *The Raven* an enigmatic bird. (CL, 573) In 1817 *The Raven* bore a subtitle, possibly composed in irritation: "A Christmas Tale, Told by a School-Boy to His Little Brothers and Sisters." In 1828 it floated quietly among the "Juvenile Poems." Swallowing the hook, Dykes Campbell proposed 1791, a date far too early. In the *Morning Post*, 10 March 1798, with no subtitle, the piece had been introduced by a letter to the editor, signed "Cuddy," suggesting that it be read *"in recitative,* in the same manner as the Aegloga Secunda of the Shepherd's Calendar," and that (this time with a nod toward the forger W. H. Ireland) it may have been written by Spenser. Referring to it as a "dream," Lamb quoted enough of it in a letter of 5 February 1797 to establish its existence and circulation by that date. (LL, I, 94)

It belongs to the general class of political fables descended from Roman satire through spatterings by Skelton, Elizabethan works like Drayton's *The Owl* and several of Spenser's brief allegories, dueling pieces by Swift and his circle and his enemies and most of his age, and even poems by the mild Cowper, but especially descended through the folk-spirit of the broadside ballads. Its first nineteen lines reminded Lamb of Chaucer. Very likely it has some blood, legitimate or otherwise, from more obvious, cruder models like *The Magpie—A Fable* in the *Morning Chronicle* for 1 August 1794.[4] That particular piece of obscenity had resulted when the team around the Duke of Portland splintered from the party of Fox to accept places in Pitt's government. Dr. Johnson complained that the typical poem in Gay's *Fables*, failing to portray generic human behavior, is not a fable, but "a Tale, or an abstracted Allegory." In Dr. Johnson's terms, *The Raven* is a tale, but it is assignable to the class of political fables in which animals act upon the motives of particular public figures.

In Coleridge's fable, or tale, swine crunch away at the mast under an old oak until they leave only one acorn. A Raven, said to belong to the witch Melancholy, buried the acorn, went off on many travels, and returned with a mate to live in the tree grown meanwhile from the acorn. Little ravens were born there. But a Woodman cut down the oak, the little ones were killed, and their mother died heartbroken. Somebody ("They") built a ship, in part from the oak, but a storm sundered it on a rock and drowned them all. The final lines as first printed and then repeated in the *Annual Anthology*, 1800, had brevity:

> The Raven was glad that such fate they did *meet*.
> They had taken his all and REVENGE WAS SWEET.[5]

This is a fable of injustice capsized. In a straight tale, allegorical or not, there would be a clearer relation between the swine and the Woodman, something definite to make up the "they" who took the Raven's all. Indebtedness to Spenser may explain some of the slack. Coleridge borrowed from Spenser's second eclogue the oak, the swine, the mast, the felling of the oak, the halting bounce of rustic couplets, and encouragement in the sport of political fabling. In Spenser's politically staid allegory of the briar and the oak, the briar scolds until the poor husbandman with sad heart fells the oak. No longer protected against wintry blasts by the holy old oak, the vain briar withers and dies. Ten years later Coleridge might have borrowed the political application.

Unobtrusive evidence against purely autobiographical interpretation of the verses lies in two letters to Thomas Poole of 1801. In March, totally without irony, Coleridge described a plan for managing a plantation of oaks in order to fatten pigs; in October, with humor but still without irony, he superimposed a figurative meaning: "... we will raise Mustard Cress; but acorns, acorns— to plant these is the work, the calling, the labor of our moral Being." [6] These passages must be considered when *The Raven* is read as the cry of a ruptured ego.

Unable to reverse the original intent, two lines added in *Sibylline Leaves* to the hem of the poem made it as cheerful as the songs for children by Isaac Watts, and much more innocuous. Was the Raven's revenge sweet?

> We must not think so; but forget and forgive,
> And what Heaven gives life to, we'll still let it live.

In a manuscript note Coleridge made the appropriate comment: "Added thro' cowardly fear of the Goody! What a Hollow, where the Heart of Faith ought to be, does it not betray? this alarm concerning Christian morality, that will not permit even a Raven to be a Raven, nor a Fox a Fox ...." (CPW, 171n)

Was this last phrase, "nor a Fox a Fox," gratuitous? If the allegory makes transparent reference to C. J. Fox, generations of Coleridgians have been unseeing. That the verses have some political burden, however, seems almost certain. Perfect correspondence of fabular and historical details is in any event not to be expected. Coleridge himself noted the main point about these partisan *jeux d'esprit,* quite inelegantly but in the spirit of the works concerned: "Unintelligible? As well call a Fart unintelligible / it tells you at [once] what it is—it is nonsense—enigmata quia non Sphinx, sed Sphincter anus." (CN, 1184) One further realizes that the fabular details first assigned political meanings may be just those details fortuitous except to the tone and action of the narrative. Tentative correspondences are nevertheless worth proposing.

If we take the Raven as C. J. Fox, we can make into Burke the Woodman "in leathern guise" with "brow, like a pent-house, hung over his eyes." (170:24–25) Burke's *Reflections,* followed by his cleavage from the Whigs and his repeated strokes in Parliament, had felled the political power of Fox, who believed that Burke had personally persuaded Portland, Windham, Grenville, Fitzwilliam, and other Whigs to desert their best friend for places under Pitt.[7] And, says the poem, "with this tree and others they made a good ship."

The oak, if it represents most narrowly the Whig party, absorbs the traditional meaning of "the British oak," the state, the constitution, and more, as in Southey's poem *The Oak of Our Fathers,* first published in the *Annual Anthology,* 1799. (I, 39–40) Southey stands in simple opposition:

> The foresters saw and they gather'd around,
> Its roots were still fast, and its heart still was sound;
> They lopt off the boughs that so beautiful spread,
> But the ivy they spared on its vitals that fed.

This larger connotation is that national oak under which Burke had perceived thousands of cud-chewing cattle (elsewhere in the *Reflections* the "swinish multitude"), indifferent to the chinking of Jacobin grasshoppers. Readers of March, 1798, who concentrated on the "old oak tree" of the opening line might have thought of the hollow oaks of the Navy, with which Duncan had won the then glorious battle of Camperdown;[8] but Coleridge's fable centers on the acorn that grew into a second oak. Lines 31–32 in the received version read: "The boughs from the trunk the Woodman did sever; And they floated it down on the course of the river." But the manuscript in the Berg Collection begins the second line of the couplet, "And floated it down": that is, the woodman (whom I take to be Burke) sent the hacked-up old oak down the river. From dissatisfaction with "they" or simply fiddling with the sound, Coleridge later (in James Gillman's copy of *Sibylline Leaves,* now at Harvard) changed the phrase to "And it went down afloat."

Fox's travels and vagaries could certainly account for the passage ending in a line Lamb called exquisite, "I can't tell half his adventures." (LL, I, 94) Indeed, except in the narrative pretense of allowing the acorn time to grow into a habitable tree, few explanations could better account for the raven's wanderings than Fox's multifarious activities.

Lamb thought still better the line, "He belong'd, I believe, to the witch Melancholy." Although opponents of Fox called him "saturnine" and his studiousness added other activities to the vices he learned from his father, Lord Holland, Fox came nearest to belonging to Melancholy, in a way fitted to Coleridge's verse, when he first joined Burke, known to caricaturists as "Don Dismallo" and "the Knight of the Woeful Countenance." (George, VI, 698, 703, 707) Moreover, Burke was caricatured with a brow "like a penthouse." It may have the significance of a joke that Coleridge altered the pertinent line into "He belonged, they did say, to the witch Melancholy!" (169:8) Conceivably "a She" with whom the Raven returned could be Mrs. Armistead, whom Fox married in 1795. It would be much more appropriate to the tone of the poem to take the She as the Duke of Portland, or some other person or persons associated in Fox's coalition with Lord North, quickly ended through personal interference by George III. Of course it is possible that Coleridge, returning once more for a suggestion from Spenser, concealed the King in the Woodman. The date of the felling of the poor Raven's oak would then go back to 1783. Substitution of the stammering George for Burke would certainly give stricter point to three lines about the Woodman:

> He'd an axe in his hand, not a word he spoke,
> But with many a hem! and a sturdy stroke,
> At length he brought down the poor Raven's own oak.
>
> (170:26–28)

By the allegorical interpretation offered here, Lamb's term for the poem, a "dream," takes on the Old Testament meaning of prophetic vision. The cry "See! See!" as the Raven "heard the last shriek of the perishing souls," then represents Fox's view of something like the foreseeable political results of the Duke of York's disastrous military campaigns, as a minimum, and probably of British defeat by France, feared more painfully by Coleridge than he thought Fox feared it. This reading would give us the poem on Fox that Coleridge must have been often tempted to put into ink. If so, he may have felt, rather than designed, the allegory. Acknowledging that the allegorical equivalents proposed may not even approximate the topical burden of *The Raven*, I present them tentatively as an illustration of the kind of meaning assuredly found there by its original readers and valuable today for sensing the texture of the verses. Little profit would accrue from the recording of further interpretations that seem possible. What I insist upon is that *The Raven* was born in political immediacy rather than in errant moralizing or idle narrative. Unlike, on the other hand, the partisan fusillade in which most of Coleridge's *jeux d'esprit* were discharged, it is not a bullet in workaday battle: it gave emotional and creative release, formed a steam-valve for his conscience and his talents, when events left him spiritually sore as they brought irresistible change to his political convictions. Aside from this piece, he identified himself to some extent with Fox's splendid isolation.

Parliamentary Oscillators, a more normal bullet, jollified the *Morning Post* on 30 December 1797 and the *Cambridge Intelligencer* one week later. (CPW, 211; *SB,* XI, 153) In the *Intelligencer* it bore the bald title, "To Sir John Sinclair, S. Thornton, Alderman Lushington, and the Whole Troop of Parliamentary Oscillators." Thornton had escaped mention the previous week, in the *Post,* but his absence had not much enlivened the title. The poem is only slightly more vital. Coleridge contrived it as a swift and naked political act in conformity with the immediate editorial policy of the *Post.* Pitt, by proposing to triple the assessed taxes, had exposed even to his commercial flock the precipice, as Coleridge's pop-up warned, "three yards beyond your noses." (212:8) Nearly every detail of the squib can be explained by reference to Parliamentary records.[9] For the political purposes involved, an oscillator was one who had previously ended on Pitt's side more often than on Fox's. As represented in Sinclair, who had once headed the splinter party of "armed neutrality," he might also have come down too often in the middle.

Looking forward with feeble hope, Coleridge was trying almost as feebly to influence the final vote, especially of metropolitan members who had opposed "with small beaks the ravenous *Bill.*" As a matter of fact, the Ayes and the Noes increased by equal numbers between the second and third readings, even though none of the named oscillators aided either increase. Did the poet hope to influence the men he named? Debate was lengthened by Fox's haranguing defense of his secession from Parliament, of his sudden (and temporary) return, and of his general character: Coleridge's attack on the oscillators, not at all pacificatory, would have been intended in part as a diversionary action at a critical moment. When Fox could be accused of returning to the debates solely from the miscalculation that Pitt's bold tax might bring down the Government, *Parliamentary Oscillators* recalled the heinous war, its nasty taxes, and metropolitan spinelessness. Foreseeing Pitt's victory, the verses had tried less to intimidate than to defame. In short, they charged the Treasury with bribing certain metropolitan members to betray their constituents.

Another of Coleridge's impulses was once more to demonstrate intellectual and moral superiority over those who disagreed with him. And yet knowledge of the political context does not restore for us the original joy of creation, as I think it does for political pieces in which the current materials merely tinge the imaginative whole. This pop-up fails to sustain imaginatively its occasionally pungent diction. It pops down. In a poetically reductive way, the author was facing facts.

Far from attempting enigma as in *The Raven*, but equally far from fighting a tactical skirmish as in *Parliamentary Oscillators*, Coleridge tried to make very clear a general moral and its current application in *Recantation: Illustrated in the Story of the Mad Ox*. Furthermore, capitalizing on the necessity of changing the final couplet for the poem's reappearance in the *Annual Anthology*, he tried to turn the moral almost diametrically opposite to what it had been in the *Morning Post* a year and a half earlier. To begin with, neither title nor text of the first version mentioned recantation. On 30 July 1798 it was called simply *A Tale*. Casual expectations are also unsettled by the structure. One more unfinished poem from Coleridge would occasion little surprise, but *Recantation*, although made into a fragment, does surprise: the first nineteen of its twenty-one stanzas form a self-contained unit, very probably—and if so quite rightly—intended as a complete poem. The original introductory note explained, should there be any doubt, that the tale "gives a very humourous description of the French Revolution, which is represented as an Ox." (CPW, 299n) The ox, underfed and overworked with yoke and chain, frisked about on its first free day in the April air. Neighbors, thinking the ox mad, pursued it with "hideous rout," in a "*hoaxing-hunt*." Declaring the ox only glad, one "sage of sober hue" urged his neighbors to stop. As Whig reporters on the period know, they did not stop. In consequence, the ox ran over its owner, old

Lewis. After one attempt to exorcise the demon, the local Parson retreated swift of foot. The poet intervenes at midpoint to declare the moral: "THEY DROVE THE POOR OX MAD." (301:60)

In the House of Commons on 17 April 1794, as reported next day in the *Morning Chronicle,* Fox typically "confessed he thought the French had been driven to this sort of bloodshed and horror." Nearer to the sage faced with a Mad Ox, Sheridan had told the Commons when the session of that year opened: "We called them monsters, and we hunted them like monsters; we drove them to the extremities that produced the evil; we baited them like mad beasts, until at length we made them so . . . ." [10] In the *Watchman* for 17 March 1796, to take one of several places, Coleridge lodged this standard charge of the Opposition, that Pitt had driven the Revolutionists to make France "an armed nation, and the greatest military power in Europe." (W, 81) In a manuscript of *The Plot Discovered,* at Harvard, he had assigned to a (hypothetical) honest member of Parliament a warning to other members in language much nearer to Sheridan's and the sage's in the Mad Ox poem: "You are hunting & goading Freedom till she runs mad and is called Anarchy." (ff. 10–11) As recently as April, in *Fears in Solitude,* he had written of the need for "Repenting of the wrongs with which we stung So fierce a foe to frenzy!" (CPW, 261:152) Like his prose, the Ox poem satirizes the argument that British arms bore the blessing of Christ because the ox had set out to gore the priest and "run against the altar." (300:38) Again like his prose, and like *Parliamentary Oscillators,* the Ox squib notes that the mending of breaches made by the maddened beast in local hedges—"Sad news for Av'rice and for Pride"—will cost a *"sight* of golden guineas!" (302:95–96) Thus, while disavowing the moral principles of any who could be persuaded materialistically, Coleridge tries to persuade by direct appeal to pride and avarice.

When the ox turns on the ninnies that have maddened him, the sage who has kept his senses urges that cowardice cease at once. He proposes that a rope be stretched in order to trip the maddened beast. If the rope fails, they must lay the ox flat with a blunderbuss. Catching the sage in an obvious lie somewhere—first he said the ox was glad, now he says the ox is mad—the crowd once more is ready to "break his Presbyterian head." In reply, conclusion, and refrain, the sage calls them to make head together: "YOU DROVE THE

POOR OX MAD." Here the fable ends. Thus far the poem defends not only the second thoughts of Coleridge and Sheridan, but the current position of nearly all the Whigs. In a general way, Coleridge remained faithful to its thesis: Pitt needlessly provoked the Jacobins until all of France went mad. A war begun unjustly became in consequence compulsory.

Two stanzas appended for readers of the *Post* on 30 July formed a half-frame for the completed poem and simultaneously declared it incomplete:

> But lo! to interrupt my chat,
>   With the morning's wet newspaper,
> In eager haste, without his hat,
> As blind and blund'ring as a bat,
> In rush'd that fierce aristocrat,
>   The pursy woollen-draper.
>
> And so perforce, my muse drew bit,
>   And he rush'd in, and panted!
> "Well, have you heard,"—"no, not a whit,
> "What! han't you heard?—come, out with it!
> "That TIERNEY's wounded Mr. PITT,
>   "And his fine tongue enchanted?"

This is the pattern of interruption that became Coleridge's trademark, made most familiar by "a person on business from Porlock" who interrupted *Kubla Khan*. Very probably the trouble we have with the allegory of the ox today results from its obviousness for the original audience. It said what every Foxite Whig had said since 1793. The two subjoined stanzas implied that the poem was just about to become brilliantly original when deflected toward a fire-new topical reference.

George Tierney had voted with Pitt in April to renew suspension of the Habeas Corpus Act, but unfriendly remarks from Pitt in the House of Commons led to a ridiculous meeting between the first minister and the inconstant Whig on 27 May at Putney Heath. According to the best accounts available, neither damaged the other physically. Tierney twice missed his opponent's thin silhouette— the "bottomless Pitt." Pitt, to the embarrassment of the whole Opposition, fired his second shot in the air. Nevertheless, to the profit of the Opposition in the battle of pasquinades that followed, the Prime Minister retired in severe illness to Bath. The many mouths that rumor opened toward Coleridge had Pitt wounded in the duel, dying of alcoholic disintegration, insane, and determined to enter the House of Lords.[11] Hence the first supplementary ending to the story of the Mad Ox: Pitt overcome.

When Fox had called upon his followers to secede from a bought Parliament, in May of the previous year, Tierney had remained in attendance. For this the offended Foxite Whigs never forgave him. Although Sheridan at first remained patriotically in attendance because of the mutinies in the Fleet, he later joined the secession and returned at Fox's side in December. On 21 April, before the poem on the Mad Ox appeared in July, the *Courier* correctly reported that Tierney voted for a suspension of habeas corpus and added that Sheridan had seconded the address to the throne. Two days earlier Stuart had cheerfully and patriotically predicted that Sheridan would move or second the speech as a sign of Whig recognition of a practical axiom: a foreign yoke would be worse than Pitt's budgets and secret committees. Stuart was just then trying to appease the Privy Council by dissociating himself and his paper from the recently arrested members of the London Corresponding Society and the treasonous Irishmen about to be brought from the Tower to what the *Morning Post* said would be a just trial. (MP, 10 March) For these reasons, when Sheridan failed to second the speech but the *Courier* reported that he had, the *Post* immediately protested against the *Courier's* attempted defamation of friends to Liberty. Verses defending Sheridan against the charge of recantation, then, would have been welcome to Stuart from mid-April on.

Coleridge would not have sprung eagerly to the defense. Since February he had been giving himself resilience against final refusal of *Osorio* by passing on to friends other proofs of Sheridan's fickleness. On 14 May he reported to George a renewed promise to refit and perform the tragedy—and expressed certainty that Sheridan would break the promise. (CL, 385, 409) Desire to please Stuart and temptation to bribe the manager of Drury Lane with flattery could have led him to conceive of fickle Sheridan as the sage who understood the ox, but no known text of the poem earlier than 1800 gives the slightest evidence of such intent. Before that date, in texts so far discovered, there is no Sheridan and no explicit recantation.

Louder cries of recanter and turncoat went up against Sheridan after the command performance of *Pizarro*, on 5 June 1799, with its patriotic speech by Rolla. Thereafter, beginning with the *Annual Anthology*, the final couplet of the Mad Ox poem read: "That Tierney votes for Mister PITT, And Sheridan's *recanted!*" Some change had been made necessary by Pitt's return to the helm, seemingly unwounded and decidedly unsilenced. The title "Recantation" moved over from honest confession at the head of *France: An Ode* to ironic summary at the head of an apology for Tierney and Sheridan and therefore of S. T. C., who was by then tenderly defensive about his own recanting and in no mood to change anything just for the sake of Sheridan. To the contrary, by the time the poems for the second number of the *Annual Anthology* were chosen and Sheridan and Tierney appeared at the tail of the Mad Ox, Coleridge thought Stuart dastardly for publishing "the most *atrocious falsehoods*" that the lying and scoundrelly Sheridan could provide. (CL, 564)

In the incongruity that he introduced the tag-end defense of Sheridan just at this unlikely moment lies the strongest hint that Coleridge perhaps had originally designed the Mad Ox poem to defend the awakened patriotism of Sheridan and Tierney. If so, he would have found the thesis inappropriate in the confusion immediately after Tierney's opposition to Pitt became public comedy. Next, according to this reconstruction, instead of industriously rounding out the poem according to his original pattern, he slapped his originally intended conclusion onto the two stanzas concerning the pursy draper, not from a desire to defend Sheridan (except so far as that meant defending himself), but from the absurdity of reprinting the erroneous couplet on the duel and typical failure to fill out the design in any other way. For whatever the testimony is worth, Coleridge noted in a copy of the *Annual Anthology*, at an unknown date, that he had written the piece when Sheridan and Tierney were "absurdly represented as having *recanted*," but thus far his note merely follows the version before him; the further explanation, that they "changed their opinion when the Revolutionists became unfaithful to their principles," is given as Coleridge's by his grandson, but the language is that of James Dykes Campbell in his edition of 1893 (p. 612), to replace words cut away by the binder.

The Mad Ox was one of Coleridge's last contributions to the *Morning Post* before he left for Germany, where he found the seed, and perhaps the whole, of another exemplum concerning French insanity, *The Madman and the Lethargist: An Example,* published in the *Post,* as discovered by Dr. R. S. Woof, on 3 September 1799.[12] These forty-five tetrameter verses purport to quote a college friend named Dick who has read how, in "old King Olim's reign," a lethargic patient and a bedfellow as mad as "the Folks in France" proved each the physician of the other. Called "Citizen" in Coleridge's notebook, "Jacobin" in the *Post,* the madman belabored his colleague, who was as lethargic as John Bull, until that snorer awoke and (in the notebook version) "half-prepared himself for fighting," just when the madman sank from fatigue into sleep. (CPW, 415:37; CN, 625 [19])

The anecdote unconscionably expands an epigram from the Greek Anthology, as given in Lessing's *Zerstreute Anmerkungen über das Epigramm,* where it is depreciated for its inconclusiveness: did the opposites heal each other, or did they exchange woes?[13] But Coleridge was translating or adapting a German source as yet unidentified. In 1799 it seemed unadvisable to write publicly that John Bull "half-prepared himself for fighting." Consequently, in the *Post* the lethargist aroused "fiercely girds himself for fighting." Yet, with all the poem's emphasis on the frothing, foaming, belaboring with fists, kicking and biting of mad France, the moral would have seemed both ambiguous and disloyal. Whether to Coleridge's pleasure or at Stuart's demand, the version in the *Post* ended with a frustrating ambiguity:

THE MORAL

The Allies and French * * *
Ye Fable-mongers in verse or prose;
By all your hopes of Cash or Laurel,
Save, O save us from the Moral.

This very nearly says, write your own poem.

The notebook version is a clean copy. In the only alteration noted by Miss Coburn, an alteration that could bear several interpretations, Coleridge first wrote that the mad Jacobin fought with "Troops of monarchs in the air," and then changed "monarchs" to "Despots." This might be a change deliberately closer to, or further from, his source; or, in keeping with similar changes elsewhere in the canon, it might represent Coleridge's growing sensitivity to his earlier identification of all monarchy with despotism. Unquestionably and fortunately, the change to "Despots" makes more graphic what the mad Jacobin envisioned.

II

When the wakeful anguish of the critic's soul is drowned in the temptation to regard the Romantics as inlooking individualists, he might well notice the great amount of Romantic collaboration, especially between Coleridge and his fellow "Lakers, in and out of place." None of Coleridge's other fireworks had the political and literary success of a fizgig he and Southey lighted together. Fourteen stanzas of *The Devil's Thoughts* enlivened the *Morning Post* on 6 September 1799. (CPW, 319) During the next thirty years the squib suffered much modification and accretion, but enjoyed revival and notoriety. Anonymous, it had so much vital cut and slash that it was attributed to Porson. It evoked imitations from both Byron and Shelley, a Satanic exercise from Lamb, a set of illustrations from Landseer, and an imitative rejoinder by R. H. Barham, *The Devil's Day in London,* which attacked Cobbett and Carlile in company with the mad conspirator Thistlewood.[14] Later, under the title of *The Devil's Walk,* Southey published a version of fifty-seven stanzas to prove, as if by sinking it into dullness, that Porson was not its author. Turning his modest side up, as he frequently did, Coleridge attributed the genius of its success to his brother-in-law.

After three stanzas by Southey telling how the Devil left his brimstone bed one morning to look over his snug little farm, the earth, the pleased demon was taken by Coleridge on a picaresque visitation of English life. Perhaps Coleridge, who never achieved Blake's clear fire in verses of protest, came nearest in these stanzas, which have as much light as heat. When the Devil saw a lawyer killing a viper on a dunghill, it reminded him happily of Cain killing his brother. When he saw an apothecary riding to work, he thought apocalyptically of Death on a pale horse. Satan felt instant kinship with a rich bookseller, for he too, as his biographer Milton accurately reported, had sat like a cormorant near the tree of Knowledge. Continuing the survey of his livestock, he knew that the nimbleness of one prize animal, a turnkey, had come only with much practice. When the same turnkey moved less expeditiously to unfetter a man, the Devil thought of the long debates on the abolition of the slave trade.

Southey dictated still a third stanza on prisons. A solitary cell in "—— —— fields" gave the Devil a hint for improving the prisons of Hell. In September, 1799, every reader could fill in the blanks without pause as "Cold Bath," although Opposition readers might get a catch in their humane throats. In a Parliamentary digression on 20 December 1798, Tierney had deplored the conditions in Coldbath Fields Prison. The next day Burdett and Courtenay spoke in the Commons of their visits to this "Bastille." One prisoner did not know why he was there, but he belonged to the Corresponding Society. By 4 January, when Lord Suffolk spoke in the upper house, the purposes of Opposition visits were clearer. The Whigs had found a double cause. A colonial officer, Edward Despard, had been dismissed by Lord Grenville on what ring out in the quiet of *The Dictionary of National Biography* as "frivolous charges." The Opposition protested all year his treatment in the "Bastille" and other prisons of London.[15] Reacting like the Mad Ox, Despard was to die on the gallows in 1802 as an Irish conspirator. The lingering of United Irishmen in the fetid prison, during several months before *The Devil's Thoughts* appeared, would presumably not have touched Coleridge as much as it touched Whigs who could not yet distinguish between trampled Ireland and some insects there who wished to crawl beneath the Gallic foot.

Coleridge's next stanza concerns a social folly he detested enough to assign it to pursy "Aristocrats" like the draper in *Recantation:* the Devil grins at the "pride that apes humility," as displayed in a cottage with a double coach house. Well-timed in the sequence of vignettes, the next stanza (originally the tenth, now numbered VIII) was the first to give a picture without its meaning: a pig, swimming downstream, was cutting its own throat. "Old Nicholas grinn'd," the following stanza explained, "And he thought of his daughter, Victory, And her darling babe, Taxation." Later versions, loosening family ties by changing "her" to "his," combined the two quatrains into one oversized stanza, which borrowed the economic whine of the Parliamentary oscillators: " 'There!' quoth he with a smile, 'Goes "England's commercial prosperity." ' " After an expansion of eleven vapid lines, Southey added an explicit couplet that sharpens Coleridge's point: "Behold a swinish nation's pride In cotton-spun prosperity." [16]

Despite some narrow topicality in the next two stanzas, their themes are clear. Meeting an old friend near the Methodist meeting, the Devil nodded a greeting: "She held a consecrated flag." E. H. Coleridge noted a possible key to this cryptic line in the Gutch notebook: "Randolp[h] consecrating D. of York's banners—." (see CN, 174 [18]) Like Miss Coburn, I investigated at some length this guilty episode of 1795, and found that it epitomized unsurpassably the union of Christianity with military ambition that roused Coleridge to the fury of *Religious Musings* and the *Departing Year*. But *The Devil's Thoughts* refers to later events: this is not the private symbolism of a Nerval, but public satire in black and white. On 4 January 1799 the *Morning Post* published a personal attack in verse, *Dr. Fungus, and the Colours,* and followed it up throughout the year with reports, often caustic, on a practice that had become standard: in the formal ceremony capping a military "field day," locally prominent and preferably beautiful ladies presented consecrated colors to the Armed, Loyal, and Volunteer Associations of each community. To the wedding of religion and war had now been joined the false advertising of bridesmaids. Besides reporting the reception of colors from some "fair hand," the *Post* often followed up with miscellaneous ridicule of the new cosmetic enhancement of loyalty, as after a *"Theatrical, Siddonian"* presentation of colors to the Guildford Volunteers: "It will scarcely be believed in this refined town, that at a late consecration of Colours, some of the Ladies made too free with the *holy water* used upon the occasion." (9 and 13 July)

When these episodes were cold, Coleridge changed the symbolic token to a "consecrated key," and Southey converted the stanza into a much clearer attack upon Catholicism. Meanwhile, copying some of the stanzas into Sara Hutchinson's book of poems (about 1809, according to George Whalley), Coleridge summarized the consecration stanza and gave a strong version of the next:

Here he meets one of the Furies, an old Acquaintance of his, with a consecrated Banner in her Hand—and gives her a familiar Greeting—

> She Tipt him the wink / then cried aloud,
> "Avaunt! *My* name's Religion!"
> [And] Then turn'd to Mister Wilberforce,
> And leer'd like a love-sick Pigeon.[17]

In the *Post* Religion turned to "Mr. —— ——," but every reader recognized the closest Evangelical friend to Pitt and Parliamentary leader for the abolition of the slave trade, who "tells you he's religious!" [18] In the *Post* the word *Religion* was thinly veiled as a blank riming with "love-sick pigeon"; the version written down for Sara Hutchinson makes the full burden quite clear: the "Fury" calling herself Religion is an avenging strumpet who will have no time for consecrating so long as Pitt's friend Wilberforce parades her as his own purchase.[19]

Encountering the burning face of a certain general, in the last stanza of all versions, the Devil hurried back to Hell in the "slight mistake" of thinking it General Conflagration. It was known before Sherman, of course, that war could be easily mistaken for Hell. Dr. Erdman believes that the original general was Sir Ralph Abercromby, the old Scottish commander who had embarked in August, and would be followed on 7 September by the Duke of York, with troops for the "Secret Expedition" to Holland: not a slight mistake, but a whopper, as Abercromby knew and defeat proved.[20] If General Conflagration appears in the poem only for convenience in closing and as a general guying of militarists, then the various names tried out in known manuscripts, Burrard, Gascoyne, and Tarleton, might as well have run unendingly through a procession of notorious high brass. As evidence against such diffusion of intent and effect in this stanza, and as a telling distinction throughout the poem, it can be observed that the stanzas which Coleridge claimed as his own tend to be particular and topical, over against the generalizing of satiric narrative in stanzas he attributed to Southey. By their particularity Coleridge's stanzas retain their sting for representatives of human vanity, folly, and hypocrisy in later days as for those particularized in 1799. This Romantic particularity contrasts with the general satire envisioned in Southey's *Common Place Book:* "A BALLAD of the devil walking abroad to look at his stock on earth,—counting the young of the viper,—seeing a navy,—a review,—going to church,—and at last, hearing the division in the House of Commons." (IV [1851], 199)

Two stanzas of Opposition envy, first claimed for Coleridge in the edition of 1834, had been oddly truant from earlier versions known to be his:

> He saw a certain minister
> (A minister to his mind)
> Go up into a certain House,
> With a majority behind.
>
> The Devil quoted Genesis
> Like a very learnèd clerk,
> How 'Noah and his creeping things
> Went up into the Ark.'
>
> (CPW, 323:54–61)

Without being adjusted for creeping, the metrical tread suggests Coleridge rather than his thumping colleague. To press this distinction to its logical conclusion, however, would be to deny to Southey the opening line of the poem: "From his brimstone bed at break of day." In two pirated editions of 1830 a footnote by H. W. Montagu on a certain "stern and stubborn" minister identified the villain topically, with support from the illustration by Robert Cruikshank, as Wellington. If the villain was Coleridge's, the creeping things followed him earlier than the Treaty of Amiens, and letters four did form his name.

Returned from the homesickness of Germany, Coleridge had thrown into *The Devil's Thoughts* his driest wit. By January, 1800, renewed hostility to Pitt and the war made him contract his energies for a sequence of partisan jabs. Lord Grenville, the Secretary of State for Foreign Affairs, stirred him to sarcasm in verse and prose for the *Morning Post*. Known most bitterly as leader of the war party and mover in the House of Lords of all the most objectionable domestic bills, Grenville was recognized also by short stature and long speeches, inflexible action and meandering style. In a prose piece of seemingly easy vigor, Coleridge carefully shredded the grammar, style, and sentiments of Grenville's most highly publicized state paper, the brusque rejection of an offer by Bonaparte of negotiation toward peace. He could have written the squib in the *Post* of 24 January 1800, wherein Taste, Grammar,

Logic, and Humanity disclaimed all connection with Grenville's "Symphonies to a War-howl."

On Christmas Day a letter from Talleyrand to Grenville had introduced a proposal of negotiations for peace from Bonaparte to George III. On 4 January Grenville released a letter above his signature and anterior to a statement for the King. Both his letter and the King's contained the unphilosophic, bullying, and syntactically vile English of the Foreign Secretary. His Majesty "seeing no reason to depart from those forms which have long been established in Europe," had asked him to return, in His Majesty's name, the answer that he could not negotiate with a body of men who had revived "warfare, of a nature long since unknown to the practice of civilized nations." When the Bourbons were restored, negotiations could resume. Even George III thought such language unwisely brusque. As a quickly notorious diplomatic absurdity, the document aroused the hopes and voices of Fox and Coleridge, who helped variously to start an extensive gabble among the Opposition; but the blunder changed no man's politics.

Coleridge's *Talleyrand to Lord Grenville: A Metrical Epistle*, published on 10 January, is an awkward political dance in fifty-seven jogging anapestic tetrameter couplets, with accessory introduction and farcical notes. It is the most opaque of his pop-ups. As in *Parliamentary Oscillators*, he tried comic rimes: "lost at," "Apostate"; "brood in us," "multitudinous"; "denied us," "Midas"; "coat is" "Boötes," and, showing that he is better at partisan satire than at comedy of sound, "sinister," "Minister." The long-windedness of the whole was originally concealed in large part by the indignation of the hour, but more creditably by the poem's buckets of scorn and bubbles of wit, the strength of its philosophic base for readers who believed in an open society, and the impromptu air of its parts.

As the official exchange revealed an *established form*, the sending of a dwarf before a knight or a giant, the *Post* respected protocol: a punning letter to the editor, signed "Gnome," preceded the anapests from Talleyrand. Gnome expressed surprise that Grenville had ignored Bonaparte, who was pretty generally admitted to exist and even to be as important as Grenville in the world's affairs. This was a regular line of the Opposition: they had blinked, as the Government told them to, but the French were still there when they opened their eyes. In a vein similar enough to be Coleridge's, the *Post* of 7 October had commented ironically on the taking of Aboukir by the *"miscreant renegado,"* Bonaparte: "How surprised then must we not be to hear of this vanished *Caitif* yet taking towns and destroying armies!" The name Gnome had a source more recent. The author of a satirical series titled *The Sylphid* had been addressed on 4 January, six days before Coleridge's pop-up, in prose "To the Sylphid," which included a prayer of "the green-eyed Gnome, whom mortals Envy call, and gods, Rodonte." We are asked to see the envy, by transfer, as Grenville's.

Thus introduced, or not introduced, came Talleyrand tripping like Grenville. Reminding his English counterpart that he had been a bishop and could be expected consequently to retain the episcopal itching palm ("Burke himself would agree That I left not the Church—'twas the Church that left me"), Talleyrand metrically ticked off similarities besides an itching palm between himself and Grenville: both stood distinct from Jacobins and American *Reps;* both admired "a form long-establish'd," such as "silent persuasion" by bribes, perjury, and theft, "the keystone and cement of *civilized States";* both took time *nobly* for a wandering style, as in this digressive epistle: for "the true line of beauty still winds in and out." (CPW, 342:44) As the *Post* had put the comparison the previous summer, "a Minister who has a *knack at raising money* will never be displaced." (9 July) Several phrases italicized by Coleridge but not in Grenville's letter came from reports of his recent speeches. Others, like the reference to Hogarth's S-curve of beauty, parodied Grenville's bland justifications of ugly Ministerial policy. They consistently attributed to him an aristocratic exclusiveness. The operative device throughout is the likening of the two statesmen by portraying Grenville in the Ministerial image of Talleyrand. Both, for example, hated newspapers and indeed printing, except as victims of taxation. Probably no other poem taken up in the present study was so completely a partisan tactic as *Talleyrand to Grenville.* Although the parody of Grenville's logic performed a respectable job in helping to keep Pitt's self-assured government aware and responsible, the poem has been kept in print only because it is Coleridge's.[21]

He could again claim the excuse of political disgust, but not convincingly, for thirty-nine severer lines on Sir James Mackintosh, a near acquaintance. Although the political philosopher from Aberdeen had turned sharply to the right since his *Vindiciae Gallicae* of 1791, Coleridge wrote *The Two Round Spaces on the Tombstone* out of a personal grudge.[22] Among other favors Mackintosh seems to have promoted Coleridge's interests with his brother-in-law, Daniel Stuart, and with the Wedgwoods, relatives by a second marriage, but the poet can be heard by May, 1800, referring to "the great Dung-fly Mackintosh." (CL, 588) Although much of his intense hatred for the lecturer on philosophy sounds like envy of a successful man, his contempt may conceivably have begun in some such unselfish motive as Mackintosh's disparagement of Wordsworth's poetry. (CL, 737) In letters and notebooks of this period, Coleridge quarrels with Mackintosh's famed eloquence; with his ordonnance—he "intertrudes, not introduces his beauties"; with his discipleship to Locke—"M. asserts the old Tale of no abstract Ideas"; and with his political reversal in 1799—"he forgets his own hypocrisy in his *conversion*." [23] Thereafter Mackintosh remained "the king of the men of talent," that is, no genius and unable even to appreciate "an eminently original man." Perhaps after all it was not Coleridge but Humphry Davy, to whom he sent the tombstone-privy verses by "way of an oddity" to fill out a letter, or some other friend or trusted correspondent, who offered them to Stuart in November for the *Morning Post*. (CL, 632) It seems unlikely that Davy or another besides Coleridge submitted the verses; but if so, publication followed a pattern as old as Gutenberg: any libelous author could foresee publication "by chance," unless he were too angry at his victim to care. Stuart later remembered that he refused to help attack his brother-in-law, but forgot that he had merely censored lines identifying Mackintosh by physical and personal peculiarities and had published the rest, on 24 November.

The lampoon reports the presence on the subject knight's tomb of two round places, in size and shape like the holes in the family house of privity, where "the Devil and His Grannam" sat every sixth of January hoping for the day of judgment so that they could get their Scotch Counsellor when he rose. Coleridge's strictures against Wordsworth's *We Are Seven* and other passages on the lonely bed of death show his horror of burial alive, of "lying in a

dark, cold place"; he nevertheless annotated the line on Mackintosh, "I trust, he lies in his Grave awake," as "a *humane* Wish,"
because the alternative for Mackintosh was Hell. (BL, II, 113; CL,
633) In short, the lampoon resembled a standard venomous type,
usually political when used in newspapers and in this case to be
taken politically by the happily uninformed reader. A reader might
also have his generic prejudice against Scotsmen tickled, but Coleridge seems to have basted Mackintosh first and despised all other
Scotsmen afterward.

For Coleridge the current satirical methods of classical—especially Roman—paraphrase, classical allusion, and lucid allegory
held little attraction. For impetus he went characteristically to
folk legends and superstitions. He neither felt nor desired appeal
to mere intellect. With the Devil's supposed appointment on 6
January to claim his own, compare not only the Devil's walk in
Coleridge's pop-up of greatest acclaim, but also the revolutionary
imp ("mad Devil") flying off with the steeple in *Parliamentary
Oscillators,* the Parson spitting over the horns of the ox to exorcise
its demon in *Recantation,* and the melancholy blackness of the
rainproof protagonist in *The Raven.*[24] In the lampoon on Mackintosh the plunge through four-beat accentual couplets, with variations of crossed quatrains and with three-beat insertions in the
latter half, is designed to give a relaxed creative pleasure that
conventional Hudibrastics or Popean couplets would have pin-
ioned.

Shortly after he sent the lampoon to Davy, as a "Skeltoniad (to
be read in the Recitative *Lilt*)," Coleridge planned, but did not
execute, a more comprehensive satire against reckless satirists like
Peter Pindar and T. J. Mathias, the author of *Pursuits of Literature,*
as well as against Mackintosh and Canning's Anti-Jacobins. (CL,
632; CN, 567) Going beyond *The Devil's Thoughts,* in other words,
the new satire would pillory low satirists, whatever their politics,
as well as turncoat and Pittite political offenders. It might be
noted that verses temporarily recovered by Coleridge at the end
of September, 1799, but apparently lost to us, can hardly be related to this satire, whether their "Pratt" be the miscellaneous
writer Samuel Jackson Pratt, whom Coleridge was soon to meet,
or Sir John Jeffreys Pratt, 2nd Earl Camden, who joined the squib-
list of the *Morning Post* when he put Ulster under martial law in

1797. "I have found," Coleridge informed Southey, "the long rigmarole Verses which I wrote about Pratt &c / but there's nothing in 'em, save facility of Language & oddity of Rhyme—." S. J. Pratt, lovable in the humane sentimentality of such poems as *Bread, or the Poor,* had fecundity but no facility; he was an "honest piece of prolix Dullity & Nullity": his name would hardly head a list of satirists like Wolcot and Mathias. (CL, 536, 553) Thelwall had written Popean couplets on Pratt's *"water-gruel* sweetness" in the *Peripatetic,* 1793. (III, 54) Much more recently, in the *Morning Post* for 25 July 1799, Mrs. Robinson had published *Lines, on Reading Mr. Pratt's Volume of "Gleanings through England,"* under the penname of Laura Maria, one of her more saccharine roles. All this sweetness may have stimulated acidity in Coleridge.

Of a satire proposed fifteen years later, we must again ask whether it was lost, transformed, or never written. When the *Quarterly Review* abused Coleridge in 1814 for dawdling instead of publishing, he threatened to "publish two long Satires in Drydenic Verse, entitled Puff and Slander." (CL, III, 532) When *Blackwood's Edinburgh Magazine* greeted the *Biographia Literaria* with calumny in 1817, he revived the threat. Still calling his counterattack "Puff and Slander," he no longer referred to Drydenic verse, which would have meant satirical heroic couplets. In telling John Morgan that he intended to prefix a chapter of autobiography covering 1816 and 1817, he rejoiced: "The Lines, I have as yet composed for Puff and Slander, are in my own opinion the most vigorous & harmonious, I ever wrote." (CL, IV, 796) E. H. Coleridge, although aware that his grandfather used language of this sort about works begun only in his head, was inclined in 1895 to identify *A Character* as a portion of the projected satires actually completed. In 1912, silent on this point, he assigned to the poem Dykes Campbell's date of 1825. (CPW, 451)

A Character is too "vigorous & harmonious" to be treated among the pop-ups, but a word can be said here concerning its date. Campbell and others after him have dated it 1825 on the supposition that Hazlitt's sketch of Coleridge in *The Spirit of the Age* evoked it. Actually the poem answers charges quite different from those made in the sketch. It accepts Hazlitt's view of its subject as a lonely waif who shunned approval by the crowd but turned also away from a reward for political services rendered, such as Wordsworth's distributorship of stamps or Southey's delivery of odes for an annual stipend. Hazlitt laments, however, not specifically political failure, but the general dissipation of his old deity's genius. He strikes only twice in *The Spirit of the Age*, and less sharply than in previous works, at Coleridge's turn "on the pivot of a subtle casuistry to the *unclean side.*" He makes nothing like a charge of venal capitulation to entrenched power, and it is this charge that *A Character* tries to parry. Venal capitulation is the charge typically represented in Byron's lunges at Coleridge, and in previous attacks by Hazlitt. Verses, letters, marginalia, the Epitaph (here a "poet lies, or that which once seem'd he")—all these attest Coleridge's awareness that he had drowned or dissolved his powers. But he was not one to remain silent at points of weakness in the opposition, and in 1825 he had recent honors, rapt disciples, and multifarious abstruse labors that he could have fluttered before readers misled by Hazlitt. *A Character*, which sticks to defense of his political integrity, was probably a satirical "fragment" seven or eight years old in 1825.

The *Round Spaces* squib arose from personal animosity. If Coleridge's distaste for another member of his circle may have been in small part responsible for a late *jeu d'esprit* that editors have entitled *The Bridge Street Committee*, it bore nobler fruit in the defense of Richard Carlile. In 1817, after clamor by Pitt Clubs and True Blue Clubs, Carlile had been arrested for publishing William Hone's parodies on Government, Creed, and Catechism. In October of 1819 he was prosecuted by the Attorney General, and convicted, for reprinting Paine's *Age of Reason*, and in the two following days, at the instigation of Wilberforce's Society for the Suppression of Vice, prosecuted and convicted for reprinting Elihu Palmer's *Principles of Nature*, a deistic and incidentally republican work from America. After further indictments he was fined £1500 and sentenced to three years in Dorchester Gaol— where he was to be kept for another three years in lieu of fines. Chiefly for the purpose of prosecuting Carlile's assistants, including his wife and his sister, who continued to print his free-thinking and Radical publications, the Constitutional Association for Opposing the Progress of Disloyal and Seditious Principles was founded, by May, 1821, rather widely and richly supported, and installed in headquarters that gave it an alias: the Bridge-Street Gang.

One of the chief promoters of the association in Bridge Street was Sir John Stoddart, a foe to Carlile and William Hone since 1815. After quarreling with John Walter of *The Times* in 1817, Stoddart had set up the *New Times* with a regular subsidy from the Treasury. The attacks of the *New Times* on Carlile and other freethinkers brought forth from Hone a burlesque mirror-image of it entitled *A Slap at Slop and the Bridge-Street Gang*, 1821 ("25th edition" in 1822). Another name for Slop is Stoddart. Brother-in-law to Hazlitt, King's Advocate and Admiralty Advocate in Malta from 1803, Stoddart was the chief influence in Coleridge's coming to Malta the next year, but it could have been he who greeted Coleridge there chillingly and it was certainly he who irritated upon his return to England by holding Coleridge's papers until a strict financial accounting could be made. (CL, 643n; III, 43) The breach may have healed enough for collaboration of some sort on a prospectus for the *Encyclopaedia Metropolitana* late in 1817.[25] Clearer evidence of renewed amicability would seem to lie in the appearance of *The Blossoming of the Solitary Date-Tree* in the *New Times* of 31 January 1818, by way of advertisement for Coleridge's lectures at the London Philosophical Society. But the healing was incomplete.

Although Coleridge's doggerel, *The Bridge Street Committee*, took the opposite side in what must have been Stoddart's bitterest campaign, it was personally punitive only if Coleridge suddenly in 1821 hated half his friends. Besides nine bishops, the Archbishop of York, Wellington, the old enemy of freedoms John Reeves, and the Duke of York's Rev. Dr. Randolph, subscribers to the Constitutional Association included two Lowthers, patrons of Wordsworth; Coleridge's friend and patron Sir George Beaumont; his nephew the Rev. William Hart Coleridge; and other such reputable friends. The head of the association would soon, without displeasing Southey, bring charges against John Hunt for printing *The Vision of Judgment*. In *Felix Farley's Bristol Journal*, J. M. Gutch currently ran editorials against both political wreckage by freethinkers and religious poisoning from radicals: he thus hit Carlile doubly on each cheek.[26] Gutch had admittedly lent Cole-

ridge too much money, and wanted too much of it back, to have
much influence on him in 1821. But even Crabb Robinson, who
generally deplored the reactionary politics of his literary idol
Wordsworth, declared his pleasure at Carlile's imprisonment.[27]

Whatever his denials, many of Coleridge's rimed fleerings arose
in personal malice, but in *The Bridge Street Committee* not even
the reference to Sir Robert Gifford, the Attorney General, could
be meant personally. At a time when the Duke of York had taken
the chair at public meetings to discuss relief, Coleridge was pained
at heart by the distresses of the poor, as can be seen even in the
esoteric middle of his second Lay Sermon. More sorely still he
felt a patriot's anguish over the bills and associations designed to
put down, as the prospectus of the Constitutional Association
declared, "the turbulence and excitement of *public meetings*" and
all "slanderous, seditious, and blasphemous publications," because
these weakened the bonds between "the humbler ranks of society
and their natural guardians and protectors." Southey's most famous
brother-in-law still detested alliances of church and state for hysterical persecution. In 1817 he had republished *Parliamentary Oscillators*, with its satiric reference to "a *Church and Constitution*
scream"; he had changed an attack of 1796 against "mad oppression" to make its object "Bigotry's mad fire-invoking rage!"; he had
added to *Fears in Solitude* the passage on England as a "vain,
speech-mouthing, speech-reporting Guild." (CPW, 157:60, 212:35,
258:57) In 1818 he had written two pamphlets in defense of what
was left of the Factory Bill that Robert Owen had drawn up for
Sir Robert Peel: the pamphlets may have helped in the reduction
of working hours for a few children. We have no reason to believe
that he would not have done more if he had known how. He
withdrew from the Philosophical Society because it would not
expel the calumniator of another member. (CL, IV, 865) Claiming
to detest Jacobins, freethinkers, Radical maligners, and all parodies
whatsoever, he wrote to the editor of the *Morning Chronicle*: "Yet
I exult in Hone's acquittal and Lord Ellenborough's deserved
humiliation . . . ." (CL, IV, 814)

His Bridge-Street doggerel parodies (if he will forgive the word)
the "Association" argument: Jack Snipe eats tripe; therefore tripe
must be considered edible. It follows, of course, that all who do
not eat tripe will be fetched below. But the Devil has been exas-

peratingly slow in claiming the culprits. "And Gifford, th'Attorney, Won't quicken their journey"; therefore loyal men must associate for the purpose:

> The Bridge-street Committee
> That colleague without Pity,
> To imprison or hang
> Carlisle and his gang
> Is the Pride of the City,
> And tis Association
> That alone saves the Nation
> From Death and Damnation.[28]

In prose Hone wrote more forcefully than this against Royal Red Hot Slop and the Inquisitional Association, less forcefully in stanzas modeled on *The Devil's Thoughts* and in other verses; but he published in many editions both verse and prose. Coleridge's principles as a gentleman prophet would not let him publish for the inflammation of the unrighteous. He opposed the hounding even of demagogues, but he could not join Cobbett and Carlile in demagoguery. Thomas Allsop, who first released the impromptu, as he called it, reported Coleridge as saying, "Carlile *may be wrong; his persecutors undoubtedly are so.*" [29]

Up at least until 1821, Coleridge related the shame of his opium addiction to the psychology of the slave, which he defined as "Hopelessness," and again as "oppressions—it is the being in a state out of which he cannot hope to rise." The condition of society in which such hopelessness could occur he called Barbarism, to distinguish it from innocent savagery: only out of Barbarism could the Tories speak of the "laboring poor," as if poverty defined a class within which an individual might be socially fixed. (IS, 35, 315, 366) Sympathy with all who felt dejection and a psychological approach to social as to all other affairs had kept his humanitarian impulses alert.

A greater degree of self-satisfaction in his last years brought with it a broad complacency, represented in 1824 by *The Delinquent Travellers*, a set of cool and assured hexameter couplets preserved for us by the conservative disciple J. H. Green. Political only in a very oblique way, their purport is to ridicule the sharpers, bankrupts, and demireps who were visiting the Continent as if under compulsion by comparing them unfavorably with the "usefullest and most patriotic" of delinquent travelers, those sentenced after fair trial to be "Of Dieman's Land the elected Gentry." [30] The previous year, in *The Reproof and the Reply*, he had taken pleasure in presenting the respectable Mr. Coleridge as a king of thieves, an irony renewed in the verses of 1824: The poet's fancy, after tentatively crossing the Channel in pursuit of countrymen who are on the move in "Tour, Journey, Voyage, Lounge, Ride, Walk," and so on, chooses instead to join the transported felons. Not in total irony, he is rejecting the fidgety progressiveness of the commercial classes for the new agrarian permanence of deportees in Australia.

Two years and one day before he died, when the Reform Bill was nearly two months old and cholera raged, Coleridge sent to Green some fifty gurgling lines slightly more complex than the Bridge-Street doggerel, under the ironic name of Demophilus Mudlarkiades, more inventively virulent against unions of Radicals, reformers, Irish Catholics, and artisans than he had earlier been against noisy associations of the propertied classes. Entitled *Cholera Cured Beforehand*, it mixed preventive medicine with political advice to mudlarks:

> Forswear all cabal, lads,
> Wakes, unions, and rows,
> Hot drams and cold salads,
> And don't pig in styes that would suffocate sows!
> Quit Cobbett's, O'Connell's and Beelzebub's banners,
> And whitewash at once your Guts, Rooms and Manners!
> (CPW, 986:39–44 and note)

Although the next two years must have made it clear that very few mudlarks were yet enfranchised, either Coleridge or his relatives and advisers saw to it that this pointed doggerel, rather than his Jacobinical sympathies with Carlile, appeared in the *Poetical Works* of 1834.

Coleridge's pop-ups vary greatly in force. *The Devil's Thoughts* retains the sharpest satiric edge, but the most readable of these poems today, from the durability of its dramatic myth, is *Fire, Famine, and Slaughter*. Both poems have genuine metrical interest, the one with its bare and driving clarity, the other by symmetry of incantation. Strictly considered, *The Devil's Thoughts* has no controlling myth at all, but an idea, a device that could be treated

like an accordion. Being in fact as expandable as a chain, the device
lent itself to collaboration more handily than the magic carpet of
The Ancient Mariner or even the Corresponding-Society carpet
of *Joan.* Slight myths, undramatic, fabular, are supported respectively by allegory ambiguous to the verge of symbol in *The Raven*
and by the more direct naïveté of *Recantation,* which Coleridge
unnecessarily weakened by the slapdash of its close. Both these
pieces keep their politics fresh by spontaneity of sound. The
Bridge-Street lines and *Cholera Cured Beforehand* continue (at
two later times) his association of political impromptus with casual
metrical experiment, as well as his concrete illustration of political
principles by rejection of current political manifestations of evil.
Other pieces by Coleridge may be cries from a rejected soul: the
pop-ups are the work of a rejecting political poet.

All seven of the poems named have more emotional coloring
than somewhat similar pieces by Swift and Prior. Not so either
Parliamentary Oscillators or *Talleyrand to Grenville,* which represent harried journalism. Although concerned with an episode
more than with the continuing issues that deepen *Fire, Famine*
and *The Devil's Thoughts,* the *Talleyrand* piece embraces more
libertarian principles than any other set of verses by Coleridge. In
the unfortunately hasty embrace it is the arid bones of the verse
itself that crack. The strengths of *Madman and Lethargist* lie in
analogy and structural core, both probably borrowed from a German as busy as Coleridge himself.

The pieces reviewed in this chapter were conceived for pay,
play, and party. These lower reaches touched bottom in his partisan epigrams. (See Appendix C.) Coleridge's talent was not for
epigram, but for prophecy, however gleefully filled with doom.
Without final loyalty to party, he could be demoniacally partisan
in attack. On the day of writing, he probably thought of each
attack as heroic, like the lectures at Bristol; he was seizing his
chance to "leap on the wall & stand in the Breach." (CL, 1001)
Usually, however, like Byron's Don José, he "got down again." As
Lamb wryly noted, there was a spirit of fun in Coleridge's most
solemn moments. Yet happily enough, despite vacillation in skirmishes of the day, the partisanship of the pop-ups is ultimately an
allegiance to humane values, felt in *The Raven* as in *Fire, Famine,
and Slaughter.*

In contrast with these *jeux d'esprit,* and as an antidote to their scorn and rancor, we might turn to two quite different contributions by Coleridge to Georgian politics. The following quatrain might seem to occupy a different world from the sarcasm of *Parliamentary Oscillators:*

> I sigh, fair injur'd stranger! for thy fate;
> But what shall sighs avail thee? thy poor heart,
> 'Mid all the 'pomp and circumstance' of state,
> Shivers in nakedness. . . .
>
> (CPW, 152:1–4)

These are the opening lines of *On a Late Connubial Rupture in High Life,* Coleridge's most dashing and most famous verses on members of the royal family. They originated in the summer of 1796 when some of the Whigs first suspected the Prince of Wales's infidelity to them as well as to his official bride. (Not even his previous marriage to the Roman Catholic Mrs. Fitzherbert, void under the Royal Marriage Act, was successfully concealed from the press.) To J. P. Estlin, a Unitarian friend, the poet wrote: ". . . I simply expressed sympathy for her without endeavoring to heap odium on her husband." (CL, 223) All newspaper readers would recognize, of course, in the poem's prayer that "some holy spell" might "lure thy Wanderer from the Syren's power," an allusion to the Prince's current infatuation with Lady Jersey. (CPW, 152:17–18) A political occasion had arisen when verses on Princess Caroline and her Wanderer would offend few persons beyond the Prince. Coleridge took the occasion so adroitly by the forelock that Lamb did not wince as he passed the verses on to Perry of the *Morning Chronicle.* (LL, I, 33)

It would seem to be of this poem, which has not been found in the *Chronicle* but finally appeared in the *Monthly Magazine* for September, that Coleridge wrote slightingly to Thelwall in mid-November that it "was written at the desire of a beautiful little Aristocrat—Consider it therefore, as a Lady's Poem." (CL, 259) Caroline's usefulness in political propaganda greatly increased with public responses to the separation; the Tories used it as a broadsword against "Prinny," the model prodigal son; from Coleridge's verses and from many, many other sketches, the Whigs later evolved the public image of Caroline as a wronged gentlewoman. That Coleridge recognized the political implications and possibilities, not as a worried Whig but as an optimist and republican, is clear from a letter of 31 May 1796, nearly and perhaps exactly the day he wrote the poem: "The reports concerning the brutality of a certain Heir apparent towards his amiable wife *distress & agitate us as men;* but open a fair prospect to the Friends of Liberty." Detestable measures had been made palatable to "people in general" because of George III's domestic virtues; revelation of his successor's vices should have the opposite beneficial effect. (CL, 219) In July, 1798, Coleridge made three last improvements to the poem, not to raise it above time, but for his own satisfaction as a poet; he headed the manuscript "To the Princess of Wales written during her separation from the Prince," and bound it tighter to a perishable event by annotating "Those plaudits that thy *public* path annoy" as "alluding to the Plaudits with which the Princess was received at the opera house."[31] Late the next year he conceived a poem of more expansive ironies to distress and agitate us as men, "on a Princess, unkissed, & foully husbanded." (CN, 605) That the work would be classed among "poems on Infancy" gives strong evidence that he meant Caroline of Wales, to whom Princess Charlotte Augusta had been born in 1796, and not some princess awaiting her first embrace. He never reprinted *Connubial Rupture,* and never wrote *A Princess Unkissed.*

Coleridge's translation of *Israel's Lament,* a dirge written by his friend Hyman Hurwitz for the funeral-day of Princess Charlotte in 1817, has been sometimes cited as a contribution to the Tories. If it counts, or once counted, either way, it leans to the other side, for Charlotte was the well-publicized secret weapon of the Whigs. They, and the Radicals, raised at Charlotte's death louder laments, as coming from a deeper wound, than the royalists. For Coleridge, the translation probably represented chivalrous, royalist fidelity without any other partisan implication. Crabb Robinson and Thomas Allsop left us evidence that Gillman twice quieted Coleridge's impulse to publish in defense of Queen Caroline when Brougham, no hero to Coleridge, was her official advocate against George's attempts to divorce, unthrone, disinherit, and deport her. (EKC, 287) It might be asked what cache of juvenilia gave up the lines that entered the *Monody on the Death of Chatterton* startlingly between the editions of 1828 and 1829, an address to death unbecoming to a royalist:

> Away, Grim Phantom! Scorpion King, away!
> Reserve thy terrors and thy stings display
> For coward Wealth and Guilt in robes of State!
>
> (CPW, 125:7–9)

Whatever the original date of these three pungent lines, the translation of Hurwitz's dirge-with-hymn on the death of George III, under the title of *The Tears of a Grateful People,* much more typically represents Coleridge's later sentiments. (CPW, 436)

Fortunately, Coleridge made far more durable use of political impulses than in poems on the tears of princesses and remote peoples, and more durable use than in any poem treated in the present chapter.

CHAPTER IX

Poems of Elevation

> ... An artist ... has got to work him-
> self into a passion .... He must make
> himself drunk somehow, and political
> passion is as good a tipple as another.
> —Clive Bell, *Since Cézanne*

The poems by Coleridge still most read and admired, aside from a few small lyrics of peculiar charm, may be separated into those attempting assimilation or suspension of disbelief by lilt, with the supernatural slowing the cadence, and those attempting persuasion by the various resources of rhetoric. The first group ignores Pitt's existence. Although a reader of *Kubla Khan* profits from acquaintance with Coleridge's views on such potentates as Catherine the Great, the poem is hardly celebrated, or open to celebration, for overt political doctrine. In this and the other two poems most eminently suspending disbelief, loved by such political objectors to Coleridge's career as Leigh Hunt, even the diction and imagery derive little of concrete significance from political feelings. The poet's homesickness after a few months in Germany is anticipated, to be sure, in the Ancient Mariner's joy at reaching "mine own countree." (CPW, 204:467) And Coleridge regarded dungeons as evil and strictly political tools, but the dungeon-grate through which the sun peered at the Mariner's guilty ship probably had not acquired its methods of security directly from Pitt, Robespierre, or Admiral Lord Hood. In view of the popularity of Robert Penn Warren's ill-grounded declaration that the sun in this poem supervises the evils of law and reason over against the lunar virtues of freedom and the imagination, let it be said at least that the poetic effect of the peering sun depends very much upon preference for the sun rather than for dungeons, a preference rather likely among readers of the poem. But *The Ancient Mariner* has neither changed nor stirred readers politically in any narrow sense. Even Coleridge's image of the windless ocean "Still as a slave before his lord" has transfixed fewer readers than the stillness of his vessel "As idle as a painted ship Upon a painted ocean." (191:117–18, 202:414) If some of the poet's own dangerous voyaging was political, his Mariner's was not explicitly so.

Repetition throughout *Christabel* gives evidence that Coleridge was not then nauseated, as slighter poems show him to have been a few years earlier, by the word *noble*. The urgency of making Christabel "safe and free" brings an even more insistent repetition, but the danger to her safety and freedom is not identifiably political. There is telling dramatic irony when Sir Leoline proclaims her safe and free. We know with terror that she is not free. And yet in the completed portions of the fragment we never learn why or even how she lacks freedom. To the Romantics, political freedom usually means absence of restraints that leaves one free to act in a certain way, a positive freedom *to*, as the language of economic regulation has it; to the poem's concern that Christabel be "free from danger, free from fear," can be ascribed none of the socialistic or other political implications of freedom *from*. (220:135, 221: 143) The freedoms at issue in *Christabel* are religious, moral, and psychological. Yet the libertarian force of political writings by Coleridge enters this poem, more firmly than it entered *The Ancient Mariner*, in the word *prison*. When Geraldine holds Christabel like an infant in the arms of a slumbering mother, "still and mild," the clang of the word *prison* concentrates all the evil of her hypocritical corruption of innocence:

> A star hath set, a star hath risen,
> O Geraldine! since arms of thine
> Have been the lovely lady's prison.
>
> (226:302–4)

Coleridge built up the impressions of confinement and necessity by diverse means throughout the poem. To take one example, *law*, a word he exercised largely in his dramas, makes a single sensitive appearance in *Christabel*. In an introductory phrase concerning the sacristan's duty of telling his beads at dawn, it was probably respect for natural law, rather than jurisprudence, that chiefly underlay the poet's extremely conscious strengthening of the senses of regularity and inviolability: "hence the custom and law began." (227:338)

It is easy to perceive, but difficult to assess, the pervasive influence of politics in the revival of interest in the Middle Ages that these poems represent. This influence does not depend upon a revived respect for feudal institutions, nor even specifically upon an admiration of what the Romantics took to have been a cohesive society, but begins in the search for a world of affections, the search for a life in which individuals were not isolated by the chopping and fencing of capitalism and Locke. Coleridge's poems of the supernatural reject enlightened selfishness.

The much larger group of important poems, the persuasive, divides by form into the stanzaic odes, like that to the Duchess of Devonshire, and the poems in blank verse, which ascend from the casually conversational through the reflective and the solemnly meditative to liturgical rapture. The blank verse of rapture was usually employed for political assault. The solemn meditations and the rapturous assaults were distinguished by Coleridge himself in 1797 in tracing his growth from the time his brother George had listened to his first measures:

> Since then my song
> Hath sounded deeper notes, such as beseem
> Or that sad wisdom folly leaves behind,
> Or such as, tuned to these tumultuous times,
> Cope with the tempest's swell!
>
> (CPW, 175:64–68)

Byron, too, recognized a duality: "Shall gentle COLERIDGE pass unnoticed here, To turgid ode and tumid stanza dear?" [1] The supernatural enters several of the more excited odes and even some of the blank verse, in that Coleridge attempts to rise by enigma and incantation into the bardic and apocalyptic. All these tumultuous poems seem to have taken as their model a volcano sloping steeply off into calm water.

Coleridge's first major effort, begun on Christmas Eve, 1794, although titled *Religious Musings* and achieving a meditative solemnity, reaches furthest among the blank verse poems into the political frenzy of the more agitated odes. As *Religious Musings* is the most ambitious effusion he ever completed, the date of its commencement could account sufficiently for the breaking off of the political sonnets. It displaced them by a higher call. In another poem he describes this one as "elaborate and swelling," which it is. (CPW, 78:2) Like most Romantic prophecy, it envisions a politically improved society, here a society much purged and at the Day of Judgment perfected.

Beginning in the season of the Nativity, the first 130 or so lines raise a hosanna to the one omnipresent Mind, or Love, whose impress lies on meadow, high grove, sea, sun, and stars, and (as demonstrated by Hartley) on the elected saints, who, having advanced from petty fears to love of God, mourn for their earthly oppressors. Out of superstition, however, which is the desire for something besides the Supreme Reality, have risen slavery and war, a "sea of blood bestrewed with wrecks." (113:124) Here begins what the Argument calls the "Digression to the present War," actually the core of the poem. The poet began to muse on God, Europe, and Peace because the war all along has been blasphemously claimed as a defense of the Lamb of God—defense by means of that "thirsty brood," Catherine, Frederick, Francis, and the German princelings. No! The War has come because "offences needs must come." (115:159)

Next, as a footnote added in 1797 explains, "the Author recalls himself from his indignation against the instruments of Evil, to contemplate the *uses* of these Evils in the great process of divine Benevolence." (CPW, 116n) A primeval "vacant Shepherd," with nothing to worry about, through Necessity fixed by the prescience of God imagined the desire for property. From property flowed the vices and virtues of human history, "Warriors, and Lords, and Priests," but over against these (yet by the law of Necessity out of them) sprang Science and Freedom, represented in society by Philosophers, Bards, and patriots. The poem comprises within itself another example of the law: Out of that nettle, War, has come this flower, *Religious Musings*.

Those I have called patriots Coleridge gives no name at all, but devotes to them the twenty-nine lines from 231 to 259. They are the benevolent, humane, sensitive few. They turn from popularly admired victors and the puppetry of thrones, with mild sorrow, to contemplate the mastery of lightning by "the Patriot Sage ... Smiling majestic," identified in a footnote as Dr. Franklin. These sensitive sages have readied themselves for a day when the miserable, at first driven by masters, have at last by eloquent speakers been led into riot. On that "fated day," the sages can and do tame the "outrageous mass" to a microcosm of order, because they have accumulated power from earlier reflection. Inly musing on a summer day, with the macrocosm of divine order wafted before them, the sages have asked themselves "Why there was misery in a world so fair." By musing as the poet muses, they stored up power. In conventional theoretic terms, the argument is this: from discovering their organic union with the living universe, the sages concluded that evil lay in artificial social arrangements, but they counteracted the doctrine of revolution against current arrangements by persuading the distressed of the possibility and necessity of growing toward a final harmony, not by violence but through the wisdom of universal benevolence. Converting the atheistic, rational argument of *Political Justice* into emotion as method and piety as end, the passage leaves unresolved the Romantic dilemma: within the organic universality of divine love, how did the evil of artificial arrangements arise? Looking to the present and the future, how can the Jacobins (in this passage uncondemned as "eloquent men ... with pealing voice") be proved inferior to Patriot Sages like the lecturer at Bristol?

Angry enough to be momentarily sympathetic with Jacobin demagogues, the poet incorporated some of their language. Lines 260–300 commiserate "the wretched Many," plundered of fruit and disbranched at winter from the tree of Knowledge: hungry assailants, prostitutes, paupers, impressed soldiers, their widows, the aged poor. Each revision washed a little, but did not efface, the wounds of "scepter'd Glory's gore-drench'd field," where the ensnared soldiers waited steaming in putrid heaps for vultures. (CPW, 120n) "Blessed Society" stretches in an epic simile as a "sun-scorched waste," coursed by the purple haze of the simoom ("emblematical of the pomp and powers of Despotism"), and by the lion, bloody hyena, and behemoth at war with serpent. (JDC, 580) Lamb protested the tumidity of these bestial sores—"Snakes, Lions, hyenas and behemoths, is carrying your resentment beyond bounds"—but the passage stands, as a whole, unsoftened. (LL, I, 8)

Stridency does not diminish as the poet assures the children of wretchedness that Retribution is nigh, the fifth seal hath been opened—that is, the French Revolution has burst upon the Rich and the "Kings and the Chief Captains of the World," who soon will be downtrodden like unripe figs shaken to the ground by storm. (121:310) With Biblical allusions throughout, the poem follows from this passage onward the teleology of the Apocalypse. The next verse paragraph begins, "O return! Pure Faith! meek Piety!" which I once mistakenly took as parallel with the recall of Alpheus in *Lycidas,* where Milton gives assurances that "the dread voice is past"; to the contrary, the apostrophe begins Coleridge's pronouncement of doom on the whoredom of religious establishments—"mitred Atheism" that has so long abused "patient Folly." (121:334, 335) Upon the fall of this Babylon, equality in common toil—that is, pantisocracy—can conduct the mystic dance of the millennium. Time closes and Paradise opens before us. Milton, Newton, Hartley, and Priestley (in chronological order) rise again. Darkness beyond time betokens the fall of the "black-visaged, red-eyed Fiend"—not, we perceive, identifiable as Pitt. (124:388) After a few lines asserting a Berkeleian idealism and a doctrine of universal redemption, the poet closes with self-dedication to the discipline of his thought in song and meditation, while divine Love rises in his soul like the great sun.

As noted on an earlier page, the controlling symbol in the poem is light, first from the surpassing brightness of the Savior, as he shines from within the oppressed who mourn for the oppressor. With Romantic assurance this light of beatitude is followed to the divine emanation, and also immanence, that gives us "Our noontide Majesty." (113:127) The poem is made further akin to others in its class by geographical vision, for the metaphors taken from exotic books of travel pass into Coleridge's poems through a unified political vision of one mysterious world, still at the time of *Religious Musings* a world to be someday pantisocratic by the unswerving will of God.

It takes an intrepid and hungry bookworm to eat through *The Destiny of Nations: A Vision,* a romantico-politico-religious patchwork of 474 lines in blank verse. The numbering emblematically includes three half-lines. As Lowes said, it contains marquetry rather than miracle. It began as 365 of the first 452 lines in Book II of Southey's *Joan of Arc*, as published in December, 1795 (dated 1796). Manuscripts make it possible to observe prenatal stages of their joint work, but nobody has set straight the embryo's ontogeny.[2] David Erdman has collated the 148 additional lines that appeared as "The Visions of the Maid of Orleans" in the *Morning Post*, the day after Christmas, 1797, when biographers have thought that Coleridge was providing Stuart with the usual moans and promises instead of copy. (*SB*, XI, 151) Basically *The Destiny of Nations* combines these two beginnings. Among alternate titles, Coleridge called it "the progress of European Liberty." (CL, 243; cf. 285, 297) Almost as much as *Religious Musings*, the fragments make up a work of prophetic exaltation and emotional discharge. But his various titles, although usually accompanying the central political concept of the progress of liberty or the destiny of nations with the modal suggestion of a vision, deny to this looser congeries the religious heights of Zion intimated in the title, invocation, and apocalyptic method of his other long poem in blank verse. He blamed the clinking abstractions of the original segment on Southey, with some justification, since he had been requested to propound a myth that explained Southey's Ambition, Slaughter, Fury, "cow'd Superstition," "mitred Hypocrisy," Oppression (on whose brow sat Desolation), and similar beasts encountered in those days when one set about to observe the victory of a virtuous France over a wicked insular enemy. Their combined work tells how Monarchy by meeting Ambition introduces carnage and all attendant evils. As Coleridge says in some lines to Charles Lloyd, he was "rudely vers'd in allegoric lore." (CPW, 156:49) His contribution, which halted all action in the poem, began and ended with the Father of Heaven, "only Rightful King." (131:3) To Coleridge was assigned, or allowed, the long pause for a "deep preluding strain." Part of his job was to create suspense by burying the thread of the story. The narrative lines in *The Destiny of Nations* (139–277) belong to the "Visions" not contributed to Southey's epic. Among lines written for the epic, manuscript portions at the British Museum show that some of the Platonic myth and metaphysics, on how we are "Placed with our backs to bright Reality," were a fairly late addition to the political theorizing and rhetoric.[3]

Coleridge's poem begins in invocation, or more strictly in a prelude to invocation. An apostrophe to "Auspicious Reverence" attunes readers to the solemn proposition ("only Rightful King") that leads into the invocation. Considering the way he tugged the segments about, it would be an act of supererogation to abstract the argument that then follows. It is more pertinent to notice some of its devices, such as the filming over of republican audacity with the paraphernalia of dream-vision; the prudential ventriloquism, as in a republican speech by the Tutelary Spirit; the augury of later wars than Joan's; the aggressive rather than prudential litotes (Joan's form "nor Sloth nor Luxury Had shrunk or paled"); the extended similes, to give an epic swell; Miltonic arrangements of syntax, which make politics seem literary; epithets like kennings, especially in an anthropological passage on Greenland; mixed symbolic and sociological interpretations of legends from distant lands; Godwinian metaphysics by personification (the Power of Justice shines from the brow of a "mild-eyed Form," to whom the poet in apostrophe says that those who have dwelt unblamed in her dwellings "call thee Happiness"); a derivative but murky myth about how Night, made envious by the rise of Love, spent ages with Chaos in her cave (Europe?), where he begot upon her the adventurous progeny of evils much adored "in Camps and Courts"; a corollary, positive myth of sorts in five extended geographical images that make up an intercontinental vision, not totally unified but more deeply pervasive than the geographical images in *Religious Musings;* and, as a later addition to the Maid's education, a lengthy exhibit of poverty, which serves the poem as an exemplum of humanitarian pity. In the murky negative myth, the abstract evils of camp and court refer back to those assembled by Southey.

Study of unpublished variants has not clarified for me the part played in the myth by fierce Hate and gloomy Hope, who engendered a Dream which roused Night to move from primeval chaos to human society. Apparently this Dream represents something like a crude anticipation of the reign of Jupiter in Shelley's *Prometheus Unbound,* a process of extinguishing intellectual light among men through tyrannous monarchy; but possibly we should believe Coleridge's later notation concerning the lines, in William Hood's copy of *Joan of Arc:* "hang me, if I know or ever did know the meaning of them." (CPW, 140n) Lamb, whom it pained to regard any of the lines as coming from the same mind as *Religious Musings*, scorned especially the narrative addition, the "cock and a bull story," he called it, that told how a publican's daughter named Joan watched a swinging signboard and with equal fascination came upon a chilled father, "Frost-mangled" mother, and their six children—"why not nine children, it would have been just half as pathetic again." (LL, I, 92–93) Like Lowes, Lamb may have felt that this "pot girl" too nearly resembled Jeanne the barmaid in Voltaire's *La Pucelle*. Despite his distaste Lamb's response informs us how a reader of that day would know at once that the two fair clouds following a pestilential vapor, pointed out for Joan by the Tutelary Spirit, represent the American and French Revolutions. (CPW, 145:421–50) For a twentieth-century reader the long passage consists of exotic vapors boiling up in the distance, like its cloud exhaled from "Egypt's fields that steam hot pestilence." Lamb, returning in his next letter to Joan of the alehouse, chaffs Coleridge's anachronism that sight of a family dying with cold roused her "into a state of mind proper to receive visions emblematical of equality"; he does not know what the devil Joan had to do with equality, "or indeed with the French and American revolutions; though that needs no pardon, it is executed so nobly." (LL, I, 99)

There is no critical defense against Lowes's complaint that the episode of the frozen family, from the feeble voice of the father to the baby with "crisp milk frozen on its innocent lips," resulted from the mere splicing of two scenes in the "Interesting Narration relative to the Campaign of 1794 and 1795," of which Coleridge ran the first installment in the *Watchman* for 19 April. (*Xanadu*, pp. 102–9) He spliced here more seamlessly than elsewhere. Approached critically, the whole poem consists of knots, lumps, and chips. Fancy shuffled the details, but imagination had not dissolved, diffused, and re-created them. The political impulses evident in Coleridge's procedure may have contributed to the rawness, as it seems a century later, in two ways, or rather may have countenanced it for two reasons. First, the poet would not wish to conceal his source from his readers; instead, the political journalist in him would wish concurring or impressible readers to see that he accused eloquently without exaggeration. More than re-using his materials, he is deliberately alluding to fact, as not only Lamb but even strangers who had read neither the *Watchman* nor its published source would recognize.[4] Second, he himself felt the modified details, the appended generalizations, and the exemplum of pity so urgently that he neither perceived the lumpiness of the result nor accepted Lamb's aesthetic aversion to temporary politics as applying to the pungency of this intensely human material, exalted by meter and metaphor. (CL, 309)

As already suggested, the poem has geographical opulence: In Lapland Fancy "unsensualises" the dark mind; along the Gulf of Bothnia "Leviathan" stirs the ocean of peace into the storm of war; from Egypt a pestilential cloud (of locusts pouring out of Exodus 10:4–19, but meaning tyranny) travels to a distant "death-doomed land"; in a still more distant land a bright following cloud overtakes the pestilential vapor; recrossing the Atlantic, the brightening cloud causes a bright form, more dazzling than Apollo when he slew the python, so to burst forth as to send shrieking Ambition and the hissing locust-fiends of Corruption into commotion like that made by a mad tornado roaring through the West Indies. In these Romantically exotic but essentially republican symbols, in the more innocent image of a white bear howling from an ice-floe toward her sundered cubs, and even (prefiguring *The Ancient Mariner*) amid the "miscreated life" poisoning the Pacific, the fragmentary poem explores our universal brotherhood under plastic God. African slavery infects life in England.

A brief guide to the political bias of geographical details in *The Destiny of Nations* is available in Southey's stanzas *To Horror* in his *Poems* of 1797. Both poets draw upon identical passages from sources widely varied but all pertinent to their Bristol lectures and their politics. Reducing Coleridge's coruscations to a mixture of plain English and threadbare poetastric diction, Southey lists almost in tabular form the scenes that horror could take him to. Except for an innocent Gothic start at a haunted sepulcher, and an innocuous visit to a tall ship sinking in a tempest, each scene partakes of Oppositional unrest: wind and snow lashing a wayworn traveler (Southey's favorite figure of misery, met also in poems by Coleridge and Wordsworth); a mariner wrecked "on Groenland's shore" while "the floating ice-hills round" echo to "the roar Of herded bears" (compare the end of Coleridge's *Destiny*); men dying amid the contagion of the battlefield; the mother clasping her frozen child to her frozen breast; the deathbed of a conqueror, when "The phantoms of the murder'd rise" (as before Catherine in Stanza III of the *Ode on the Departing Year*); and the "impaled Negro" awaiting the "blasting gales of Pestilence" (which, as Coleridge often tells us, come from Egypt).[5]

Both *Religious Musings* and the stiffer shards of *The Destiny of Nations* reach back through eighteenth-century meditative and persuasive blank verse toward the cadences of Milton. The century of Coleridge's birth also cultivated, or allowed to grow with less and less pruning, odes to arouse and odes to sublimate political emotion. There were, for Coleridge to modify, as the late Humphry House simplified it, "the Gray-like Ode precedents and the Darwin-like periphrastic precedents."[6] The architecture of the Gothicized Pindaric provided exactly the gusty, storm-receiving tower suitable for the political impulses in Coleridge's temperament. The *Ode on the Departing Year,* the first of his "splendid Tirades" inhabiting a ruined castle of this order, had general precedent in the populous race of political odes in the newspapers. It had more specific provocation from certain odes offering biased predictions for the coming year. The Poet Laureate, Henry James Pye, earned part of his annual cash, perhaps the part he took unpoetically in lieu of a butt of sack, by an officially optimistic "Ode for the New Year." The Laureate's official ode was carried annually in most newspapers and periodicals, including those of the Opposition, which gleefully named them "Christmas pyes." In this morass lay challenges to originality and to Jacobin response.

In the *Morning Chronicle,* typically, *An Ode for New Year's Day, 1794* greeted readers on 1 January, ahead of Pye, with the Opposition view: "Howl ye fiends of black despair." The next year Robert Merry, flamboyant mentor to Perdita, hounded 1795 through stanzas of predicted desolation, slaughter, tyranny, and the "armed Rich," but closed with the prospective tomb of War itself, dimly seen yet gaily decorated with the flags of Peace and Liberty. On 17 January *Felix Farley's Bristol Journal* followed Pye's ode, which it had printed on the third day of the year, with an unsigned *Ode for the New Year,* "addressed to His Excellency Earl Fitzwilliam." Although the ode hailed Fitzwilliam as "Ireland's hope," it was no more faithful than Merry's ode to the cheerful and forgiving Tory-Pyed type. Ahead lay another wretched year under Pitt. Other variations on the standard type appeared where Coleridge would have seen them. Benjamin Flower, who commissioned Coleridge's ode—first titled *Ode for the Last Day of the Year, 1796*—had carried in the *Cambridge Intelligencer* Pye's odes for 1794 and 1795; on 27 December 1794 he had printed Cowper's poem beginning "Thankless for favours from on high" as "Verses Written at the close of the Year." By a first step the Opposition countered Pye's fawning and happy odes with dire predictions; by a second step, they could look back toward the miserable year under Hanoverian George just brought to a bloody close. In this mood Samuel Whitchurch wrote a *Farewell to the Year 1794*, which anticipates Coleridge's ode of 1796 not only in measuring the bloodiness of such a year of massacre but also in giving pride of place to "the bloody Tygress of the North." Coleridge could have seen the journalistic quatrains of this *Farewell* in Thelwall's *Tribune*.[7] Unless Cottle and Griggs are a year too early in their dating, Coleridge had certainly learned no later than the last day of 1795 to look both ways at the change of years, for on that evening he was desired "to drink only one wine glass of Punch in honor of the departing Year—& after 12, one other in honor of the new year." (CL, 174)

He wrote the ode partly to share his "indignant grief" and partly as a catharsis of strong public emotions, inspired particularly by the death on 17 November of Catherine of Russia. (CPW, 149:15; 160) Hysterical prophecy is in him, and must get out. When public events stung him into poetry, he had to tell "intemperate truth" in contrast with what Collins' *Ode on the Poetical Character* called "Truth, in sunny vest array'd." The ode on 1796 seemed literary enough, and not too intemperate, to prepare for publication as a separate quarto on the same "last day" it appeared in the *Intelligencer*. The journalist labored successfully to confine his passions within the oscillatory form of a regular Pindaric ode, even though his labeling of Strophes I and II before Epode I, with Antistrophes I and II accompanying Epode II, was not precisely Hellenic. But Lamb, asking irreverently what these things meant, suggested that any laws of strophe and antistrophe too rigid to allow change toward more sense and better taste would be about as worth following as the laws of the Medes and Persians.[8]

Lamb's sarcasm and Romantic principle prevailed: the form

relaxed licentiously with subsequent changes in the text. It may have been fear of reprisal that made Coleridge remove a topical passage of several lines, which told how the "boastful bloody son of Pride"—presumably Pitt—sent an ambassador with "treacherous dalliance" to sue for peace, and then stiffened the terms when Charles Louis of Austria gained a victory on the Rhine. Fortunately the removal of this passage, which destroyed the regularity of the ode, improved its structure organically. Throughout all changes, the disposition of forces remained basically the same: Invocation to Providence, and announcement of occasion; call to men to turn from private emotions and social misery to "Weep and rejoice" at the labor pains of Nature; call to the slaughtered to haunt the tomb of that slaughteress whose death had just stunned Ambition; vision of the Year, which introduces the Spirit of the Earth; call to the God of Nature—by the Spirit, now assisting the bard—to avenge the warfare, treachery, hunger, and slavery of the Year; and prophecy by the bard himself, in the anguish of his wisdom, revealing how Destruction hurries upon Albion. With the poet cleansed from "vaporous passions," which are specified in the versions of 1797 and 1803 as Fear and Anguish, his ode subsides into the calm of a postlude. Far from seeking pastures new, he recenters his soul in "meek self-content."

The original title, to accord with a new Oppositional mode provoked by the Laureate's annual "Ode for the New Year," was "Ode for": ode for the last day of 1796, its simple meaning of an ode fitted for publication on that day overlaid with an ironic meaning. Like the toast, it was given "in honor of the departing Year." Thereafter, Coleridge entitled it *Ode on the Departing Year*, meaning an elevated poem on a certain serious subject of public concern. By choosing to reprint from the edition of 1834, which was supervised by the poet's nephew, the grandson E. H. Coleridge has propagated, though I hope not perpetuated, what is in effect the typographical error of *Ode to the Departing Year*.[9] This "to" for "for" makes less effective, first, the opening apostrophe to the creative Spirit whose "inwoven harmonies" have been unraveled by 1796; second, the device of a vision in which the train of the Departing Year sweeps through the ode like Bede's swallow through the mead-hall; third, the turn to address Albion in Stanzas VII and VIII and finally to address the poet's inner being; and

fourth, worst of all, the strategic whole, which analyzes a personified collection of events—not in tête-à-tête, but with attempted
ode-like formality. Into the whole is sharply and intricately set,
in Stanza IV, the apostrophe to the personified collection of events
making up the Departing Year. From the apostrophe, Coleridge
faltered into a footnote, lest the reader miss the distinction between
the actual, slaughtered Year, addressed in Stanza IV, and its image
in the vision, described elsewhere in the ode. "To" for "for" in
the title blurs all such distinctions.

Beyond all other models, Coleridge emulated Thomas Gray's
bloodiest imagining, *The Bard: A Pindaric Ode*. In defense of his
predictions of British woe, he reminded correspondents that in
ancient days (as they could learn from Gray) bard and prophet
were one. He told Cottle that some persons thought his ode
superior to *The Bard*. (CL, 309) Gray may have been his excuse
for the twenty-odd personifications, which have only slightly
warmer blood than those in *The Destiny of Nations* blamed on
Southey. Despite queries from Lamb, Coleridge retained incon-
gruities and oxymorons based on the practice of Gray and Collins,
like "mad Avarice," and looser methods of reconciling opposites,
as in the impetuous solemnity of the poet's response when his
eye caught the wavy folds of the train of the Departing Year: "I
rais'd the impetuous song, and solemnis'd his flight." (CPW,
161:12) This solemnity in impetuosity he then felt in *The Bard*. A
few years later he discovered the temporary effect of such poems
as Gray's to lie in their being "generally & not perfectly understood." In his own ode he had tried to emulate the passionate
vagueness through which his model continues to affect readers,
said Coleridge, so long as "no criticism is pretended to"; later he
understood *The Bard* so perfectly that he saw through it: "*The
Bard* once intoxicated me, & now I read it without pleasure." (CN,
383)

Although it contains the impetuosity of transition and precip-
itation of fancy that Coleridge admired, Gray's ode altogether
lacks, to put it mildly, passion for public life, even in its docu-
mented history from Plantagenets to Tudors. Essentially it is a
narrative ode with extensive quotation from such curses pronounced by the druidical bard as "Ruin seize thee, ruthless King!"
and "Weave the warp, and weave the woof, The winding-sheet of

Edward's race." Taking from Gray all his stanzas could hold, Coleridge had to leave the narrative approach behind. Wisdom has been accorded to speakers framed within odes since the First Olympian of Pindar, and Coleridge assigns to the informing Spirit his direct threat against "the thankless Island"; but he recedes into no narrative except of the unmediated vision, by which he authenticates the source of his wisdom as bard: "Long had I listen'd, free from mortal fear," when lo! "I saw the train of the Departing Year!" [10] He strips the past tense from Gray's method, adopts its visionary fervor, and steps forth in his own guise as unbridled genius. He replaces the irony in Gray's foreshadowing of recorded history with a more stirring moral charge to his readers, who stare with him into an actual darkness and are already disposed to worry about the doom he prophesies.

He who thus declares his country to be hated by other nations, and furthermore to have been disclaimed by heaven, otherwise shows himself a lover of the hills, valleys, showers, and sheep of England, and notes that the wild Ocean still "Speaks safety to his Island-child." (167:130) He is a kind of Auden or MacLeish (of 1940) who denies guilt in the promotion of tyranny—"I unpartaking of the evil thing"—but feels his burden as a member of the responsible class. (168:154) The incantation Coleridge admired in the odes of Gray and Collins, and for which he strove, is drowned in the howl of his political passions, except when the Apocalypse is evoked, rather weakly and too tunefully, for the introduction of the Earth-Spirit:

> Throughout the blissful throng,
> Hush'd were harp and song:
> Till wheeling round the throne the Lampads seven,
> (The mystic Words of Heaven)
> Permissive signal make . . . .
>
> (CPW, 164:74–78)

On the other and stronger hand, one of the most apocalyptic of all the images in Coleridge's political poetry comes in the present Stanza VIII: Destruction, a vast dragon-like beast, soothes her fierce solitude by dreaming of central fires thundering up through nether seas, but she leaps on her perilous couch and mutters distempered triumph whenever the predestined ruins of England pass as a reflection in her lidless eyes. After a rising shrillness of eight stanzas, the ode purges its turbulent prophecy in a quiet epode of thirteen lines. Its pity had meanwhile got rather stormy, as Coleridge admitted to Bowles. (CL, 318) By pursuing Destruction into the manuscripts, we can identify her with the "old Hag" of the millennium, the "eyeless drudge, black Ruin." In an early manuscript of *Religious Musings*, at line 321, he had described Ruin as

> Nursing th'impatient earthquake, and with dreams
> Of shatter'd cities & the promis'd day
> Of central fires thro' nether seas upthundering
> Soothes her fierce solitude—
>
>   (B.M. MS. Add. 35343, f. 66)

The original readers of the *Ode on the Departing Year* would not know that Coleridge was stealing from his own left hand; but they probably understood without this information that he was predicting for the British monarchy not merely defeat but annihilation in the storm whose beginning "alludes to the French Revolution." (CPW, 121n)

In the quarto pamphlet, his preface in the form of dedicatory letter assured readers that Thomas Poole would *"know*, that although I prophesy curses, I pray fervently for blessings." (CPW, 1114) When he replaced the opening of the address to Albion, "O doom'd to fall, enslav'd and vile," by its reading after 1803, "Not yet enslaved, not wholly vile," he must have felt the relief of a judge mitigating sentence, but its effect in context is hardly milder than before the change. Where the original version attributed foredoomed vileness to future enslavement, the final version leaves the source of enslavement ambiguous, but makes his country's partial vileness present and certain.

He could slash without hesitation at the acknowledged vileness of Catherine. If the Greek epigraph castigates her indirectly, the reason for indirection was not hesitancy but artfulness. When Cottle's printer omitted the epigraph from the proofs of the 1797 edition, Coleridge raged: "The Motto—! where is the Motto?—? I would not have lost the MOTTO for a kingdom." And he explained his emotion: "twas the best part of the Ode." [11] The quotation comes from a key speech of Cassandra's in *Agamemnon*, where it is broken by twenty-odd lines that Coleridge omitted. The quoted lines open with Cassandra's cry at the horror of her own vision, and close with a prediction that future tears will tell how true the prophecy. The omitted lines revile Clytemnestra, monstrous, lecherous murderer of her mate, in anticipation of Coleridge's Stanza III (of the final version), which in similar language reviles the "insatiate Hag" Catherine. It had to be pointed out to him, by Thelwall, that one line on the Empress "had more of Juvenal than Pindar." (CL, 307)

The greatest of Coleridge's political poems is *France: An Ode*. Despite its wizards, "Priestcraft's harpy minions," "factious Blasphemy's obscener slaves," and writhing dragons, it flows with clarity of exposition. (CPW, 247:95–96) Overt dignity of rhythm and pattern replace the mystical knots of the *Ode on the Departing Year*, to which the later poem is, in style as in idea, "a kind of Palinodia." (CPW, 168n) Talk with Wordsworth has thinned out the personifications. The poem first appeared in the *Morning Post* for 16 April 1798, as "The Recantation, an Ode. By S. T. Coleridge." An introductory note revealed what disquiet Bonaparte's invasion of Switzerland had stirred among those who styled themselves advocates for Freedom. An editorial note praised Coleridge not for thinking the conduct of France atrocious, which everybody did, but for publicly denouncing what he had formerly praised and for avowing his past misjudgment, which few lovers of Freedom had yet shown the courage to do.

Here we may once again, as in the overturn of Godwin, regard Coleridge as a leader of the retreat toward the right, not for the whole society but for a small group who had taken up a given position on the left, to the lee of extremists who had martyrdom as an aim or physical need as a drive. Granting our ignorance of one stanza editorially excised, Coleridge seems in *France* to have gone slightly ahead of Stuart. Since Coleridge's editorials and articles for the *Post* usually coincide with the drift of editorial policy, it may be that he took to verse to persuade Stuart as well as their readers. For five years the Opposition had dared ministers to prove the one charge that might justify their war, the frequent but unproved charge that France was disposed toward "unprovoked interference with the Governments of other Countries." (MC, 5 Aug. 1794) Coleridge had believed Britain, not France, guilty in the failure of negotiations. He did not in *France* acknowl-

edge, and perhaps did not realize, the victory that Grenville's diplomacy had won over his mind the previous September, when the
French Directory returned Baron Malmesbury with insults. Now
proof lay on the table, as *France: An Ode* acknowledged, although
it gave no credit to Grenville or Pitt. In this ode and in the almost
contemporaneous *Fears in Solitude* Coleridge had to charge the
British with impiety and their clergy with indolent hypocrisy as
a political transition to his patriotic rejection of French blasphemy.
Like his editor and the Opposition generally, he became more
strident against the established regime whenever he needed continuity in transition from a position that had become untenable.

As Dr. Erdman's studies make quite clear, the *Morning Post*
was currently in retreat on the issues of domestic freedom. The
United Irishmen had made every form of treason and sedition
unattractive. Besides the suspension of habeas corpus for which
Tierney voted, there were more direct threats to freedom of the
press. In early March, Stuart was summoned before the Privy
Council; in late March, Perry of the *Morning Chronicle* was
sentenced to Newgate for three months. It does not seem likely
that Coleridge uttered the recantation of *France: An Ode* out of
a sudden desire to put himself right with the Ministers, but his
renunciation of government as a source of freedom follows from
current events in London as well as from French betrayal of
Swiss liberty.

The ode reveals, on the other hand, a more general cause
behind Coleridge's response to the invasion of Switzerland: an
intellectual and emotional dissatisfaction with the materialism
and empiricism of Hartley and Priestley, and with all doctrines
appropriated by the French; a deep spiritual thirst not satisfied
by doctrines of natural right and reform. In March, when the
annuity from the Wedgwoods had made his detachment from
ephemeral quarrels possible and morally necessary, his letters
had begun to argue the importance of moral, independent action
by individual citizens and the unimportance of party leaders and
the governments they misshaped. (CL, 395) The invocation to
Clouds, Ocean-Waves, and Woods that opens the ode is not merely
conventional. The last stanza returns, for reasons not thinly aesthetic, to an evocation of the first stanza. I "shot my being through
earth, sea, and air," possessing all, for "O Liberty! my spirit felt

thee there." (CPW, 247:103–5) The last stanza thus reviews the
affirmation of the first that Liberty resides only among free natural
elements, "every thing that is and will be free." (244:18) In short,
the ode seems to begin and end in despair of government. The
poet seems neither to hope for political reform nor any longer
to trust it.

The second, third, and fourth stanzas trace his voyage to this
unregimented shore. These three are the stanzas concerning France
in what is fundamentally an Ode to Liberty. They do not mitigate
his former allegiance to Gallic freedom; rather they emphasize
his perseverance in isolation from his fellow countrymen. The
second stanza proves his perseverance by holding still the Opposition view of the origin of the war in Britain's collusion with the
Continental despots, "Like fiends embattled by a wizard's wand."
(245:29) If he is antedating, as he may be, when he claims to have
hoped and feared from the moment France stamped her foot and
gave "that oath, which smote air, earth, and sea," antedating is
poetically justified for the metaphor of the smiting circles, which
have radiated from the Bastille and the Bill of Rights to make
their impact at the foundation of other countries, in an international
version of the leaden circles that were to spread from Big Ben to
Mrs. Dalloway and then to strangers thus encircled in her life. So
Gallic liberty has encircled mankind. The stanza proceeds to its
close: All associations and affections made the poet love the hills
and groves of Britain—but not enough, O Liberty! to make him
damp thy holy flame.

Stanza III continues his apologies for the French Revolution.
Although worried when dissonance strove with the sweet paeans
of delivered France, he reproached his worries. Neither the scream
of Blasphemy (at the altar of Reason) nor the wild dance of
drunken passions (around the guillotine) shook him from his
unpopular belief that beyond these storms the sun was rising.
Stanzas II and III successfully strengthen the venerable antithesis
of light and darkness with the sonant contrast of harmony and
discord. Sight and sound together present a single impression of
self-torn France. Stanza III tells also how the poet dreamed that
France would "compel the nations to be free," in the time before he
felt the unpleasant tension since brought by Bonaparte to the
paradox of enforcing freedom. (246:62)

Stanza IV, beginning "Forgive me, Freedom!" specifies as the cause for his dream's abrupt ending the loud lament of Freedom in Helvetia. The placing of Switzerland's icy caverns and snow-strewn mountains against smooth English hills and groves heightens the reversed contrast, both aesthetic and ideological, between the "bloodless freedom of the mountaineer" and the "low lust of sway" that has brought first Britain and now France to yell in the hunt. About 1808, in Sir George Beaumont's copy of the 1798 quarto (now in the Pierpont Morgan Library), Coleridge glossed the final couplet of the stanza, "To insult the shrine of Liberty with spoils From freemen torn; to tempt and to betray," as "alluding to Venice, and Holland." [12] If the Beaumonts needed a gloss in 1808, it is not surprising that lay readers today interpret the spoils, temptation, and betrayal as adequate references to France's abuse of Switzerland. Three chronological groups are discernible: the immediate readers, who felt the force of supplementary atrocities in Venice and Holland; the intermediate, who remembered enough to sense inappropriate reference to Switzerland; and the later, for whom the stanza coheres around one subject and one event. But close readers should avoid a false conclusion; the poem does not make the liberty of its morally centered Swiss succumb to mere temptation. The uncentered Venetians and Dutch succumbed.

The fourth stanza of the original manuscript has been lost since Coleridge, Stuart, or some inconceivable sub-editor of the *Post* took the precaution of excluding it and informing readers that it "alluded to the African Slave Trade as conducted by this Country, and to the present Ministry and their supporters." (CPW, 247n) To examine the trace left behind is to feel relief that something was excluded, for the final stanza opened by asking Africa, "Shall I with *these* my patriot zeal combine?" and answered no, not with these dwellers in murk, these whining, mangling (Ministerial) hyenas. Unquestionably Coleridge further improved the poem when he got rid of a stanza that had made the French share with the Ministry his full contempt. The lost stanza is of interest for the poet's spiritual history, but unity would be lessened and the tone lowered by recovery of a stanza castigating Pitt. In its final form, as a result of dropping direct references to the slave trade, the opening of the last stanza utilizes an historic irony fascinating to Coleridge. He had earlier noted it for further use:

"At Genoa the word, Liberty, is engraved on the chains of the galley-slaves, & the doors of Prisons.—" (CN, 206) With this he mated a further paradox, more fitting and yet more imaginative than having France compel the nations to be free:

> The Sensual and the Dark rebel in vain,
> Slaves by their own compulsion! In mad game
> They burst their manacles and wear the name
> Of Freedom, graven on a heavier chain!
>
> (CPW, 247:85–88)

To the stanza otherwise annihilated these lines owe part of their excellence and even their existence. From the linked subject of France and Liberty why not omit Africans compelled into slavery? Jacobins who follow Reason slavishly are "Dark" enough, and self-compelled. The force of the implications in "own compulsion" and "Dark" reached the poem through the rejected stanza on the slave trade.

Thus political decisions, extraneous and in the aesthetic view wholly accidental, contributed to the final shape of the poem. Like the original political impulse and the "impure" purposes in communication, the decisions can be called no more than contributory, but they helped determine the area in which poetic unity could be achieved. Before altering the first lines of the last stanza for partly political reasons, Coleridge must have desired the improvement in unity. Contrariwise, a consideration purely aesthetic has been of little direct value to readers. Slightly wasp-waisted with tetrameter lines but largely avoiding a quick return of rimes as in the occasional trimeter of the *Ode on the Departing Year*, every stanza in *France* has the same complex pattern of ten rime-sounds repeated in the same order in twenty-one lines. Such uniformity not even the Babbitts can call Romantic hysteria. In the result, we have a poem keen in ironies and forceful, although unromantically cautious, in its affirmations.

Logicians will ask what Switzerland has lost by the overthrow of her government if she retains, with or without suffrage from government, the mountains and streams where Liberty dwells. There would seem to be a bald contradiction between denial of governmental effect on natural freedom and lament for the change of government at the core of the Alps. Slightly burlesquing

Aristotle, we can say of the contradiction that its efficient cause was Coleridge's malaise over the associational beliefs he had gloried in at Cambridge; that its material and final causes lie in the nature of poetry, especially Romantic poetry; and that its formal cause, a concept of national morality, makes it less contradictory than it seems.

First as to the poetic method. What we feel as the greatest strength in Coleridge's prose is the power of fine discrimination between two or three related matters, and next we admire its considerable power of analyzing wholes: these powers the poems generally lack. On the other hand, confusions and inconsistencies that mar the prose could be pruned and fused in poems, where Coleridge compelled discordant elements, by verbal necromancy, into the blurring he liked to call the "reconciliation of opposites." But blurring as a poetic method does not require equal blurring of thought.

Against Southey, as one who had found confusion if not contradiction in the handling of personal and national liberty, Coleridge penned an answer for the edification of the Beaumonts:

Southey in a review made some (me judice) *unfounded* objections to this last Stanza—as if I had confounded moral with political Freedom—but surely the Object of the Stanza is to shew, that true political Freedom can only arise out of moral Freedom—what indeed is it but a Dilatation of those *golden* Lines of Milton—

> "Licence they mean, when they cry—Liberty!
> For who loves that must first be wise & good." [13]

He was asking readers of his annotation to believe that he felt in 1798, and that the poem declares, virtue to rest in him, and in any Swiss patriot who will rise to it, and not in Nature except as the individual half-creates and actively uses it. But the poem does not quite say this, even after later changes.

When the poem seemed once more timely, in October, 1802, the *Morning Post* reprinted it with an Argument that attributes to the first and last stanzas some of the metaphysical subjectivity apparent that year in *Dejection: An Ode.* In a step beyond the poem, the Argument of 1802 denies explicitly that the feelings and "grand *ideal* of Freedom" can be realized "under any form of human government." It attributes the feelings and ideal not directly to the elements but "to the individual man, so far as he is pure, and inflamed with the love and adoration of God in Nature." (CPW, 244n) Except in degree of subjectivity, he had retreated in 1798 very nearly to this position of reliance upon individual morality, for he had been unable to find anywhere a moral nation to restore his optimism by supplanting apostate France. As he argued in a reasoned letter of March to his brother George and in *Fears in Solitude*, as well as in *France*, rulers even more than other men will be "as bad as they dare to be"; and government accomplishes little at best; hence necessity and hope must combine, under the guidance of Nature, for independent moral action. (CL, 395) The ode itself goes no further toward subjectivity than to declare, as its author later glossed it, "that true political Freedom can only arise out of Moral Freedom . . . ." With slight allowance for hyperbole, we can interpret it structurally as holding that a poet who once believed in the political doctrines of the French Revolution, and in French actions based on those doctrines, has learned from the violation of Helvetian liberty that all usable freedom depends upon political morality, absent whenever the individuals making up a nation have broken their life-giving bond with Nature. Admirers of English Romantic poetry gladly make a further allowance for the discrepancy between the earlier hesitations and retractions by the actual Coleridge and the fulfillment of climactic effect in the poem by having a nearly infallible bard rehearse aloud, for Heaven to hear, how he stemmed the tide even of his own rising palpitations until the invasion of Switzerland exposed forever the polluting nature of the flood.

It is worth going through the poem again briefly to observe how four motives, Liberty, light, sound, and the elements of Nature, are woven throughout. The first stanza addresses the Clouds, Waves, and Woods; notes the singing of birds and the music of the branches; traces the poet's way through glooms, led by moonlight; and addresses again, but more expansively, Waves, Forests, Clouds, Sun, Sky, entire Nature: all things truly free. The music of birds and wind in the first stanza becomes in the second the matins of the poet as priest praying for a continued dawn of French freedom; in the third it becomes the music of deliverance, then the scream of blasphemy, the wild dance of drunken passions, and general dissonance; in the fourth, the loud lament of Freedom, the harsh sounds of bleak Helvetia's icy caverns and stormy wilds, and the yell of France joining the pack and insulting the shrine; early in the fifth, the clanking of manacles and chains, the false strain of the victor, and the cries of harpy minions and obscener slaves. In the second stanza Liberty is a light, a flame, tended by the poet-priest: in the third, Liberty is the sun still rising; in the fourth, bloodless freedom in the mountains gives way to the bloodstained streams and snow; in the fifth the name of political Freedom is graven on the chains of the self-enslaved, while true Liberty—like the being of the poet— possesses concretely the winds in the pines, the playfully murmuring waves, and the sea-cliff's verge. The expansiveness returns quietly to earth, sea, and air: "O Liberty! my spirit felt thee there!" Once more, as in earlier poems, first the volcano and then the slope into calm. But with what a superiority of craft, what a difference even from the *Ode on the Departing Year*. Yet, again, who could believe that the themes of sound and light are more than utensils when compared with Liberty and the soil? The latter belong to the causes formal and final, as well as material, of the poem that lives.

It follows from comparison with *France: An Ode* that the *Hymn before Sunrise in the Vale of Chamouni*, which Coleridge translated, stole, tortured, stretched, and gradually re-formed from a poem by Friederike Brun, stands in 1802 at the end of his flight from faith in government as efficacious rearranger of society. In this comparison, it is not incidental that the *Hymn* hails "sovran Blanc" as "sole sovereign of the Vale":

> Thou kingly Spirit throned among the hills,
> Thou dread ambassador from Earth to Heaven,
> Great Hierarch!
>
> (CPW, 380:81–83)

Here in "Hierarch" the divine right of kings, after a century of movement toward God-intended sovereignty of the people, passes momentarily from human hands. The poet had ceased, at least temporarily, to acknowledge any political intermediary between the giver of all laws and the individual human subject. By such political metaphors as "kingly Spirit" and "dread ambassador," almost the only phrases in the poem for which the late A. P.

Rossiter found no source in Brun, Stolberg, or Bowles,[14] the hope
of rearranging government as a means of procuring freedom comes
to an end. In relation to human government, the *Hymn* had arrived
at anarchic individualism. The only evident way to move was
toward an organic theory of the state as natural agent between
Nature and man.

Meanwhile Coleridge had written an ode more specifically
political but less poetic. The *Ode to Tranquillity*, a sort of political
ode announcing an end of political odes, lacks tranquillity. Its
four stanzas pick and fret at the society they claim to have renounced. Aloof like a hermit, the poet says, he scans the "present
works of present man— A wild and dream-like trade of blood and
guile." (361:30–31) When the poem appeared in the *Morning
Post* on 4 December 1801, its first two stanzas, afterward dropped,
made the other four seem tranquil by contrast. Significantly, the
list of things that "Disturb not me!" filled the first stanza to bursting,
and the declaration of indifference had to be held over to disturb
the opening of the next stanza. The year had been a tiresome
confusion of treaties between enemies to allow a pause for battles
and treachery among allies. The caldron had produced two gigantic
bubbles: Pitt had resigned and Parliament had ratified a treaty
of peace with France. "What Statesmen scheme," negotiations,
were going on everywhere. The second stanza depreciates *France:
An Ode* with a scant admission, "Some tears I shed When bow'd
the Swiss his noble head," but denies that any later events impinge
upon tranquillity. A poem thus determined upon calm nevertheless
devotes an ingenious metaphor of five lines to the prediction that
war will erupt again. The fights and treaties, "Live Discord's
green Combustibles, And future Fuel of the funeral Pyre," now
hide the fire they soon must feed.

The Ovidian epigraph, *Vix ea nostra voco* (which Coleridge
had from Sir Philip Sidney), was attached in the *Morning Post*
of 1 December to Sapphics he adapted from Stolberg, as presumably meaning, "I can hardly call these verses mine"; applied to the
Ode to Tranquillity three days later, the epigraph suggests some
such meaning as "The joys of tranquillity are hardly characteristic
of Britons at war with Bonaparte." (CPW, 979; CL, 769; CN,
1011n) In any event, the words also carried, and still carry, a
cryptic admission that the personal quiet claimed in the ode had

fled on arrival. Coleridge had addressed the stanzas to tranquillity, as a boast and a challenge, lest tranquillity leave him. Later he made a still more strenuous assault. Introducing the decapitated version of the poem in the opening essay of the *Friend* in 1809, he asserted with fervor: "But all intentional allusions to particular persons, all support of, or hostility to, particular parties or factions, I now and for ever utterly disclaim. My Principles command this Abstinence, my Tranquillity requires it." (p. 12) Dissatisfied even with his own rancor, he had turned to pursue abstinence from political partisanship and similar excitements; he failed, and tranquillity eluded him. Nevertheless, when he removed the two most fretful stanzas from the *Ode to Tranquillity,* he eliminated politics almost completely from the little impassioned verse left in him. The content of *Dejection: An Ode* swerves from the poet's own life toward politics merely to pay his disrespects to "the poor loveless ever-anxious crowd." (CPW, 365:52) Yet it was not politics that Coleridge was giving up, so much as poetry.[15]

Meanwhile, in fact contemporary with *France: An Ode* and illustrating the degree of tranquillity he had then possessed and was attempting to regain at the end of 1801, there had been two controlled utterances in blank verse, *The Nightingale: A Conversation Poem,* and a greater work that concerns students of politics in poetry, *Fears in Solitude,* which bears an explanatory subtitle, "Written in April 1798, during the Alarm of an Invasion." Coleridge dated a manuscript version more specifically as 20 April, at Nether Stowey, which meant either his cottage or the nearby hills which form the scene of the poem. By unwonted tameness it gained his description as a "sort of middle thing between Poetry & Oratory—Sermoni propiora[?]"—translated humbly, after Lamb, as "properer for a sermon." [16] Let us call it a middle thing between a torrential effusion like *Religious Musings* and a "conversation poem." The conversation poems lack that suggestion of a poet talking to himself which is winningly present in *Fears in Solitude,* the suggestion of intimate disclosure within the self, which actually widens the imagined audience beyond a conversational circle. Homiletic, *Fears in Solitude* avoids the excesses of all the political poems written before 1798. Its metrical texture is finer than that of either conversational or hysterical extremes. Its author has shaken off the plague of personified abstractions. The pestilential cloud from Egypt travels here from *The Destiny of Nations* to symbolize—half-consciously to satirize—British expansion, which has borne to distant tribes the pangs of slavery and "deadlier far, our vices"; but the language and the landscape are otherwise simple. (258:51) Avoiding the portentous myths and proud flesh of earlier political eruptions, the argument of *Fears in Solitude* gains unobtrusive force through an antithetical, epigrammatic balance and thrust in the sentences; by use of monosyllabic and colloquial words; by a marked pattern of vowel and consonantal sounds, bold in initial and internal alliteration; by a rocking and sliding variety in the pauses; and, in its general progress, by rapid changes of pace. A simplicity and ease of movement, eroding the antithetic precision, dissolves the individual line-units into flowing paragraphs, with the freedom newly discovered by Coleridge and Wordsworth. Betrayed by the Revolution, they have found a liberty in which a poet can have faith.

Misleadingly, the social "we" of this poem sounds more democratic than Liberty's jealous priest in the odes. Rather, the poet is here trying to involve all orders of society. The common danger joins all in a common blame. Not merely rulers and wealthy, but all, have drunk pollutions lewdly and effeminately from the cup of wealth. Barterers and perjurers, every one, "We gabble o'er the oaths we mean to break." (CPW, 259:72) Among clergymen, custodians of oath-making as they should be of the message that might stem destruction, the indolent mutterers admittedly outnumber the rank scoffers. A list to show the extent of perjury, "Merchant and lawyer, senator and priest," rocks antithetically, two in one line and four in the next, again two, then four, to another trenchant phrase: "All, all make up one scheme of perjury." This culling and packing of political passions must have brought as much glee to the poet as the earlier damning of Pitt and his cronies to eternal cousinship with Beelzebub. The darker imagination returns for a moment, from somewhere near *Religious Musings*, with the "owlet Atheism," flapping obscene wings and hooting "Where is it?" at the glorious sun, but the new counter-mythical techniques quickly overcome it.

"Thankless too for peace," begins the next verse paragraph. Here Coleridge treats the "ghastlier workings" of war and their blasphemous adjunct, the naming of God in mandates for the death of ten thousands, with just enough solemnity to lend sobriety to the rest of the paragraph's satiric bite. We all know, and many of us have been, the spectators lashed in these lines with impassioned wit, civilian *aficionados* who quibble with each other over "our dainty terms for fratricide," the exact technical phrases for the tools and tactics of victory or defeat, as if the soldier were dead without a wound and translated without a death into Heaven. The lines are Shakespearean. Indeed, the passage refutes Hotspur in his own vernacular while condemning on more humane grounds than his the popinjay who daintily told him all about gunpowder and would, but for these vile guns, himself have been a soldier.

Avoiding abrupt transition, the verse ascends to a prediction of evil days sent by "all-avenging Providence." Yet it allows still another short leap upward to the next paragraph, or movement, which begins in prayer to God to "spare us yet awhile!" After a picture of English mothers dragging their babes in flight, sentimental to a century hardened by democratic and totalitarian atrocity, the paragraph makes a partial recovery in urging islanders to be men, to repel those who promise Freedom wherever they conquer, "themselves too sensual to be free." They are urged, when victory has come from resurgence of national virtue, to be humble and ashamed of having stung the foe to frenzy.These lines contain Coleridge's clearest and most assured presentation in verse of the dependence of freedom in a nation upon the virtue of its people. Government is not a cloak to be put on and off. His argument is Judaic: a people who believe in God can fail to repel infidel invaders only if they join battle steeped in sin, deserving heavy punishment as the necessary means of restoring them to submission under retributive God. The religious argument for a reversal of national behavior comes more persuasively in a poem both meditative and trembling, as *Fears in Solitude* is, than in exhortatory poems that quake with intolerance.

The next movement begins as if to summarize and close: "I have told, O Britons! . . . Most bitter truth, but without bitterness." (261:153–55) It calls for a bipartisan end to the delusions of the Opposition, which, as if government were a removable cloak, blames the wickedness and folly of the whole on "a few Poor drudges of chastising Providence," as well as to the delusions of the "drudges," the entrenched, who dote with mad idolatry and

declare all who will not worship their idols to be therefore enemies
of the country. Hitting the Tories on both cheeks, Coleridge mod-
erates his blows by the patriotic air of humbly seeking after truth
and dividing his curse between the parties. Despite this rhetorical
sophistication, he is feeling his way honestly into a vitalistic theory
of government.

Such an enemy as Tory delusion invents, says the transition to
a lower key, have I been deemed. Again the poet finds room for
a basic theory transitionally political. All his sensations, all his
ennobling thoughts, have come in association with the lakes, hills,
clouds, dales, rocks, and seas of his and God's Britain. Loving God,
knowing father, brother, friend, wife, and child on this island,
How—"How shouldst thou prove aught else but dear and holy"?
And how can a reader speed through this hypermetric line of
monosyllables? Simply by observing the solemn tread of the previous line: "O native Britain! O my Mother Isle!" (262:182)
Here the student of politics in poetry will care less for the patriotic
sentiment than for the metrics that dignify it. With this movement
ends what a writer less interested in Coleridge's political conversion than in his philosophic idealism called "somewhat intemperate
politics, pamphleteeringly expressed." [17] In a pause for reversal
the poet prays that his fears may be as vain as the gust that has
subsided in the dell. Because *Fears* is a poem of clarity and
general calm, where the forebodings of disaster have lacked the
pleasure-giving ingenuity of the prophesying in the *Ode on the
Departing Year*, the movement of the verse smoothly regains a
sense of blessings to come. The poem recalls its author from his
bodings and sends him homeward through the sunny dales to
the particulars that bind him to the isle: the church-tower, elms
around the mansion of his friend, his own cottage, babe, and wife.
His heart, softened by nature's quietness, has been made worthy
of "thoughts that yearn for human kind." (263:232) These final
words, "human kind," enforce a point suggested in the more theoretical paragraph preceding it, that only by the narrowness of the
individual's associations, the "bonds" of love, the "limits" of the
rocky shores, can he win to a sense of boundless brotherhood.

About 1815, Coleridge added five lines of dissatisfaction with
organized utilitarian life after Waterloo. It may be that the added
lines, by the accident of the poet's failing powers, flow less freely

than the lines into which they are set, which he called "too tame even for animated Prose," but the discrepancy is not too great for successful contrast with the dell made of liquid *l*'s in the opening:

> A green and silent spot, amid the hills,
> A small and silent dell! O'er stiller place
> No singing sky-lark ever poised himself.

Against this peacefulness of connotation and fluidity of sound, place the annoyed sputter of the new lines:

> All individual dignity and power
> Engulfed in Courts, Committees, Institutions,
> Associations and Societies,
> A vain, speech-mouthing, speech-reporting Guild,
> One Benefit-Club for mutual flattery . . . .
>
> (258:54–58)

Despite his disparagement of the "middle thing," or perhaps as the beseeching modesty of his disparagement tends to prove, Coleridge saw that the poem does not lack elevation. Yet the return to satire against his countrymen in crisis, heavier in the somewhat topical insertion than it had been in the passage on dainty terms for fratricide, confirms his disparagement. The heavy insertion suggests more definitely than his quite habitual abasement that he did not recognize in the poem what we find there: By its novel simplicity of style and structure, the subdued articulation of its movement, and its approach through subjective mood to public theme, *Fears in Solitude* is a representative Romantic poem.

CHAPTER X

The Plays

> For the writer the great test is, how
> much truth can he force through the
> sieve of his opinions?
> —Irving Howe,
> *Politics and the Novel*

Like the other literary forms he practiced, Coleridge's plays show
his irregular transit from hesitant republican to independent Tory.
His first attempt, Act I of *The Fall of Robespierre,* may be regarded
as a hastily contrived study of freedom and demagoguery.

By the doctrine of Necessity that Coleridge held concurrently
with his revolutionary enthusiasm, demagogues are those through
whom offenses needs must come. In the poem addressed to Miss
Brunton with a copy of *The Fall of Robespierre,* she was not
asked to think of Louis XVI and beheaded aristocrats, but of
Robespierre and his accomplices: "In ghastly horror lie th'Oppressors low— And my Heart akes tho' Mercy struck the Blow."
(CL, 65) The victim partly lamented is "the Tyrant" made up
collectively of "Oppressors"; Miss Brunton is asked to take it as
the Mountain, with Robespierre at the peak.[1] To some extent
intellect checked passion, but Coleridge's disappointment with
Robespierre belonged to an emotional identification with him that
later generations have been unable to grasp—have apparently
dreaded to touch. His poetry dealing with Robespierre should be
read in the light of John Poole's story, convincing in essence,
that Coleridge reacted with shock to the news of the tyrant's fall.
His companion Southey "actually laid his head down upon his

arms and exclaimed, 'I had rather have heard of the death of my own father.' " [2]

The play itself clearly condemns Barrere, who had waited criminally long before betraying the tyrant, and allows him and other characters to assign to Robespierre that worst sin, Ambition, but it does not commit itself further about Robespierre's motives. After a few months' further thought, Coleridge analyzed Robespierre as having been too intense, too eager, too enthusiastic, but as early as 1795 he had difficulty condemning enthusiasm, and concluded in Robespierre's favor that "it is not the character of the possessor which directs the power, but the power which shapes and depraves the character of the possessor." (EOT, 9) Even in 1809, writing for the then Tory *Courier,* he could not say that Robespierre "had disclosed any plan of permanent usurpation, and at this hour it remains uncertain whether the monster died a fanatic or an impostor." (EOT, 632)

The Fall of Robespierre was topical rather than historical. Coleridge wrote accurately in the poem to Miss Brunton: "Red from the Tyrant's wound I shook the lance, And strode in joy the reeking plains of France!" (CPW, 65:25–26) For "plains of France" read topically *des chambres et des places de Paris.* Few belletristic works signed by major writers can ever have come hotter from the chronicled events. Robespierre was executed on 28 July 1794. By mid-August, rumors had reached the London newspapers. On 18 August the *Morning Chronicle* was able to confirm the rumors and to print the last Parisian speeches needed for the writing of *The Fall of Robespierre.* Reports of these speeches, of 23–28 July, appeared in *Felix Farley's Bristol Journal* for 23 August. Shortly before this date Coleridge and Southey must have returned to Bristol from a week's walking tour, during which they had explained Pantisocracy to Thomas Poole. Originally Coleridge, Southey, and Robert Lovell were each to have written one act, but Southey found it necessary to take over the third act from Lovell. The few dates on surviving letters seem contradictory, but Coleridge started for London about the end of August, with Southey's two acts completed and not more than one day's work left on his own. After vicissitudes with publishers, he dated the dedication at Cambridge on 22 September; copies were ready at the beginning of October.[3]

In the collaboration on *Robespierre* Coleridge certainly provided the tug of brain. Southey's two acts hardly deviate from the newspaper accounts of the principal speeches. The uncreative "transversing" of news in his two-thirds, apparent by inspection, was confirmed by Southey in a letter to Henry Nelson Coleridge: "It was written with newspapers before me as fast as newspapers could be put into blank verse." [4] Although Southey was capable of imaginative phrases, his best departures from the news may have come from Coleridge. Dulany Terrett pointed out in his Harvard dissertation that the "crownèd cockatrices" described by Tallien in Act II had been anatomized by Coleridge (with Linnaean precision and republican frenzy) in a letter of 6 July to Southey.[5] For Act I Coleridge relied on the characterizations of Robespierre, Barère, Tallien, Couthon, and St. Just built up in newspaper reports that commented also on actions in the Convention, Tribunal, and Committee of Public Safety, but he attempted to recreate what must have occurred in private prior to the public events. Here he had Shakespeare's *Julius Caesar* in mind, somewhat as the actual conspirators took Brutus as their ideal. Meeting ancient Barère at Brussels in 1829–30, T. C. Grattan heard from him accounts that resembled in content and atmosphere, in treachery and general fearfulness, the opening soliloquy of *The Fall of Robespierre,* in which Barrere thinks of his last "secret conference" with Robespierre, when "He scowl'd upon me with suspicious rage." [6] St. Just is something of a hero, a just man, in the play; Barrere is the demagogue and opportunist, as the live (and long-lived) Barère had been consistently portrayed in the newspapers. Opposition papers, taking their cue from Sheridan, had been referring to Pitt as the "English Roberspierre" [*sic*] and "British Barrere." [7]

To some extent the play thus provided a countermining of Pitt in its portrayal of intrigue, censorship, and violence in Paris. Its authors also had the republican desire to identify the true friends of Liberty and whatever betrayers of the Revolution there might be among the leaders of France. The alignment of forces and the motivations closely resemble those suggested in *Felix Farley's Bristol Journal* for 23 August. Coleridge's Tallien conforms remarkably to the portrait given in the same paper one week later: "*Tallien,* who is at present supposed to take the lead in the French

Convention, is a man of talents greatly above mediocrity, of polished manners, elegant accomplishments, and a fine person. Were we to compare him with an ancient Roman, Antony would be the man. He loves women, conversation, the pleasures of the table, and all the more refined amusements. . . . Under the auspices of such men [as Tallien and Sieyès], a better order of things may be reasonably expected." Coleridge gives Robespierre opportunities to assert his "steel-strong Rectitude of soul," but Act I carries the theme that ends the play: Freedom must be restored by violence in the removal of a man whose tyranny in the name of Liberty is corrupting the state. (CPW, 499:117) Awe at horrors performed in a cause the two authors supported, along with fidelity to fact as they understood it, prevented the play from showing by bald contrast its central lesson: how demagogues who maneuver for power in the name of Liberty fall before patriots for whom Liberty is genuinely the axis of all motivation. To his brother George, Coleridge admitted that under the tutelage of Locke and Hartley he could conceive "the point of *possible* perfection at which the World may perhaps be destined to arrive," but insisted that his own voice could be heard in the lament by Tallien's mistress, Adelaide, that domestic affections had all been "sacrificed to liberty's wild riot." (CL, 126; CPW, 501:201)

Astonishingly, Adelaide has the emollient effect on Coleridge's Tallien that Thérésa de Cabarrús, by unusually strong agreement among historians, had on the actual Tallien. Thérésa had entered Paris secretly as Tallien's mistress, soon to be his wife; Robespierre had signed a warrant for her arrest. Robespierre denounced Tallien publicly, but English newspapers missed the vital significance of his speech, and the conspiratorial details of the closet would have been hard to come by in Bristol.[8] Mostly, if not altogether, Coleridge must have worked up the scenes from hint and instinct.

Adelaide was probably created for her song, later titled *Domestic Peace*, to a greater extent than the song was designed for Adelaide, however much it was shaped for her. The "cottag'd vale" in which Domestic Peace resides, far not only from "the pomp of Sceptered State" but also from "the Rebel's noisy hate," and within listening distance of "Sabbath bells," admittedly gives a strong anti-political hue to Pantisocracy; Adelaide anticipates by two years her author's protest that "local and temporary Politics are my aversion." (CPW,

71:5–8, 501:217–20; CL, 222) But it was to advertise the play about French politics, and not to describe the poem, that Benjamin Flower published Adelaide's Pantisocratic lyric in the *Cambridge Intelligencer* of 25 October 1794 as "SONG," with the advertisement in brackets: "[From the FALL of ROBESPIERRE, an Historic Drama, by S. T. Coleridge.]."

Adelaide, her song, and the rest of Act I demonstrate Coleridge's fears for the direction of events in France. They illustrate, too, that need for a negative purpose which he explained to Southey: "Wherever Men *can* be vicious, some *will* be. The leading Idea of Pantisocracy is to make men *necessarily* virtuous by removing all Motives to Evil—all possible Temptations." (CL, 114) Defending the play against charges of Jacobinism was to sharpen still more Coleridge's skill at restraining, counterbalancing, and contradicting impulsive political utterance. Meanwhile, he reminded Southey that it was financially astute to affix his own name singly to their publication, as he was already notorious in Cambridge, where Southey was not yet so. Although he may have practiced just the opposite, Coleridge assured his collaborator that he gave "the *true* biography" of the play to any man who praised it. (CL, 106) He does not specifically mention a danger of prosecution for seditious utterance. His main point, perhaps the one that silenced Southey, is that they would become doubly ridiculous from public admission that it took both of them to write a play no better than *The Fall of Robespierre*.

Even if *The Fall of Robespierre* be discounted as journalism in more than one sense impertinent, Coleridge had not long practiced tumid stanza and turgid ode when he attempted the cadences of blank verse that had been sanctified by the Elizabethans to dramatic use. In this form spiritual autobiography proved less fitting. The distribution of speeches among characters imagined as in conflict requires some degree of objectivity. Personal detachment could be further expected because Coleridge tried playwriting more for money than for fame or communication. Not only Coleridge but most English Romantic poets tried to write for the stage because the directors of Drury Lane and Covent Garden diffused the aroma of well-spiced financial reward. This aroma kept most of the poets in a state of uncertain judgment, a kind of emotional agnosticism, over their attempts at Shakespearean depth,

Shakespearean richness of language, and Shakespearean royalties. Shakespeare invited them to soar, but audiences demanded clarity and entertainment. Cash, by subtler means than the physical vastness of the legitimate theaters, discouraged lyric subjectivity. Nevertheless, despite Coleridge's promptings to give a designated audience what it wanted, *Osorio* of 1797 (with its revision as *Remorse* in 1813), the fragment of *The Triumph of Loyalty*, about 1800, and *Zapolya*, 1817, preserve strong intimations of the political moods of their author as well as the political temper of the age. Indeed, when the concept of politics is taken widely enough to include its metaphysical and psychological bases, Coleridge's most significantly political belletristic works can be taken to be his blank verse effusions, with their passionate exposition of political beliefs; the odes, with their shaping of political excitement; and the dramas, with their considered application of political principles.

How he applies these principles can be seen in his extensive use and conscious delimitation of the words *Nature* and *Natural* and his characterization of heroes as naturally commanding in *Osorio* and *Zapolya*. Although the pertinent references to Nature are reduced from fourteen in *Osorio* (of which more later) to ten in its reconstitution as *Remorse*, Nature retains its controlling force in the theme, as in an addition that has the heroine declare of the disguised hero: "No, I have faith, that Nature ne'er permitted Baseness to wear a form so noble." (CPW, 865:9–10) Like this passage, with some indication that conventions a century old have been assayed before being retained, *Zapolya* assumes that "Great Nature" chooses and endows the truly noble hero. (914:410) Although not typical of its code of political morality, generally stringent enough for Cato, *Zapolya* allows its noblest figure to accept the contemporary view of military looting: trophies wrested valiantly from a valiant foe are "Love's natural offerings to a rightful king." (889:168) A later passage washes military plunder even whiter by making it a defense against aggression.

For the "commanding genius" of Coleridge's prose, there is a dramatic senior, the "commanding spirit," inspired by the Titanic heroes of Schiller. We are told that a painting of the hero in *Osorio* shows him meeting a paid assassin "Calm, yet commanding"; in fuller praise worked up separately and modified for *Remorse*, he has a "spiritual and almost heavenly light In his commanding eye—his mien heroic, Virtue's own native heraldry!" (558:203; 866:54–56) Wallenstein, in Coleridge's direct translation of lines in *The Piccolomini,* has "a commanding spirit," the "commanding intellect," fitted to "the station of command" (*"Geworden ist ihm eine Herrscherseele, Und ist gestellt auf einen Herrscherplatz."*— *Die Piccolomini* I.412–13). A noble follower of the great Wallenstein believed it in accord with Nature *"Dem Herrschtalent den Herrschplatz zu erobern"* (I.441). In *Zapolya,* after Napoleon had cast a lurid glow over both spirit and station, one evil character recommends another even more evil on Schiller's now-soured principle: "Let the commanding spirit Possess the station of command!" (894:324–25)

Early in February, 1797, upon Sheridan's suggestion that he write "a tragedy on some popular subject," Coleridge began *Osorio.* (CL, 304) Besides Shakespearean tragedy and what Coleridge conceived to be the requirements of Drury Lane, with starring roles for Kemble and Mrs. Siddons, he kept in mind the "material Sublime" of Schiller, especially the "chill and trembling" exacted by *The Robbers.* (CL, 122) In *The Orphan* of Otway he studied warmer and tenderer sentiments. To complete his five acts, classical in number if not in content, he worked until October. His setting is Granada under Philip II, after the defeat of the Moors in 1571 and "during the heat of the persecution which raged against them." (CPW, 519) The background, the theme of remorse following upon envy, and most of the names seem to derive from Robert Watşon, *The History of the Reign of Philip the Second.* (CN, 210n) But Coleridge's Alhadra is notably absent from that source.

A brief outline of the play will show the extent to which Coleridge chose, first, to suppress the political conflict implicit in the setting, and second, in the opposite direction, to suggest political themes through the characterizations. The outline can only hint at the more explicit presentation of political and kindred themes, sometimes faithful to characterization, sometimes indifferent to it, in what one is tempted to call the arias.

Osorio, of "proud forbidding eye," younger son of Lord Velez, persists in courtship of Maria, who is plighted to his brother Albert. Ferdinand, a Moor, has reported three years since that Albert was killed by pirates, but Maria will not believe it. There is further evidence, however: Osorio, in return for saving Ferdinand's life, had exacted a promise to murder Albert, and the grateful Moor had brought back Albert's portrait of Maria, in a locket bestowed by her, as evidence to Osorio that the job was done. When Francesco, the local Inquisitor, comes to inquire about a suspected Moor who has made reference to the death of Albert, Osorio assures him that Ferdinand is a Catholic. For recompense, Osorio requests Ferdinand to pretend a power of necromancy in order to call the portrait up before Maria, as supernatural proof of Albert's death. Fearful of a second arrest by the Inquisitor, Ferdinand recommends for the post of necromancer a nearby hermit, known by him and the audience to be Albert, courageously disguised as a Moor despite the proscription of Moorish dress. Albert hopes to reduce his brother to the anguish of remorse. Acting the sorcerer, he shows Maria a miniature of his attempted assassination instead of her portrait.

Immediately arrested for sorcery by Francesco, Albert is thrust into the Velez dungeon. Not yet recognizing his brother Albert, but realizing that Ferdinand and the hermit in collusion have deceived him, Osorio entices Ferdinand into a cavern and murders him. He then goes to poison Albert in the family dungeon, where they are joined by Maria, to whom Velez has given the dismaying alternative of Osorio or a convent. At last, recognition of his wronged brother brings to the cold misanthrope a spasm of remorse. Too late, for a party of Moors, collected by Ferdinand's widow, arrive to execute revenge on an unusually cruel Christian.

As has been long recognized and often stressed, the necromancy and some extremities of *Osorio* come from the Sicilian's tale in *Der Geisterseher*, a fragmentary romance in which Schiller drew scenes, ironies, and lessons from the diableries of Cagliostro and his rivals in black daring. But Coleridge went to *Der Geisterseher*, or to a popular translation of it, *through*, as it were, the Sturm-und-Drang of Schiller's first drama, which had staggered him. "My God! Southey!" he had asked after midnight, "Who is this Schiller? This Convulser of the Heart?" (CL, 122) He borrowed a little from the prose tale largely as a way of exaggerating the distance, which by intention is not otherwise very great, between *The Robbers* and *Osorio*. Of *Die Räuber* Coleridge almost certainly knew only an English translation of the stage version, probably that issued anonymously by Alexander F. Tytler (later Lord Woodhouselee) in 1792, slightly corrected in an edition of 1795.[9]

So closely did Coleridge note both trappings and fundamentals that his departures are significant. In Schiller's play Francis de Moor, the villain, tried to convince Amelia, the ward of their father, that his brother Charles was dead. Returning incognito, Charles decided that Amelia still loved him. In both tale and drama, where Coleridge provides a portrait, Schiller employed a ring as false evidence of the good brother's death. Old Count de Moor, the father, supposed to have been killed by an aged servant, was actually kept alive by him in an ancient tower. These elements form the basis for details given political overtones by both playwrights. Like the residence of the Velez family, the Moor castle included a suitable dungeon. Even the conflict between Moors and Inquisition in Osorio may have been touched off associationally by the surname of Schiller's protagonist. The Robbers contained a usable malcontent, Spiegelberg.

Schiller provided even stronger guidance for the major figures. Divided against himself at the beginning of Act II, wicked Francis looked forward in anguish to repentance and remorse; by the end of the act, his misanthropy was complete. The career of his nobler brother Charles also resulted from misanthropy, impetuous rather than brooding. Coleridge assigns all the misanthropy to Osorio, none to Albert. Schiller could permit Charles to decide that Amelia still loved him, because Charles would be "driven by perfidy, and the supposed inhumanity of those most dear to him" (in the words of Tytler's Preface to the edition of 1792), into misanthropy, crime, and despair. Charles is not so blameless that others must be blamed merely for contrast. Albert must doubt Maria's fidelity, because Coleridge risks no divisions of soul in his hero. The aim of popularization, aided perhaps by psychic defenses, leads the English imitator to a melodramatic paring and severing of Schiller's psychological themes into good against evil, a cowardly misanthropy against majestic tenderness. Although two scenes in Osorio do suggest a struggle of conscience within the title character, sympathy is called away to the brother, who sacrifices further revenge to achieve solely his victim's self-dividing remorse. Albert has prayed only in a dream that the poisonous tooth of remorse, "the punishment that cleanses hearts," will sink into whoever has wronged him. (CPW, 533:328) Remorse, as the author later pointed out to Southey, "is everywhere distinguished from virtuous Penitence." (CL, III, 434)

Most suggestions of Coleridge's indebtedness to *The Borderers* of Wordsworth have ignored influences common to both plays, but Dr. L. F. Christensen has noted cogently that Osorio acquires in the last two acts the pride of Wordsworth's Oswald.[10] And yet pride must have been part of the original conception, however amorphous that was. The review of *Remorse* in the *Morning Chronicle* of 25 January 1813, reprinted in the evening *Courier*, was able to quote Coleridge's long-considered views on his title character. The figure he supposed central to the play was "a man of originally strong understanding, and morbid feelings; whose reason points out to him a high and severe standard of unattainable perfection, while his temperament urges him on to a violation of all the ordinary distinctions of right and wrong; whose pride finds consolation for its vices in its contempt for the dull virtues, or perhaps hypocritical pretenses of the generality of men: whose conscience seeks a balm for its wounds in theoretical speculations on human depravity, and whose moody and preposterous self-love, by an habitual sophistry, exaggerates the slightest affront, or even a suspicion of possible injury, into solid reasons for the last acts of hatred and revenge." As long as the play was a raging success, its author could be encouraged to describe a fullness and consistency of characterization that actors and audiences were struggling to comprehend. Concerning Osorio's pride, however, we can go back at least as far as Coleridge's undated but early Preface, where he professed to have "had most clear & psychologically accurate ideas" of a "man who from constitutional Calmness of appetites is seduced into Pride & the love of Power—by these into Misanthropy or rather a contempt for Mankind. . . ."[11]

Osorio is not, like the later *Zapolya*, organized around an intelligible political theme. Coleridge saw it as unveiling several stages of remorse and exposing the inadequacy of each in turn; he might have ordered it so, had he coaxed Osorio into its true center, but instead he allowed the more sympathetic characters to upstage the villain in nearly every scene. If Coleridge had seen Schiller's own preface, with its defense of the truth to Nature in his admixture of vice and virtue in the erring but noble Carl Moor, he profited only in his unsentimentalized portrayal of the oppressed but fierce Alhadra. Genuine passion against tyrannical injustice, not trumped up to satisfy Sheridan, helped make Alhadra the strongest figure in the play. Several long speeches contain vignettes of pathos, Coleridgian in melancholia more often than Schilleresque in passion: "I saw a skull; a poppy grew beside it, There was a ghastly solace in the sight!" (584:33–34) Yet Alhadra is frequently onstage to demonstrate successfully, as well as to proclaim, that "Great evils ask great passions to redress them." (528:231)

Cloaked by the distance of time and place, the public theme of victory of the persecuted meek over the tyrannically powerful stands in *Osorio* close behind the personal theme of remorse: The only worthy power is power over self. Schiller's play had oppugned the *ancien régime*. Before surrendering by a final humanitarian act to an officer with eleven children to feed (in the version known to Coleridge), Charles gave a last charge to his fellow robbers: "Go, serve a gracious king, who wages war to vindicate the rights of man!" (p. 218) Until 1799 *The Robbers* was denied a license for performance in London "owing to supposed political dangers." [12] In *Osorio* opposition to the established regime comes mostly by indirection and implication. Opposed to the absolute tyranny of the Inquisition, Albert could have returned to "the heroic Prince of Orange." (544:185) Instead he remains under tyranny, as required in order to have any plot at all. Besides the passage of thirty lines included in the *Lyrical Ballads* as "The Dungeon," there are dungeon-plaints throughout, in a spirit combining the humanitarianism of Howard with politics of the Opposition. Occasionally the plaints rise from pools of sentiment with a steel succinctness. Ferdinand thanks Osorio: "Now, but for you, a dungeon's slimy stones Had pillow'd my snapt joints." (535:5–6)

Francesco, repellent to both principal women, represents the union of established church with military force. If the "ghastly punishments" perpetrated by the "holy brethren" belong less to routine anti-Catholicism than to the lower, theatrical German craze of the day, the "foul officers" who invade a private residence (*horrescet Albion*) and hold there Alhadra's "babes and husband" have anti-Ministerial import, unmistakably. (523:109, 527:195)

They awaken memories of the thief-takers left by "the unnatural Villain" Dundas with Horne Tooke's unprotected daughters. (CPW, 151:46) The "knells and masses" of the Church become intertwined, through "a few odd prayers," with the hocus-pocus of wizardry. (545:211, 552:43–56) A philosophy different from that of the Holy Church, taught by Albert to Maria and belittled by the villainous Osorio as "some newer nonsense," we may take perhaps as tinged with the Socinian rationalism of the Unitarians, not then fully renounced by Coleridge. (536:30) *Der Geisterseher* would seem to demonstrate the sanctified stability of the Church; to the contrary, Coleridge allows his Moors to make unanswered denunciations of the "Christian tyrants" and their "pious policy." On balance, the author does not seem to include himself among the guilty. The eloquent anti-Christian speeches of Alhadra, usually accusatory in their pessimism, culminate in the closing pronouncement of the play, that the multitudinous oppressed have it in their power to conquer their oppressors.[13]

The key tone of *Osorio* is "Nature." In opposition to Osorio's "faith in universal villainy," Nature gives instruction in forgiveness by demonstrating to pure minds the essential uprightness and benevolence of man. (591:188) Ferdinand's worship of Nature has no effect on the action, but is central to the theme. (529:245) Maria would choose to love "that Almighty One" residing in "every gale that breath'd, and wave that murmur'd" rather than to stagnate in the "tame and credulous faith" of a convent. (577:291–92, 578:299) Both Schiller's Francis de Moor and Coleridge's Osorio erred in blaming their treachery and cynicism on fate. Francis hated Nature for burdening him unnaturally with the hideous deformity of lacking the capacity for affection. The "sickly moralist" Osorio respects the "goodly face of Nature," but justifies his lack of benevolence by believing all men, in their rampant evil, equally with himself deformers of Nature. (558:214, 583:12) A materialist, he cannot comprehend natural gratitude. (537:62) That Osorio usurps the "wealth, power, influence" of his brother comes more from personal and literary than from political impulses, but the language of Osorio's misanthropy recommends by inversion the majesty of the people. I do not argue that *Osorio* is a Trojan horse heavy with concealed politics. Rather it is a Cassandra, cramped by the attempt to make prophecy salable, but revealing some emotional and theoretical fountains of Coleridge's early political partisanship.

In summary, Sheridan was instigator of the play, anti-Ministerial journalism its background, Schiller its chief inspirer, and Watson's history of Philip a major source, the difference beween Schiller and Watson being that Coleridge absorbed from the one out of personal, poetic, and political affinity and found the other an unusually interesting quarry where he could dig among the stones. Resolutely he dug first within his own breathing envy and hacking remorse, but self-pity eased him away from conscientious anguish and centered the play in the injured and oppressed. Very possibly the political themes gained some of their prominence as an "objective correlative" to these internal churnings. Escape from self and attack on aristocratic privilege and cruelty could be positive and negative of one X ray. As a curb on the purely biographical approach to Albert and Alhadra, however, those who would press psychological interpretation to its limit should find in Coleridge's later support of the aristocracy a fuller personal gratitude than seems likely under any reading whatever. Or have we doomed psychology to explain all by sin and guilt?

A reader who proceeds directly from *Osorio* to its more successful recasting as *Remorse* encounters a new title, new names for the dramatis personae, and new opening lines. Partly, at least, the changes for easier entry were supervised by master carpenters at Drury Lane. The change of title clarifies the intended dramatic center; only one character, Alhadra, retains her original name; an expository opening scene tells what has gone before and anticipates the story-line to follow. The characters perorate less. To the speeches there are twenty-five sizable revisions. Alvar (formerly Albert) still recites the humanitarian and anti-utilitarian lines separately published as "The Dungeon," but "The Foster-Mother's Tale" returns from the *Lyrical Ballads* to *Remorse* only as an appendix to the second edition.

Despite these improvements, the political matter is essentially unchanged. Alvar has a "kingly forehead" and other concrete features of nobility not specifically noted in Albert. (CPW, 866:52) The role of the Inquisitor is briefer and fiercer. The new introductory scene opens with a speech of patriotism resembling the key tone of the roughly contemporaneous *Zapolya:*

If aught on earth demand an unmix'd feeling,
'Tis surely this—after long years of exile,
To step forth on firm land, and gazing round us,
To hail at once our country, and our birth-place.
Hail, Spain! Granada, hail! once more I press
Thy sands with filial awe, land of my fathers!

(820:4–9)

Although the author's return from Malta has not made a personal
imprint on these lines nearly as marked as the conventional imprint
descended from Greek and Elizabethan plays, the patriotic implications have become fairly complex, here and throughout. Coleridge would have noted as he revised that the lapse of years had
changed the force of many lines he retained. For the audience of
1813 the Spain of the play, made more attractive in this new
passage than it had been anywhere in *Osorio,* could be at once
England and the scene of Wellington's Peninsular campaigns. The
tyranny of the Inquisitors, once suggestive of the lords temporal
and divine who upheld Pitt, could now oddly shadow forth Napoleon. That reviewers could think the play unfriendly toward Spain
was an accident of its origins. By small amplifications *Remorse*
makes clearer the dramatic and political significance of Osorio's
association with the oppressive Inquisitors and Albert's association
with the oppressed Moors; but these are improvements in form,
not changes of substance.[14] Coleridge did not systematically alter
the play to make its allusions current. What he most wanted from
the audience, in fact, after fifteen discouraging years, was the
£400 he got. (CL, III, 437)

Most of the variant issues among the three editions of *Remorse,*
all in 1813, reflect the practices and dilemmas of actual production
in the theater. There was especial uncertainty over how and by
whom Ordonio should be killed, and one version by oversight
leaves him alive. The producers made cuts beyond those reflected
in printed editions, and changed the remaining language enough
to cauterize the wounds. The prompt copy of W. H. West of Drury
Lane, now at Harvard, and a Warren and Wood prompt copy
for the Philadelphia and Baltimore production, in the New York
Public Library, reveal not only impatience with elaborate speeches,
philosophic and otherwise, but also caution concerning religion
and politics. Alhadra's denunciations of Christian cruelty, as at

I.ii.200 (in the final version), were cut rigorously and no doubt righteously. The lament in the dungeon, V.i.1–35, passionately transcending Godwin, was reduced in London to one line: "Merciful heaven was this place made for man." The lines on martyred Belgium, IV.ii.59–61, added by Coleridge as a matter of topical interest, were insecurely lodged in a longer passage which shrank in London and vanished in Philadelphia (and probably in New York, where *Remorse* was performed in November, 1813). Ironically, it was about this time that the poet himself excised "Belgium's corse-impeded flood" from the *Ode on the Departing Year;* but there, as in the lines to Tooke, Belgium had disgraced England, not France. (CPW, 151:31, 165n) Other political passages shrank in the city of the playwright's residence and disappeared in theaters beyond the Atlantic: for example, Alvar's recital of his acts and sufferings in wars of liberty against oppression. (II.ii.5–25) No actor anywhere was required to recite Alvar's lines on "some Lapland wizard's skiff," but politics were not responsible for the escape. (CPW, 849:59)

For clarity, action, suspense, and antiquing, rather than for politics resembling Coleridge's old animosity against Dundas, Drury Lane interpolated a new scene, in which the Inquisitor is apprised of the sorcery to come. It is not clear that Coleridge was a party to the improvement:

Act 3ʳᵈ. Scene 1ˢᵗ
The Court before Lord Valdez Castle
(Monviedro & a Spy (ENTER O P.)

Mon. Fear not the name of Spy–This disclosure is meritorious
Spy. Had it been any ordinary crime your reverence! I had remaind silent! but sorcery
Mon. It is most foul yea inexpiable!–
Spy. Don Ordonios trustiest servants have been placed, at the Sorcerer's bidding: their preperations are just finished, and I can place your Lordship where unobserved you may be a Witness of the Whole
Mon.— Tis well – Collect the other servants of the Household. Two of our familiars are in waiting when the profis [proof is] completed, I will give the signal and let them follow me
Spy This way may it please your Reverence

Exeunt

Coleridge would not have cared about the sparse punctuation, but he would have protested against "placed" and "place" occurring so close together in the spy's explanation of arrangements, and he might have objected to the misspelling of "preperations." [15]

Translating two of the three parts of "that accursed Wallenstein" for Longmans chilled Coleridge's interest in Schiller sufficiently for Shakespearean diction, exposition, and definition of character to reign unopposed, except by Coleridge's infirmities, in the fragment of *The Triumph of Loyalty*, which achieved its 372 lines in November or December of 1800—"written purposely vile," he said. (CL, 662) Boredom with the drudgery of translation, even more than renewed desire for theatrical success, drove him to produce the fragment, perhaps at first surreptitiously, to revise *Osorio*, and possibly to conceive in a general way of the drama on Hungary that became *Zapolya*.[16]

Distinct hazards forbid the measurement of political winds in *The Triumph of Loyalty*. It is a fragment, less than one act. Within that narrow room the characters display their costumes and their ruling passions without philosophic embroidery. The fragment shows us clearly enough a hero's loyalty to sovereign and country despite arbitrary recall from opportunity for further heroism, and presents that loyalty in a favorable light. But what the whole was intended to make of this presentation might depend upon such imponderables as Coleridge's view of Queen Elizabeth's Essex, for he based his play upon Lessing's summary, in *Hamburgische Dramaturgie*, of a Spanish play about Essex. (CN, 869, 871 and note) After summarizing Lessing's summary, Coleridge increased our uncertainties by deviating from the source in a skeletal outline and then departing from the outline in the full-dress fragment.

Although the recent misfortunes of British armies sent against the French would have made thwarted generals seem topical enough, and indeed a glut on the market, the materials given to us through Lessing and through Elizabethan history eliminate the necessity of our finding a recently recalled military patriot or of recognizing in Coleridge's Earl Henry the Whig hero of 1794, Earl Howe, who died in retirement in 1799. If Coleridge remembered Howe in his recalled patriot, the memory seems unbelligerently nostalgic. Howe's obituary in the *Morning Post*, on 6 August, had been notably coy concerning events "painful to recollect"; but *Embarcation*, a song on 7 October, recalled the paper to its duty toward Whigs, and succeeding issues emblazoned regularly Howe's name, deeds, and monuments. (Not incidentally, some of the blazoning advertises Thomas John Dibdin's musical entertainment at Covent Garden, *The Naval Pillar*.) It should be observed that Coleridge's Earl Henry has suffered recall from military success through the "private enmity" of the "politic Chancellor," who to Coleridge or to a Lamb in the imagined audience could be Pitt or a combination of Pitt and Howe's particular enemy, the second Earl Spencer. (CPW, 1062:15, 1066:163) Of course the Chancellor embodies at least in part an Elizabethan figure, either William or Robert Cecil, and I am willing to allow something for the internal needs of the drama, without reference to extraneous events. Belief that Howe gives breath to the Earl Henry of 1800 would lead us to speculate on possible explanations for the reminiscence: that Coleridge thought of himself as having been more nobly committed to politics in 1794–96 than later, that he preserved more deeply than he realized his earlier relentless opposition to the nation's established leaders, or that he could not decide what political views he wished to stress.

References to current issues, as distinct from current events, represent patriotic emotions often evident in Coleridge's journalism of 1800. Choice of a plot with a military hero as protagonist guides him straight toward defense of a brave soldiery. Ironic treatment of the Chancellor's generosity in pensioning soldiers exposes his calling home of veterans, which is made into a spiteful curtailment of communal glory. (1066:147–70) The poet has changed since 1796, when he would have called it curtailment of plunder. Interest centers in the heroic general, not in faceless privates. The proved and applauded heroism of the central character, whom Coleridge imagined as ennobled by the acting of John Philip Kemble, is baldly military. Earl Henry lacks, of course, the ambition that rots the Chancellor. But his callow, splenetic brother, Don Curio (whose shoes Coleridge dreamed of filling with Charles Kemble), is permitted unreproved disappointment at recall after "One glorious Battle." (1069:248) Although it is the play's fool who calls Don Curio "very valiant," a courageous foil swears to Curio's having "a Hero's soul." (1067:184, 1066:148)

The main conflict of the completed act sets the righteousness of the loyal hero over against the vileness of a headlong demagogue who appealed to "deluded citizens," the "unreasoning Multitude." (1063:43, 63) Manrique, Lord of Valdez, the demagogue and a pretender to the throne, was poisoned before the action begins. He has a role analogous to that of Elizabeth's Robert Dudley, Earl of Leicester. If Coleridge was thinking of Leicester, it is the more notable that his Valdez did not merely intrigue among noblemen, but carried treachery to the further point of making his claims plausible to the multitude. Since Valdez is dead, the lesson for the audience is that heroic Earl Henry acts on completely opposite principles.

Earl Henry's loyalty begins in love, or physically inspired passion, for the Queen (imagined as Mrs. Siddons), but the severity of his code transcends all personal passion. To his choleric brother he admits offense: "For you've not learnt the noblest part of valour, To suffer and obey." (1069:237–38) Supported by the title, this glorification of suffering and obedience may enunciate the intended theme. The Chancellor by "pernicious influence" brought the Queen to have the pretender, Valdez, confined without trial and secretly poisoned. Obviously Earl Henry expresses an ideal of the playwright's: "I would have pledged my life on the safety of a public Trial and a public Punishment." (1063:60, 72–73) Beyond this passage, however, the dramatic appropriateness of the speeches makes it uncertain, and even unlikely, that the fragment contains much of Coleridge's usual ventriloquism on political topics.

Abandonment of *The Triumph of Loyalty* released the name Valdez, which Coleridge then substituted for the Velez of *Osorio*. The transfer helps to support a minor conclusion: from Adelaide to Zapolya, the names in his plays lack symbolic or even representative value. Out of the wreck Coleridge salvaged *The Night-Scene: A Dramatic Fragment*, slightly revised in the playwriting year 1813, if we trust his own dating in *Sibylline Leaves* and thereafter. (CPW, 421–23)

Presumably the fragment of the *Triumph* continued, although unidentifiably, in the foggy lists of actable manuscripts that came profusely from Coleridge—lists came, not scripts—following the financial success of *Remorse*. His attempts "to *imitate* W. Scott" in "making Hay while the Sun shines" failed progressively. (CL, III, 431) Partly from financial expectancy, more from the desperate fear of narcosis that spurted him toward production and publication at this time, but in any event painfully and courageously, he completed the manuscript of *Zapolya,* which he submitted to the managers of Drury Lane, without success, in March, 1816. Among the wishful lists of plays in progress during the previous year, *Zapolya* seems to appear now as a tragedy, now as "a tragic Romance," again as a "dramatic Romance," and perhaps still again in indeterminate guise.[17] With all these opportunities, he failed to call it even once a romance of statesmanship. But it is that.

By the subtitle, "A Christmas Tale," he seems to have sought the protection of unreality, or more particularly the non-historical remoteness of *A Winter's Tale,* of which his own "dramatic poem is in humble imitation." (CPW, 883) Besides license for ignoring the neoclassic unity of time, he found in Shakespeare's romantic tragi-comedy a kind of pastoralized courtiership, as well as "serious trouble" in the theme and actions of tyranny over feminine innocence. Under Romantic remodeling, with a touch of Sophocles and Aeschylus, the public implications of a tyrannic act are much more evident. Coleridge seems to have had in mind also *The Tempest,* especially what he had described in a fairly recent lecture as its display of "a profound veneration for all the established institutions of society, and for those classes which form the permanent elements of the state." [18] Thomas John Dibdin turned Coleridge's published but unperformed play into "A Grand Melodrama in Three Acts," entitled *Zapolya, Or the Warwolf,* advertised in the *Morning Post* during February, 1818. Far from desiring flight into mere entertainment, Coleridge had hoped to tiptoe into profundity. According to the notice in the *Theatrical Inquisitor* for February, Dibdin made so few changes that the melodrama remained "too serious," or more politely, "too poetical," for habitués of the Surrey Theater.

For the operation of symbolic fantasy in "Christmas" plays, one might peep into a morality by David Garrick, first published in 1774: *A New Dramatic Entertainment, called A Christmas Tale.* Garrick, in the manner of *Die Zauberflöte,* has the good magician Bonora call forward into virtuous love and liberty those who have previously been swayed by the ugly magician, Nigromant, and thus have been until now "By tyrant pow'r and lust confin'd." Coleridge drew his warning against tyranny, much more public and political than Garrick's, from the severe error, severely rectified, of French blindness to tyrannic ambition. He wrote with a patriotic intent not unlike that clumsily built into such crudities as the popular Christmas pantomime of later years—may it not run forever!—*Where the Rainbow Ends.* The revival of medieval romances, with their supernatural and their superstitions, seems to furnish the link between Garrick's kind of allegoric fantasy and the jolly-season ghost story of which Dickens' *A Christmas Carol: A Ghost Story of Christmas* is the heartiest example. For the nonce Byron had discouraged naturalistic silliness by pointing satirically to Wordsworth's demonstration in *The Idiot Boy* that "Christmas stories tortured into rhyme Contain the essence of the true sublime." (BP, I, 316:245–46) Half-fantasy was safer.

Even more than the Germanic hurly-burly of *Osorio,* the Christmas patri-miming of *Zapolya* provided a dramatic tradition and current theatrical atmosphere into which Coleridge could brush his own political coloration. The ideological storm of the Revolution had opened most literary forms to satiric or hortatory political uses, but traditional veins had not all been equally worked. Loyalist theorizing in a never-almost-never land appealed to Coleridge's sense of reconciling extremes within an imaginatively organic whole.

As for the overtly political form of *Zapolya,* Emerick typifies the usurper that every demagogue would choose to become. Raab Kiuprili is the courageous, clear-eyed patriot, a soldier who has brought to the nation "large acquests, Made honest by the aggression of the foe." (CPW, 896:389–90) Casimir is the well-meaning dupe forceful enough to be corrupted by a military demagogue into positive misdeeds. The words *tyrant* and *patriot* occur even more frequently than in the *Robespierre* play of 1794. Other characters call Emerick little else but tyrant and usurper. The young man whose throne he usurped denounces him as a fratricide who "fill'st the land with curses, being thyself All curses in one tyrant!" (935:328–29)

A lapse of years severs *Zapolya,* after the manner of *A Winter's Tale,* into two parts. Coleridge labeled these parts with a pointed finger: "The Prelude, Entitled 'The Usurper's Fortune'" and "The Sequel, Entitled 'The Usurper's Fate.'" The political language is generally more shrill, less sonorous, than in the first act of *Robespierre;* take an example, not as Miltonic as it first looks: "these will flee abhorrent from the throne Of usurpation!" (889:163–64) Even Kiuprili is not nice as he denounces his son Casimir's allegiance to Emerick: "a bought bond-slave, Guilt's pandar, treason's mouth-piece, a gay parrot, School'd to shrill forth his feeder's usurp'd titles." (890:195–97) Emerick is allowed Cobbett-like language in stating the case for usurpation. Does a patriot's conscience also demand, he asks Kiuprili,

> That a free nation should be handed down,
> Like the dull clods beneath our feet, by chance
> And the blind law of lineage?
>
> (893:304–6)

As noted on an earlier page of this chapter, the beguiled Casimir answers in terms his author would have used without irony twenty years earlier, when Bonaparte was seeking wheels for his chariot: "Let the commanding spirit Possess the station of command!" (894:324–25) But the father has already given the answer regarded as appropriate by the author when the European Phaëthon had run his course. "Recant this instant," the prophetic Kiuprili has ordered his son, "and swear loyalty, And strict obedience to thy sovereign's will . . . ." (891:225–26) All Casimir's arguments for a leader proved by deeds and chosen by the people are but the "shallow sophisms of a popular choice," worthy only of schoolboys' themes and "the mad whirl of crowds Where folly is contagious." (895:354, 369–70) Taken in context, Kiuprili's speech has a further validity, dramatic as well as ideological, because Emerick claims with self-contradiction to be both popular choice and legitimate heir to the throne. Kiuprili argues that a man who really believed himself legitimate heir would avoid justification based upon an unmeasured approval by the unconvened and uncounted populace. Despite the extreme alteration of political taste since *Osorio* which is illustrated in Kiuprili's dicta, Romantic judgment has remained almost as constant as Coleridge claimed: the author of both plays felt the same about a character like Emerick who could refer to native soil as "dull clods."

Perhaps it was easier in a "Christmas tale" than it would have been in a genre excluding fantasy to have Sarolta recognize instantaneously the nobility in Glycine: "Thou art sprung too of no ignoble blood, Or there's no faith in instinct." (903:73–74) Similarly, while Bethlen serves by pastoral convention his princely term as rustic son of a mountaineer, Sarolta adjures him to "still believe That in each noble deed, achieved or suffered, Thou solvest best the riddle of thy birth!" (914:415–17) The argument is not arbitrarily aristocratic, not oligarchic. It was by such nobility as Sarolta describes that every peasant and fisherman in Scott's novels became a king in disguise. Dickens would soon mean the same thing when he called himself a gentleman. Glycine's own love, more than the transcendence of Bethlen's royal blood or the affinity of one chieftain's child for another, made her assert to Zapolya, in a manuscript addition never published by Coleridge, that a "something round me of a wider reach Feels his approach." (940:96n)

To the disgust of the judges at Drury Lane who were asked to consider the play for production, several speeches went even further in "their *metaphysical* dullness." (CL, IV, 721; cf. BL, II, 212) Their displeasure extended to one of the richest pieces of poetry in the play, Casimir's recollection that Sarolta had instinctive knowledge of Laska's treachery:

> And yet Sarolta, simple, inexperienced,
> Could see him as he was, and often warned me.
> Whence learned she this?—O she was innocent!
> And to be innocent is Nature's wisdom!
> The fledge-dove knows the prowlers of the air,
> Feared soon as seen, and flutters back to shelter.
> And the young steed recoils upon his haunches,
> The never-yet-seen adder's hiss first heard.
> O surer than Suspicion's hundred eyes
> Is that fine sense, which to the pure in heart,
> By mere oppugnancy of their own goodness,
> Reveals the approach of evil.
>
> (939:70–81)

This passage, toward which much in the play has been leading, justifies Samuel C. Chew's praise of *Zapolya* for its "Love and beauty and ripe experience." [19] Psychological criticism today might interpret the length of Casimir's explanation as embarrassment by the author over Sarolta's infallible perception both of nobility in Glycine and of base treachery in Laska. Criticism would thereby reduce to a pinprick one of the keys to the play. *Zapolya* has been widely known for Glycine's song, "A sunny shaft did I behold," which Coleridge adapted freely and triumphantly from the *Herbstlied* of Tieck.[20] It should be better known for speeches that carry the larger burden of joy in innocence.

Sarolta's instinct for divorcing evil from good serves Rudolf Lutz's reading of *Zapolya* as a symbolic presentation of Kant's *Vernunft* over against *Verstand*, with the accompanying antinomies of *Geist* against *Natur* and of course imagination against fancy.[21] But hardly more than *Osorio* does *Zapolya* denigrate Nature. Although he went much further than Kant toward belief in the reality of Platonic ideas, and faith in man's capacity to know reality, Coleridge departs naturalistically from the antinomies of Kant, and even from the need for reconciliation as by Schelling, in making Sarolta's innocence "Nature's wisdom." [22] However Germanic in its Transcendentalism *Zapolya* may otherwise be, the naturalism is English. Sanctifying Nature, the play glorifies a God-given wisdom diffused through a virtuous people, available to the true patriot like Kiuprili, and at last comprehended by Casimir, but never accessible to the mechanical experience of a Locke, a Mackintosh, an Emerick, or a Laska, any more than to the minor character Pestalutz, an assassin.

Another speech in *Zapolya* unacceptable to Drury Lane opens wide the political door. First asking just how the commanding spirit comes to be identified and chosen (instinct seems not to be universally viable), Kiuprili goes on to define the practical duties of the patriot:

> By wholesome laws to embank the sovereign power,
> To deepen by restraint, and by prevention
> Of lawless will to amass and guide the flood
> In its majestic channel, is man's task
> And the true patriot's glory! In all else
> Men safelier trust to Heaven . . . .

(895:363–68)

Observe the guided ambiguity by which two connotations are scooped into the word *majestic*. The narrower meaning begins in "sovereign power," which here denotes the power of the single sovereign; the broader connotation arises in the desire to see "lawless will" curbed the noblest and firmest way. The rhetoric of this passage is designed to persuade the disinterested patriot that a firmer royalist faith would bring him greater peace of mind.

In one of his most reprinted pieces of journalism, the comparison of France and Rome, Coleridge traced with severity a curve that he fancifully decorated and prettified in *Zapolya:* "... the most abject disposition to slavery rapidly trod on the heels of the most outrageous fanaticism for an almost anarchical liberty." (EOT, 487) Such stark extremes could have no conceivable place either in a pastoral illusion or in reality presentable to freeborn Englishmen. But the action of *Zapolya,* set declaredly in Illyria, spiritually occurs in France. To take a minute piece of evidence, the French tyrant slept little, notoriously; sensual as he is, Emerick makes himself by policy an "early stirrer." (938:37) Less concrete in application than Wordsworth's odes of Thanksgiving, *Zapolya* nevertheless celebrates the overthrow of Napoleon. In so far as Coleridge considered the popular palate, he tried tincture (to adapt a metaphor of Wordsworth's) for a public satiated from cayenne and garlic.

Political power is not ultimately justified in *Zapolya* by divine or hereditary right, but by law. Upon the death of "royal Andreas" the duped Casimir still agrees with his father that legal process must come from "the States convened" and convened forthwith, "the States Met in due course of law." (892:254, 280; 896:413–14) In these passages *States* seems to be equivalent to *estates,* in the sense of constituent orders of the body politic, convened either directly or by representation. If so, Coleridge may share here, like Emerick, some of the confusion that led theorists to speak of the necessary separation of powers and at the same time of the ultimate sovereignty of the people. At the time of *Zapolya,* of course, he believed that the lower classes had virtual representation in Parliament, by a common Tory theory that he once attributed to Paley. (EOT, 88) Twenty years later in the action of the play, when in brief stage directions Emerick *"falls"* and *"Dies,"* the "assembled chieftains" simultaneously, offstage, depose the tyrant and withdraw from him the protection of the law. (948:322) These chieftains will comprise "the assembled council" that will now give the "awful sanction of convened Illyria" to the new king, the legitimate son of Zapolya known earlier in the play as Bethlen Bathory. (949:352, 357) Although Coleridge may have taken from Palma or some other historian of Hungary a sense of the chieftains as executive representatives of geographical "States," *Zapolya* certainly presents Illyria as a unified and determinate nation.[23]

The usurper who blinded Casimir and oppressed Illyria especially lacked respect for the purity of womanhood. Disrespect for woman's purity had become one of the worst charges Coleridge could bring against a character, male or female; he brought it against Emerick's basest followers as well as against the usurper himself. Emerick's downfall occurs when, if not altogether because, he attempts to seduce Sarolta, whom Casimir has kept isolated and inexperienced. A cryptic message of warning to the husband captures the spirit, as it summarizes the major action, of the last three acts: "The royal Leopard Chases thy milk-white dedicated Hind." (937:9–10) Like Glycine, an audience capable of sympathetic response to the play expects a king to "protect the helpless every where," widows and orphans above all. (909:261) Kiuprili makes it as clear as high noon that the true patriot, like the true king, may be distinguished from the false because he takes no bribes, bears no false witness, outfaces the rights of no orphan, leaves no widow's plea undefended. (890:204–17) The stress of the play lies on Zapolya and her son less as queen and prince than as widow and orphan. Repentant Casimir, who too long joined in the pursuit of "a patriot father, A widow and an orphan," asks forgiveness for the sake of his bleeding country and his "innocent wife." (940:83–91, 946:270) His good wife pronounces the final, familial, anti-Godwinian lesson:

> E'en women at the distaff hence may see,
> That bad men may rebel, but ne'er be free;
> May whisper, when the waves of faction foam,
> None love their country, but who love their home;
> For freedom can with those alone abide,
> Who wear the golden chain, with honest pride,
> Of love and duty, at their own fire-side:
> While mad ambition ever doth caress
> Its own sure fate, in its own restlessness!
>
> (950:390–98)

This close of the playwright's domestic romance of statesmanship closed also the poet's twenty-year defense of the affections against Godwin.

Whatever might have developed from the relations of mistress and slave in *Diadestè*, "an entertainment in one Act," the confused fragment in prose that survives (partly, as it happened, on the verso of announcements for Coleridge's lectures on Shakespeare and Milton in 1811) holds nothing for the student of politics.[24] The Faustian play he conceived and described with the astrologer Michael Scott as protagonist would probably have contained politics, at least in the Aristotelian sense; but he composed none of it.[25] Until some Samuel Ireland attributes a new and actual play or fragment to Coleridge, *Zapolya* closes the account.

CHAPTER XI

A Character

I said, I knew a very wise man so
much of Sir Chr——'s sentiment, that
he believed if a man were permitted
to make all the ballads, he need not
care who should make the laws of a
nation.

—Andrew Fletcher, *An Account
of a Conversation*, 1704

Along with religion, love, friendship, and introspection, politics
must be reckoned as an important impulse toward Coleridge's
poetic creating, and a valuable quality in the finished (and some
of the unfinished) creations.

An attempt to sum up metrically all his political activity, from
musings in blank verse to quipping paragraphs of prose, was made
by Coleridge himself in *A Character*, for a time uncertainly titled
"A Trifle." These tetrameters, or octosyllabics with license, much
influenced by Swift, emerge from the cloudiness native to Coleridge into the noonday clarity of Swift's verses on his own death.[1]
Collier thought *A Character* humiliating with its self-portrait of
the artist as tomtit. But then Collier, a forger and cheat, could not
understand honest self-respect. As remarked earlier, the poem
takes the form of a defensive apology for its author's political
integrity. Hazlitt, too, would think the apology mean and opium-
drenched; it bends, quite unlike the brass of Hazlitt's low bow:
"Mr. Blackwood, I am yours—Mr. Croker, my service to you—
Mr. T. Moore, I am alive and well." Coleridge could neither have

continued to praise Napoleon publicly, as Hazlitt did, nor have refrained from too much apology for wishing to do so.

Irony and zest brace the plaintiveness of the opening lines:

> A BIRD, who for his other sins
> Had liv'd amongst the Jacobins;
> Though like a kitten amid rats,
> Or callow tit in nest of bats,
> He much abhorr'd all democrats....[2]

Though every day brought new feathers, and the tit declared himself a bird of Phoebus' breed, a harmless poet, those on the side of Church and Court still called him bat, and the bats hailed him Brother Cit, or, "at the furthest, cousin-german." To put an end to these ambiguities, he denounced the vermin whom he had, "for his other sins," lived among.

> He spared the mouse, he praised the owl;
> But bats were neither flesh nor fowl.
> Blood-sucker, vampire, harpy, goul,
> Came in full clatter from his throat,
> Till his old nest-mates chang'd their note
> To hireling, traitor, and turncoat,—
> A base apostate who had sold
> His very teeth and claws for gold....
>
> (452:23–30)

They said he had abandoned the leathern wing to feather well his nest; they predicted he would soon play Count Goldfinch or Sir Joseph Jay. "Alas, poor Bird."

Despite his success in achieving the range of ingenuity necessary to Swiftian weight of argument in homely narrative, Coleridge at this point abandons the allegory. Henceforth it is plain "Alas, poor Bard." Writing for his own conscience, serving a party solely by chance (and not even by the chance that his newspaper employers served the party), the bard neither received nor expected reward. What claim had he, Coleridge asked in the sturdiest antithetical verses he ever wrote,

> Who swore it vex'd his soul to see
> So grand a cause, so proud a realm,
> With Goose and Goody at the helm;
> Who long ago had fall'n asunder

But for their rivals' baser blunder,
The coward whine and Frenchified
Slaver and slang of the other side?—

(453:62–68)

The bard signed his name complacently as ΕΣΤΗΣΕ, "Punic Greek for 'he hath stood,'" despite squeakings of the bats to the effect that he had bartered his conscience for bays. After joking without wit that the "circlets of green baize" worn by the bard were only his garters, the poem, or patched fragment, ends by denying charges of venality in a tone to make Hazlitt gruffly weep:

Ah! silly Bard, unfed, untended,
His lamp but glimmer'd in its socket;
He lived unhonour'd and unfriended
With scarce a penny in his pocket;—
Nay—tho' he hid it from the many—
With scarce a pocket for his penny!

(453:84–89)

When all praise is exhausted, the verses lack the pliant regularity of Swift's. The colloquy with Jacobinical bats lacks the dramatic movement of the trivia exchanged over Swift's decease. The colloquialism stumbles over un-ironic Latin and false Greek. Coleridge's self-depreciation seems more egoistic by comparison, for Swift's wry portraiture of friends, avoided by Coleridge, leaves a final impression of sociability. Most of all, the poem lacks Swift's source of strength in ultimate pride of accomplishment.

And yet, if Coleridge had not held together two incompatible chief ministers and had not rallied a whole nation until even a Walpole retreated, he had not malingered. He had raised an excited voice against Pitt's invasions of English liberties, perhaps to some effect; he had brought an elevation to the policy of at least one newspaper, and some increase in its circulation and influence. Shocked from his original confidence in inevitable progress and rational reform, he had not retreated into a Nature free of political strife, but had tried for thirty years to bring that Nature to the attention of statesmen who needed to comprehend the laws of growth. Did he seriously believe that his honesty as a journalist had led (in Fox's mind, at least) to the rupture of the Peace of Amiens, and had driven Napoleon to order his arrest and to have him chased at sea? Probably. His daughter Sara thought it feasible,[3] Napoleon certainly hounded unfriendly journalists, some of the agents Coleridge named were in the unlikely right place at the right time, and in general Coleridge's anecdotes are verifiable far more often than they are reputed to be. In any event, he regarded his political notoriety and influence as coming from his articles in prose, not from his odes or fables. Here, in a later age, we have followed the path of politics through the odes and lesser poems, and now reach a different conclusion.

When we first come upon the poet in the boy Coleridge, he is occupied in pleasing his elders by returning to them the political sentiments they have given him, and given him partly in metrical forms. He returns the sentiments in forms similar but never identical to theirs. Pity, swelling the books, pamphlets, and periodicals of the day, makes all the fibers of the youth's being vibrate now all together and now in discordant opposition to the pitiless. At Cambridge, Frend, Wakefield, and a few other keen and discontented elders unfold for him the greater fun of daring a more sharply defined opposition to the Establishment. Humanitarian and libertarian politics have the honor of calling into the unruly student's verse for the first time that unimitative accuracy of report on personal thoughts and feelings which we call the artist's sincerity. Thereafter this sincerity had to contend also with the editorial needs of a partisan newspaper.

If *Christabel, Kubla Khan,* and *The Ancient Mariner* are poems of escape, politics form a large part of what they escaped from. Regarded somewhat more positively, each of the three is a demonstration against the times, by a young poet whose writings in prose and verse had been mostly political. Just as Romantic medievalism rejects the isolating individualism of Locke, so the evocation of the supernatural in *The Ancient Mariner* rejects the commercial spirit and refutes the utilitarian doctrines of Coleridge's day. Extending from partisan opposition to Aristotelian theory, politics were an expansive, amorphous part of Coleridge's "one Life within us and abroad." As poet, he did not wish to divorce the ethics of politics from the ethics of love.

Sir Leoline complacently embraces the foul Geraldine, and assures all listeners—in the face of Bard Bracy's prophetic dream and poetic instinct—that "arms more strong than harp or song" will crush the serpentine evil that threatens them. The Bard is a dreamier but surer guide than the Baron: he knows when the garden has a snake in it. Although political information has helped us to distinguish between a poet's divine creation and a khan's mundane decree, we would follow politics too slavishly if we attempted to explain or illustrate the situation of Bard, Baron, and snake by reference to a trying experience deeply felt by Coleridge, the situation of Bard, England, and Pitt. Nor should we seek in the insensitive murder of the albatross either a particular political crime or a crime particularly political. Aside from the inaptness of emotional texture when practical politics are read allegorically into such poems, we can feel justified in our current fear lest the Palace of Art resume too many administrative functions. Yet we may retain a distaste for verse that advises us on where to plant our footsteps, without believing that a poem suspected of reference to life outside the poem should be cut dead. The study here completed has sought, in part, to establish the political life as one corresponding actuality for the imagined worlds of Sir Leoline and of the Mariner who learned to love "All things both great and small."

Coleridge's periods of producing impassioned poetry roughly coincided with his political excitements (excluding his later unpoetical years), and the bulk of his verse had both a political inspiration and a conscious political purpose. The "Character" could look back on glories accomplished. He had written great poetry of political assessment, as in *France: An Ode;* more often he had versified a partisan position *pro tempore,* or in deeper verse combined politics with religious passion, as in *Religious Musings* and *Ode on the Departing Year.* He had usually reached and expressed underlying political principles, whether in a *Talleyrand to Grenville* or *Fears in Solitude.* He had put experiments like his anapestic modification of Stolberg, *The British Stripling's War-Song,* to a use that fed his family and at the same time registered a transition in his politics. Poems concerned with immediate events remained fluid while the situation was fluid: witness *France* as well as the lesser *Recantation.* But usually he regarded his own completed poems as artistically unavailable for impromptu fitting to a political situation, a debasement that he forced Renaissance poems of Fulke Greville, Samuel Daniel, and others to undergo.

He moved almost steadily away from the slightly inspired

journalism of *The Fall of Robespierre*. His last substantial poetic work, *Zapolya*, came from a psychologist who had studied for two decades the yearnings, joys, suffering, pride, and self-laceration of his own mind; it came also from a poet not only alertly indebted to Kant, Jacobi, and a miscellany of German metaphysicians, but long steeped in political lucubrations by the medieval Fathers more than by neighbors like Hooker and Burke. With a final quiet but sure affirmative, *Zapolya* answers a question we can justly—and it should be safely—regard as important: "Did the prophet in some sense believe his prophecies?"

For the most part, as *A Character* puts it, "whate'er he wrote or said Came from his heart as well as head." (452:47–48) He had communicated his horror at social injustice, needless misery, and political procedures standing upon might without any stooping to mere right. He had not willingly closed his eyes. The Home Office had set spies upon him. A tomtit bard, he had acquired a dossier. Unlike other political poets of the day, he had avoided having Lord Eldon declare any of his works ineligible for legal protection against piracy because written to undermine public morale, but he had labored and rimed and quipped in the eternal political struggle to keep the other man honest and responsible. He had honestly and bravely sung his recantation. Because of his influence many readers, like Southey, Wordsworth, and Hazlitt in his own day, have adhered more fervently to the ideals of land, people, dedicated endeavor, freedom, enlightenment, and mercy. For mercy is one of those things publicly applicable that a poet can diffuse for the common welfare.

The Last Leaf
of the Gutch Notebook

Many Coleridgians have tried to guess what political heroes the poet almost but not quite celebrated in verse. The starting place has been the excruciatingly illegible penciled list among the hindmost entries in the Gutch Memorandum Book. The prevalent temptation, since Brandl succumbed in 1896, has been to read into the abbreviated hieroglyphics the names of persons on whom Coleridge might have intended to write poems. Actually, the list provides a tentative order for "effusions" in the volume of 1796. It differs markedly from later lists. (CL, 243, 298) Probably it is a proposal of order jotted about July, 1795, as a memorandum "to speak to Cottle concerning Selections &c." (CN, 297)

The list begins, omitting Pitt, with the order laid down in the *Morning Chronicle:* Erskine, Burke, Priestley, Fayette, Kosciusko, Bowles. Under these names Coleridge inked the numbers 1 to 6. The next name is Stanhope, but the figure 6 appears under Bowles, not, as given in the published notebooks, under Stanhope. Soon after Brandl's transcriptions were published, the late Arthur Beatty read the first word on the next line as "Wakefield." Professor Coburn and I have also independently arrived at this reading. After the next name, Schiller, come two sets of difficult initials or abbreviations. Brandl read "Th. C." and "J. M.," for which he proposed Chatterton and Milton as subjects. Professor Coburn reads "Th. C." and "J. H." Accepting Chatterton, she proposes as his companion the very unlikely Hort of *To the Rev. W. J. H.*, the second poem in the volume of 1796. Neither the *W. J. H.* nor the first poem, the *Monody to Chatterton,* was designated as an effusion. Thomas Clarkson and Joseph Hucks have been temptingly suggested, but the list is almost certainly a tentative order for effusions ready to print, and the Coburn readings are in this case probably wrong. Of these two sets of initials, which bear the inked numbers

9 and 10, I fear the second may be "O. M.," for the poem *To an Old Man* (Effusion 16 in 1796), or even possibly "A. M." for *Autumnal Moon* (Effusion 18), and the first an abbreviation, say "Th. L.," for Effusion 14, beginning "Thou gentle Look." (CPW, 47) Professor Beatty, examining the notebook when the pencilings may have been more legible, recorded the following decipherment: "Thel[?]" and "Gon[or Gd n?]." One would assume the first to stand for Thelwall and guess the second to represent Godwin. Like the initials for Clarkson and Hucks, these readings would appeal to me more than unpolitical effusions, but Beatty may have assumed first and deciphered afterward. Notwithstanding the range of these readings and their relationship to the series in the *Morning Chronicle,* Sheridan is notably absent. Coleridge, if not all the decipherers, omitted Southey. (Brandl read "Southey" for what is unquestionably "Burke.") Stanhope is here; Sheridan, Southey, and probably Godwin are not.

The next item has always been transcribed as "Robespierre," by inheritance from one decipherer to the next, but it is hardly more than "Ros," and probably stands for *The Rose* (Effusion 27). If it is an abbreviation for Robespierre, unlikely as that is, it could refer to the forty-four lines *To a Young Lady with a Poem on the French Revolution,* the eighth item in the volume of 1796 and by that time firmly associated with *The Fall of Robespierre.* The next, numbered 8, abbreviates *Genevieve;* next, I am sure, comes "Brock." for *Brockley Coomb* (Effusion 21, composed in May, 1795); then "Kiss," and finally, numbered 11, 12, and 13, "Prostitute" (Effusion 15), Pitt, and Siddons. Who knows how these last three got together? Probably it was not the politics once thought to dominate Coleridge's list. Even what seems to be "Wakefield" may be something like "Own Heart" (Effusion 19), since all the other hieroglyphs represent completed poems. In summary, we have accounted for Effusions 1 through 21 of the 1796 volume, except 6 (Sheridan), 11–13 (borrowed from Lamb, and like the Siddons signed "C. L."), and the uncertain 16, 18, and 19. Then we skip five miscellaneous effusions (or four if "Kiss" refers to 26 rather than the more likely 28), and account for two more. I can hardly hope to have Wakefield left over.

For sources of this discussion, see A. Brandl, "S. T. Coleridges Notizbuch aus den Jahren 1795–1798," *Archiv,* XCVII (1896), 333–72; CN, 305 and note; B.M. MS. Add. 27901, f. 89ᵛ. My efforts were aided by the staff of the British Museum, an ultraviolet photograph, the kind permission of Mr. A. H. B. Coleridge, and Professor Abbie Findlay Potts, who was responsible for the return of the Beatty transcriptions to the University of Wisconsin.

Coleridge's Pseudonyms

Hints concerning Coleridge's attitudes toward his primarily journalistic verse can be gleaned from the signatures he originally affixed. Much of his newspapering was completely anonymous, but several of the poems were signed in full, and most of the other verse, with an increasing ratio of the prose, bore some guise of his initials. A few items with the initials scrambled can be assigned to him uncertainly. More and more he spelled out the initials S. T. C. in corrupt Greek as "ESTEESI," "ΕΣΤΗΣΕ," or as a word, "Εστησε," which he explained in a rugged poem of self-justification: " 'Tis Punic Greek for 'he hath stood!' " (CPW, 453:73) Like "ΕΣΤΗΣΕ," most of his pseudonyms were intended to incorporate a significance at least partly political. He signed his first verses in the *Morning Post*, after the fashion of the Della Cruscans, as "Albert," from the admirable brother in his *Osorio*. (MP, 7 Dec. 1797) *To the Snow Drop*, in praise of Perdita Robinson, bears in the manuscript an introductory note signed "Zagri," from the Moresco martyr to oppression in the same play. Zagri, like a model Romantic, "dared avow the prophet." (CPW, 356, 529:255) As shown earlier, the published poem to Mrs. Robinson was signed "Francini."

Five items, scattered over a full year, bore "Laberius" as signature: *Parliamentary Oscillators; Fire, Famine, and Slaughter;* one non-political poem; and two epigrams. (CPW, 213, 239, 252, 953, 977) Just possibly "Laberius" was suggested by a versifier in the *Morning Chronicle* of 8 August 1794 who signed himself "Librarius"; improbably but conceivably it darts an associative glance at Coleridge's labial gape (from a blockage either adenoidal or so in effect). Whatever its secondary suggestions, the pseudonym refers almost certainly to a liberal among the *equites Romani* named Laberius, who may have seemed ironically akin for his mimes, for his comic and satiric poems, or for his epic employing uncommon words. Laberius is known most widely of all through the legend that Caesar reduced him to acting in his own

farces. Probably the legend led Coleridge to assume the name out of
bitterness toward the satiric depths he had fallen to, but a footnote in
Conyers Middleton's life of Cicero had spread the opposing view, ranged
for a time by Hobhouse against Byron, that Caesar "made Laberius,
who was an actor, a knight, not a knight an actor." Is it mere coincidence
that Coleridge drew Middleton's Cicero from the Bristol Library (with
the assistance of Cottle's name for the second volume) immediately
after he first signed the name of the "celebrated mimic actor" to his
Parliamentary Oscillators?

To join Middleton in making an accomplished artist and hero of
Laberius would take from the pseudonym the self-deprecating Socratic
irony, slightly Romantic in its divided judgment, that Coleridge usually
embodied in his pseudonyms. Later, one of the favorite personae "mask-
ing his birth-name" was "Idoloclastes Satyrane." Of Satyrane, the man
of nature in Book I of Spenser's *Fairy Queen,* John Wilson was to record
in *Blackwood's* shortly after Coleridge died the view which may have
been Coleridge's, that he represented Natural Heroic Activity, as "a
good Knight, but a savage, and not a Moral or leading Champion." (1835,
XXXVII, 54) In *A Tombless Epitaph,* Coleridge wrote similarly of
Satyrane's—that is, his own—"wild-wood fancy and impetuous zeal."
(CPW, 413:1, 4, 5) The addition of "Idoloclastes" declared him con-
sanguineous with Luther. Although pride and embarrassment varied
in relative intensity, self-consciousness over his political squibs never
vanished.

In Germany, with heart at home, he signed two small poems as
"Cordomi." (CPW, 313, 314) In the guise of dwarfed forerunner and
editor of *Talleyrand to Lord Grenville,* he signed himself "Gnome."
(CPW, 341) If Coleridge wrote the sonnet to Lord Stanhope signed
"One of the People" in the *Morning Chronicle,* a printer's devil must
have provided the pseudonym. (CPW, 89) More to the pattern, Coleridge signed as "Civis," in the *Courier,* a sonnet adapted from Fulke
Greville to denounce "yon Corsican" as a creature of Talleyrand. (CPW,
1116) His emblematic author for *Cholera Cured Beforehand,* written
in contempt of leveling at the time of the Reform Bill, was "Demophilus
Mudlarkiades." (CPW, 986) This procedure, the inventing of a contemptible persona as author of a transparently ironic set of verses,
reverses his usual practice, by which an ironic pseudonym undercuts
self-protectively a set of verses put before the public for admiration
and concurrence.

"Cassiani, jun.," the signature for *The Mad Monk,* may represent
merely a current interest, imbibed from Wordsworth (who may have
begun the poem itself, later jerry-built by Coleridge); but Giuliano

Cassiani, who had died in 1778, asserted premonitory Italian nationalism in several poems among his elegies, and wrote somewhat in the vein of *The Mad Monk*. (CPW, 347) There had been in fact an austere hermit of the late fourth century in Egypt, thought mad, named Johannes Cassianus. It was Coleridge's practice, when meeting his journalistic commitments with Wordsworth's juvenilia, to affix pseudonyms. He thought of Wordsworth as a hermit, and could in "Cassiani, jun." have heaped two lyrical balladers, with the poem's mad monk, Cassianus, and Cassiani, all in one. Richard Garnett puzzled at some length in 1898 over Coleridge's signature of "Nicius Erythraeus" for the *Morning Post* appearance of *Lewti* and *The Old Man of the Alps*. But *Lewti* is now known to be reworked from a juvenile poem of Wordsworth's, and the pseudonym therefore supports internal evidence that the other poem, never reprinted by Coleridge, is at least partly Wordsworth's. The ponderous movement of the caesuras; the tale of a maid who dreamed of a home—in one of Coleridge's quiet dells, admittedly—when her love would return from the wars; the casual news of his death, which "left her mind imperfect"; the stoic prayer of her old father when the mad daughter drowned; the exasperating device that has parallels midway in *Simon Lee* and other ventriloquistic poems by Wordsworth: "Kind-hearted stranger! patiently you hear A tedious tale"; all these suggest a Wordsworthian precursor of the *Lyrical Ballads*. (CPW, 249–50:75, 89–90) This speculation leaves us wondering, more or less as Garnett wondered, how "a learned, loquacious, sarcastic, but otherwise harmless Jesuit" signifies aid given by the hermit of the Lakes to a London drudge. Yet it is important—for anybody who has come this far with me—to distinguish between pseudonyms that point to aid in authorship and pseudonyms that dally with the vocation of political journalism. The signature "Aphilos" of March, 1811, and the pseudonyms related to doggerel passed among friends (and uncollected as yet) are alike in indifference to politics. (CPW, 417) As for those like "ΕΣΤΗΣΕ" that lay claim to constancy, Coleridge wrote in serious and basically honest humility as early as 1802: "Let him that stands take heed lest he fall—." (CL, 867) And names like Laberius and Francini avoid a boast of sovereignty such as Byron might make.

On "Laberius" see the notes to *Childe Harold* IV.cxli, 1st and 2nd issues of the 1st edition, 1818, pp. 217, 226; George Whalley, "The Bristol Borrowings of Southey and Coleridge, 1793–8," *Library*, 5th s., IV (1949), 125, 129; Middleton, *A History of the Life of Cicero*, 6th ed. (1755), II, 334n. On "Civis" see J. D. Campbell in *Athenaeum*, 25 Apr. 1903, p. 531. On "Nicius Erythraeus" see Garnett, "Among My

Books," *Literature*, 22 Oct. 1898, pp. 374–76; CPW, 248, 256; D. V. Erdman in *SB*, XI (1958), 154–56. On "Groscollius" see CPW, 1142; CL, 390 and note; *Athenaeum*, 10 Dec. 1798, p. 825; J. B. Beer, "Coleridge at School," *N & Q*, CCIII (1958), 114–16. On "Satyrane" see C. E. Mounts, "Coleridge's Self-Identification with Spenserian Characters," *SP*, XLVII (1950), 522–33.

The Epigrams

Coleridge's bits in verse and prose will never be identified with complete accuracy. If his shorter political epigrams have been even half-properly identified, however, he barely dabbled in that genre.

The first of what he called "Critiques on Sir W. Anderson's nose" for the *Morning Post* in 1798–99 drew upon *The Nose*, forty lines on Lord Mayor William Gill written by the cleverest of Bluecoat boys in 1789. (CPW, 8, 958; CL, 552) This joke became routine, almost compulsory, both for Coleridge and for the Opposition generally. In 1794 he had suggested that Southey lampoon for him the red-nosed Pittite mayor of Cambridge. (CL, 110) Elected Lord Mayor of London on 18 October 1797, Anderson had promised the Livery in his speech of acceptance to harden the City toward support of Pitt, and he had been carrying out his promise, in order to preserve King, country, and "glorious Constitution." The Opposition despised him as sycophant and alarmist. Coleridge pretended to believe that Grenville's second note to Talleyrand was "composed originally by some emigrant priest, and translated into a *resemblance* of English by Mr. Windham or Alderman Anderson." (EOT, 252)

Unless Coleridge was slow to learn of the baronetcy awarded Anderson on 5 May 1798, he may originally have intended some other aldermanic M.P. in Pitt's pocket for the couplet on "Naso Rubicund, Esq." sent to Southey on 30 September 1799. (CL, 536) It appeared in the *Morning Post* on 7 December as an epigram "On Sir Rubicund Naso, a Court Alderman, and Whisperer of Secrets." Besides the idiomatic pun in the rime with "so ruddy your nose," Coleridge's readers would find an apt reference to bribery by George Rose, secretary to the treasury, in "talk where you will, 'tis all *under the Rose*." (CPW, 958) The Livery had come far toward George III since the mayoralty of John Wilkes in 1774, and some distance since the beginning of the war with France. Anderson's successor, Sir Richard Carr Glyn, kept the mayoralty firm for Pitt. But the chief need for deriding red-nosed mayors and aldermen was probably to offset, even if weakly, the Ministerial satires on the famous glow of Sheridan's drunken nose. Even in a colored print of 1788, concerned with Mayor Gill, prominence went to Sheridan's Bardolphian beacon; and pertinent conditions had in every way worsened. (George, VI, 533) A famous political ballad of the Commonwealth bore the refrain, "Under the rose"; and even then noses were a political liability: to judge by Cavalier ballads, Cromwell's nose was ruddier than Bardolph's. (See *Political Ballads ... during the Commonwealth*, ed. Thomas Wright [1841], pp. 49–50; *Cavalier and Puritan*, ed. Hyder E. Rollins [New York, 1923], pp. 71–72.)

As one would expect, unless one thought Coleridge would give more of his mind to it, the most effective of the epigrams, politically, attack Pitt personally. Not sufficiently retailored from the German to fit the new victim, they merely abuse him. From the notebooks we learn that the epigram *On the Sickness of a Great Minister*, ending in the *Morning Post* "No! Ministers and Quacks! them take I not so young," was first translated by Coleridge as "On the Recovery of a Harlot," ending "No! Whores & Doctors—no—I fetch *them* not so young!" (*MP*, 1 Oct. 1799; CPW, 957; CN, 625 [17]) *On a Report of a Minister's Death* had been effective in Lessing's version; Coleridge increased its wit by avoiding Pitt's name but adding a homophonic refrain, repeated when the report of death proves false: "Pity, indeed, 'tis pity!" (CPW, 956) From Lessing also came the quatrain applied to Pye's *Carmen Seculare*: originating in satiric defense of true poetry against pinchbeck, it was enlisted in the partisan campaign against Pye's purchased loyalty. (CPW, 959; CN, 625 [18])

Coleridge's original contributions to the field are too few to allow evaluation or even identification of his motives, except for his desire to earn (or to get) bread and cheese, mostly by personal lampoon. A punning partisan couplet of slightly generalized politics has been among his collected works since 1877: "To be ruled like a Frenchman the Briton is loth, Yet in truth a *direct-tory* governs them both." (CPW, 953) One of the pieces signed "Laberius" expands an epigram from the Greek Anthology to six lines *On Deputy* ——, much to the disadvantage of the deputy's "idiot face." (CPW, 953) I have been able neither to ascertain the political use of this tweak nor to be sure why Coleridge was almost always less epigrammatic in brief flicks of the hand than in longer poems. The epigram that J. P. Collier said Coleridge wrote on the first Earl of Lonsdale, adapted from a German source, probably had little stimulus from politics, for persons of all parties could have said of this Tory defrauder of the Wordsworths what the epigram says: "We know nothing good but that he is dead." (CPW, 971; *Old Man's Diary*, I, 35) Remarks all too similar could be made about the epitaph applied to Hazlitt. (CPW, 962)

Two epigrams published on 2 and 3 September 1799 in the *Morning Post* and reprinted in the *Annual Anthology*, 1800 (the first adapted from a German original), execrated the United Irishmen as next below "the greedy creeping Things in Place"; they were locusts and wild honeys that John the Baptist was welcome to return for. Coleridge was much readier to believe the Irish in treasonous alliance with the French, as exposed by Dundas and the Committee of Secrecy in 1799, after the aborted conspiracy under Wolfe Tone of the previous year. The people (at that time), yes; but united traitors, no! Although they contain none of the damp chat against tolerance of Catholicism that makes his later *Sancti Dominici Pallium* a sodden debate, Coleridge was not excessively passionate when he scratched a line through the two epigrams and declared them "Dull and profane." (CPW, 959; JDC, 652) Typically, in the *Courier* for 31 August 1811, one of his anti-Catholic additions to the *Allegoric Vision* was "an Hibernian variety of the Centaur genus, composed of a deranged man and mad *bull*." Incidentally, however, by all those endearing and more mature charms, Tom Moore got to be, in 1827, "Erin's sweet melodist." (CPW, 464) And a belated sense of fair play made him ask God to forgive him for signing the letters to Mr. Justice Fletcher, against Catholic Emancipation, as "An Irish Protestant." (MS in the Berg Collection, at the end of Letter 1; see EOT, 682; W, 186, 255–56.)

Bertram Dobell identified as John Taylor Coleridge the owner of a commonplace book who therein attributed to "S. T. C." two epigrams sharper than any that S. T. C.'s daughter Sara was able to find. One, greeting the news in 1806 that a new Garrick had been found in the boy-actor Billy Petty and a new Pitt in Henry Petty, Chancellor of the Exchequer at twenty-two, replied that the latter was "a very *petty* Pitt indeed." The second is a keener version of an epigram on the death of Fox in the turncoat *Morning Post* of 26 September 1806, which roused young Byron to a reply. Resolved at last to do like Pitt, said the epigram in the *Post*, "For once to serve his Country, Fox died too!" (CPW, 970) E. H. Coleridge thought that his grandfather might have veiled his initials in one line of the *Post* version: "Let Sense and Truth unclue." Dr. Erdman has challenged the ascription. (SB, XI, 160) Coleridge could have turned in contempt on Fox, whom he later regarded as unpatriotic and indirectly a Liberticide; but he could not easily have written: "Pitt in his Country's service lived and died." More than twenty years later he wrote that Pitt "(his measures and notions,

I mean) was and still is the object of my almost unqualified aversion."
(UL, II, 408)

That Coleridge produced the whole batch of his known epigrams—
and we can throw in the conjectural ones—merely by clearing out his
desk for Stuart, as he said, seems exactly descriptive. (CL, 876) It is
not charitable to believe that he translated most of them for any other
reason. Generosity might lead a critic to take these thimble-sized
squibs as some of the political vindictiveness Coleridge told Tom
Wedgwood he ground out with displeasure. But heart and soul combined could not make of him a productive epigrammatist, that is, a
passionless wit. When Napoleon fell to Elba in 1814, the merchants of
Bristol, then England's second largest city, entered into a jealous war
of gigantic illuminations and transparencies, some up to thirty-five
feet in height, to be exposed on 29 June, Proclamation Day, for all to
see and newspapers to describe. All were to have the most intoxicating
allegories and the most exultant mottoes that Bristol wits could conceive. For his affluent friend Josiah Wade, Coleridge conceived the
theme and details of a transparency to be designed by the artist most
nearly great among their friends, a representative Romantic painter,
Washington Allston. *Felix Farley's Bristol Journal* described it on 2
July: "Mr. *Wade*, next door to the Custom-House, a large transparency
14 feet by 12, a vulture with human head, chained to a rock (Elba)
Britannia clipping its wings with shears, on one blade of which was
Nelson, the other Wellington." One colored engraving, advertised on
4 June as given free to every purchaser of a ticket or share in the Lot-
tery, was simpler but more literary in its symbols, even if anti-Romantic.
It depicted "Buonaparte chained to the Rock of Elba, overtaken by
Justice, and a Vulture feeding on his heart proves him to be the *modern
Prometheus.*" Coleridge's symbols would have seemed more ingenious
than original, but doubtless his use of the vulture to represent the
enemy would be much to the taste of victorious English shopkeepers.
According to Cottle, he offered Wade alternate captions, a quatrain
describing the allegory and a couplet to add another turn of metaphor:

> We've conquered us a Peace, like lads true metalled:
> And Bankrupt *Nap's* accounts seem all now settled.

> (CPW, 972)

This, I am saying, is the best Coleridge could do in epigram. To com-
pete before those who were (in the language of the Merriam diction-
aries) honoring the occasion by refraining from business and by ex-
uberant merrymaking, Coleridge wrote a sober quatrain, given here
from *Farley's:*

We've fought for Peace and conquered it at last,
The rav'ning *Vulture's* leg seems fettered fast,
Britons rejoice! and yet be wary too,
The chain may break, the clipt wings sprout anew.

(For "wings" read "wing"; see Cottle, *Early Recollections* [1837], II, 144–45; CPW, 972; CL, IV, 565; *Bristol Mercury*, 4 July 1814, where the *Farley's* version is repeated.)

Coleridge's talent, I repeat, is for prophecy, not for epigram or epigraph.

On the epigrams in general, see Dobell, "Coleridgeana," *Athenaeum*, 9 Jan. 1904, p. 53; O. Ritter, "Coleridgiana," *Englische Studien*, LVIII (1924), 368–89; Lewis Patton, "The Coleridge Canon," *TLS*, 3 Sept. 1938, p. 570; and current studies by R. S. Woof. "As gay Lord Edward," sometimes attributed to Coleridge, was claimed by James Lawrence, *Love: An Allegory* (1802), p. 46, and *The Etonian out of Bounds* (1828), II, 156.

On Anderson and Gill, see Edmund Blunden in *Coleridge*, ed. Blunden and Griggs (1934), pp. 58, 63; MP, 5, 20 Oct., 20 Dec. 1797, 2, 17 Jan., 13, 19 Feb. 1798, 7, 24 Dec. 1799; *The Times*, 28–30 Sept., 6, 11, 14, 16, 19 Oct. 1797; *City Biography* (1800), p. 45; SPJ for 1800, p. 80; MS notes on the lord mayors by John J. Stocken and Samuel Gregory, in the Guildhall Library. Gill returned to notice with his death on 26 March 1798.

Lines Composed
in a Concert-Room

The stanzas of unequal length and varied structure making up *Lines Composed in a Concert-Room* contain perplexities disproportionate to their moderate poetic importance. Like the stanzas and the metrics, the diction and sense seem to have been nursed in rational convention, but to have grown into independence, or at least into eccentricity, by kicking emotionally through the original order and restraint. The poem could serve as a case for negative Romanticism, by its rejection of the mechanical without achieving the organic. (CPW, 324)

Fully understood, it would add to our knowledge of Coleridge's curve of allegiance from French revolt to British continuity. Partly understood, it probably illustrates his skill at adapting surface meanings to changed conditions. It is written as if spoken in discontent at a soloist's vocal concert, apparently provincial:

> Hark! the deep buzz of Vanity and Hate!
>   Scornful, yet envious, with self-torturing sneer
> My lady eyes some maid of humbler state,
>   While the pert Captain, or the primmer Priest,
>   Prattles accordant scandal in her ear.
>
> (CPW, 324:9–13)

The speaker, addressing a "Dear Maid," would much prefer to escape from this artificially scented atmosphere and get among the folk and the "things of Nature." When the poem emerged in the *Morning Post* of 27 September 1799, eighteen lines included at the end, not inharmonious with the whole, anticipated a day when a world freed of these "vile and painted locusts" shall be "made worthy of its God." (CPW, 325:56, 58)

Of uncertain date, the verses may possibly have been addressed to

Fanny Nesbitt in 1793 or to his choice among the Brunton sisters in 1794; as Coleridge usually altered names of private persons before addressing them in print, we learn nothing definite from the "dear Anne" of line 29. It is scarcely conceivable that the theme, tone, or any basic details of the poem arose, as Dykes Campbell thought possible, from any occasion with his dear sister Ann, who died in 1791; the intimacy of a few lines, and a designation of the addressee as "gentle woman," suggest that it may have been partly adapted about 1796 for his wife Sara. Its origin is irrevocably occasional, with such specific details of setting that Sara could not have been appeased by the displacement of a different dear. It has of course been made into something not directly dependent on its occasion. We may throw out any likelihood that it is dramatically objective without a source in personal experience, but we must allow a bare possibility that "dear Anne" is an alias to dissociate Sara from acidic stanzas. There is a noticeable absence of the Pantisocratic vale, although convenient opportunities for it abound.

Several editors have been tempted to suppose that Lamb referred to the third line, "Heaves the proud Harlot her distended breast," when he warned and asked in July, 1796: "Have a care, good Master poet, of the Statute de Contumelia. What do you mean by calling Madame Mara harlot & naughty things?" (JDC, 623; CPW, 324:3; LL, I, 37–38) The setting seems to be provincial; more specifically, on or near a coast with "weedy caves." H. M. Belden, in *MLN*, XXII (Nov., 1907), 218–20, identified its landscape specifically with the ash-tree dell at Nether Stowey, 1796–97. Therefore, the poem may be thought to reject some "laborious song" less famous than Mara's or Banti's; but of course Lamb could have meant "Madame Mara" as a generic term rather than as an identification. Or he may refer to verses now lost. We have not yet found proof that the *Concert-Room* existed in 1796, in whole or in part.

In general theme, the poem condemns the haughty, artificial, vain, scented, hating and hateful concert-sitters; it proposes a contrast highly flattering to the simple tunes and marches of the old blind musician who played at country dances, and equally favorable to the ballads of the folk and the varied musical utterances of Nature. The theme and its details make any original date outside 1794–96 seem unlikely, and yet leave almost uniquely appropriate September, 1799, when Coleridge and Southey visited Exeter in company with their wives and walked south as far as Dartmouth. Coleridge was in high spirits, as his letters show, ready to have his writing pens repaired for vigorous use against the Ministers. The last three stanzas in the *Post*, not included by Coleridge in reprintings of the poem, concluded in a couplet riddled with blanks, presumably of cautious self-censoring by author or editor:

> Leaving un—— —— undebas'd
> A —— world made worthy of its God.

The vile and painted locusts, whom human feelings shall rise against and purge from the earth (in the uncensored portion of the final stanza), must be the whole class represented at the concert, and not merely such performers as the long-breathed singer of "uptrilled strain." The persona speaking in the poem by no means admires coloratura, but his attack bears chiefly upon the "gaudy throng" that chooses artificiality over "Nature's passion-warbled plaint"—thus described in inappropriately artificial phrase. In general, however, the simplicity of diction and absence of metaphor conform with Coleridge's satiric style of 1799 rather than earlier.

As long as the original date goes undetermined, it cannot be known with certainty how far the stanza before the last exemplifies Coleridge's pliant capacity for adapting passages and whole poems to changing beliefs and circumstances. In solitude apart from concert-goers, with the white arm of the dear maid around his neck and her kiss upon his cheek, the speaker would tell her "what a holier joy," a *holier* joy,

> It were in proud and stately step to go,
>   With trump and timbrel clang, and popular shout,
>   To celebrate the shame and absolute rout
> Unhealable of Freedom's latest foe,
>   Whose tower'd might shall to its centre nod.
>   (CPW, 325:47–51)

On 24 September 1799, readers of the *Morning Post* would have to take "Freedom's newest foe" to be France and the "absolute rout" to be Suvorov's victory over Joubert at Novi. They might not share the apparent spirit of the lines. The King's speech had asked them to admire Suvorov and the wise Emperor Paul who had sent this dragon south to eat Frenchmen; the *Post* in turn had encouraged readers to continue in abhorrence of both Suvorov and Paul—and of the King's Ministerial speeches. Still, it may be said, no other "newest foe" than France, and no other "absolute rout" than Novi, was apparent. And yet nothing else in the poem makes much sense if the "vile and painted locusts" of the last stanza are the French.

If the speaker wishes to leave his imagined solitude with the maid to go in "proud and stately step," what is keeping him? If his imagination got him out of the concert, why can it not grant him the "holier joy" of joining the popular shout? Supporters of the English Government will not hold him back. Will readers who last year approved of the recantation of S. T. Coleridge weep if Bonaparte is shamed? What accounts for this anonymous poet's stridency and strain? Paradoxically, it could be only this: neither Coleridge nor readers who subscribed morally to the *Morning Post* had the slightest temptation to find a "holier joy" in celebrating any campaigns Suvorov had won or any he would ever win. The original readers could have made a sorry truce with the poem by divorcing the last two stanzas from each other and agreeing lamely with lines 46–51 that it would be better to shout with the mob over Suvorov's victory, better even that, than to vegetate in an aristocratic hothouse of song. Had not France become almost as great an enemy to Freedom as Russia and Austria? This topical poet and his readers could not let themselves celebrate, but they could think of activities much worse.

E. H. Coleridge cited the letter to Poole of 16 September, which refers to Novi. That letter, in which Coleridge blasts his brothers and other inhabitants of Devonshire as bigots who believe in slavery, a point of view that "makes Pitt & Paul the first among the moral Fitnesses of Things," praises a provincial poet for "the merit of being a Jacobin or so" and comments very dubiously indeed on the success of Emperor Paul's General Suvorov: "The Victory at Novi!—If I were a good Caricaturist, I would sketch off Suwarrow, in a Car of Conquest drawn by huge Crabs!! with what retrograde Majesty the Vehicle advances! He may truly say he came off with Eclat—i.e. A *claw!*—" (CL, 529) He is hardly ready to make Suvorov the hero of an "absolute rout." Nor is the tone of the stanza any nearer to the tone of a letter sent a month later to Southey, when Masséna's recent reversal over the Russians at Zürich gave Coleridge "such an Infusion of animal Spirits" that he wrote of the victory with conscious blasphemy as "the Resurrection & Glorification of the Saviour of the East after his Tryals in the Wilderness" and playfully defied Ministerial censors by repeating "dear dear DEAR Buonaparte!" (CL, 539) In short, Coleridge's attitude in the autumn of 1799 was quite out of keeping with the spirit in which the published stanza on trump and timbrel would then be taken.

If we had to assume that the last eighteen lines were composed in September, 1799, the most satisfactory interpretation would align them with the whole poem: Aristocrats and their equally vile and painted entertainers must and shall be swept to oblivion (lines 52–58); consonant with this moral truth, it would be holier to leave the concert-room, with its distended subtleties of breast and song, and to shout with the mob, who exercise their honest, simple lungs in the celebration of what they take to be the rout of "Freedom's latest foe" (lines 46–51), in a situation either actual and recent or hypothetical and prophesied. This interpretation would emphasize the opposition of natural simplicity to sophisticated intricacy. But the vigor of the shame-and-shout stanza belongs to emotion neither shammed nor fancied.

The undue violence of the stanza might suggest that it had been designed to celebrate an earlier defeat of some Continental power, perhaps in the spring or summer of 1795 when rout of the allied despots seemed acutely "Unhealable." In truth—however unusually extreme the violence of expression—until France became "Freedom's latest foe" in the recantations of 1798, no other country with military power seemed so clearly the latest foe of Freedom as the poet's own. If we have discovered that the nodding of Britain's "tower'd might" was once predicted here, then the assertion in *France: An Ode*, that the poet "sang defeat To all that braved the tyrant-quelling lance, And shame too long delayed and vain retreat," has one more actual passage of poetry to refer to, and merely neglects to say that Coleridge had not until then (April, 1798) sung it publicly. (CPW, 245:36–38) It seems very probable that the verses were patched up or newly applied in 1799, and almost as probable that the poet's impulse of creation was politically opposite from the public application. Although there is no Pantisocratic vale, which makes a date of 1794–95 less likely, the subjunctive conveying a sense of restraint on celebration (a holier joy it *were*) probably indicates that the rout had not occurred at the time of writing, that the nodding of towered might lay in the holier future when a New Order would ring out the Old. The reason for publishing in 1799, by this interpretation, was simply Coleridge's battered desire to meet the terms of employment under Daniel Stuart. In addition, even with words blanked out, he could call adherents to the aristocracy "harlot & naughty things." Even though readers might take its larger implication to be that the Revolution had betrayed the hopes of man for a better Europe, the poet could know how the stanzas suited his present hope: that the commanding genius of Bonaparte, bringing new strength, would be indirectly the means of purifying the Revolution. As often, the poet was too uncertain to desire partisan clarity in journalistic use of the poem.

In conclusion, three tesserae can be picked up from the scattered mosaic. (1) Line 48, "With trump and timbrel clang, and popular shout," is repeated as the penultimate line of *Zapolya*, Part I, in Zapolya's vision of the day when her son will return in triumph to their palace. If the blanks at the end of the Concert lines replaced such adjectives as *unsceptered, kingless*, or *priestless*, line 48 was moved to a quite different context in *Zapolya*. (2) Line 54, "Were armied in the hearts of living men," lacks a riming companion; and "nod," "God," rime seven lines apart. Were two or more lines dropped? (3) In 1828 Thomas C. Grattan (*Beaten Paths*, 1862, II, 117) heard Coleridge recite a fragment that contains a version of line 38:

> —and oft I saw him stray,
> The bells of fox-glove on his hand—and ever
> And anon he to his ear would hold a blade
> *Of that stiff grass that 'mid the heath-flower grows,*
> Which made a subtle kind of melody,
> Most like the apparition of a breeze,
> Singing with its thin voice in shadowy worlds.

Notes

For all works cited, unless otherwise noted, the place of publication is London.

Chapter 1

1 For abbreviations used in documentation throughout this volume, see the list on pages ix and x.
2 *Political Disquisitions; Or, An Enquiry into Public Errors, Defects, and Abuses,* 3 vols. (1774–75), III, 10.
3 CPW, 114n. Here and hereafter readings from the *apparatus criticus* at the foot of a page are designated, like other notes, by *n.*
4 Although this is a study of the degree to which Coleridge's poems are concerned with the disposition of worldly power, it has probably been influenced more than the documentation suggests by such arguments as those in Newton P. Stallknecht's *Strange Seas of Thought* (Durham, 1945), Adolph A. Suppan's "Coleridge: The Shaping Mind" (unpub. diss., Univ. of Wisconsin, 1947), and the current studies of John Beer and Lucyle Werkmeister, to the effect that Coleridge paid great and early attention to such otherworldly writers as Plotinus and Boehme. Like David V. Erdman's *Blake: Prophet Against Empire* (Princeton, 1954), the study has been necessarily concerned first of all with what has been most ignored: current situations and topical allusions.

Chapter II

1 *Reflections on the Revolution in France* (8th ed., 1791), p. 144. For representative recent appraisals of Burke's conservatism, see Charles Parkin, *The Moral Basis of Burke's Political Thought* (Cambridge, 1956), and Peter J. Stanlis, *Edmund Burke and the Natural Law* (Ann Arbor, 1958).

2 Gerrit P. Judd, *Members of Parliament 1734–1832* (New Haven, 1955), pp. 31–33; Betty Kemp, *King and Commons 1660–1832* (1957), pp. 97–110.

3 See Robert Preyer, *Bentham, Coleridge, and the Science of History* (Bochum, 1958), pp. 51–62.

4 Frend, *An Account of the Proceedings in the University of Cambridge . . .* (Cambridge, 1793), p. 92. J. B. Beer tries unsuccessfully to delay Coleridge's Unitarianism until after Cambridge, in *Coleridge the Visionary* (1959), pp. 76–81.

5 Charles Lamb, *Works*, ed. T. Hutchinson (1908), I, 498. See also Ben R. Schneider, Jr., *Wordsworth's Cambridge Education* (Cambridge, 1957), pp. 42–47.

6 CL, 269; *Monthly Repository*, VIII (1834), 656.

7 *A Moral and Political Lecture*, p. 7, altered in *Conciones ad Populum; Or, Addresses to the People* (Bristol, 1795).

8 J. L. Lowes, "Coleridge and the 'Forty Youths of Bristol,'" *TLS*, 11 Oct. 1928, p. 736; Joseph Cottle, *Early Recollections* (1837), I, 13–26. For recent studies of the lectures, see Lucyle Werkmeister, "Coleridge's *The Plot Discovered . . . ,*" *MP*, LVI (1959), 254–63; John Colmer, *Coleridge, Critic of Society* (Oxford, 1959), pp. 9–30. For closer attention to detail than Colmer gives, see Dulany Terrett, "Coleridge's Politics, 1789–1810," unpub. diss., Northwestern Univ., 1941.

9 G. H. B. Coleridge, "Biographical Notes: Being Chapters of Ernest Hartley Coleridge's Fragmentary and Unpublished Life of Coleridge," in *Coleridge: Studies by Several Hands,* ed. E. Blunden and E. L. Griggs (1934), p. 42.

10 See Colmer, pp. 65–67, 213–18. D. V. Erdman has independently identified the essay as Coleridge's.

11 BL, I, 145, 262; Elizabeth, Lady Holland, *Journal* (1908), II, 237–38.

12 Aspinall, *Politics and the Press* (1949), pp. 88–89, 104–5, 202, 208; see HCR, 37.

13 A. S. Link, "Samuel Taylor Coleridge and the Economic and Political Crisis in Great Britain, 1816–1820," *JHI*, IX (1948), 323–38.

14 *A Letter to William Smith, Esq. M.P.* (1817), p. 7, reprinted in *Essays, Moral and Political* (1832), II, 10.

Chapter III

1 CN, 71, 91, 114, 158, 272 [v], 296.
2 CN, 124, 134, 143, 272 [a], and note.
3 The MS, in the Henry W. and Albert A. Berg Collection of The New York Public Library, is quoted here with permission.
4 O. Ritter, "Coleridgiana," *Englische Studien*, LVIII (1924), 382.
5 EOT, 562; *Remarks on the Objections Which Have Been Urged against the Principle of Sir Robert Peel's Bill* (1818), p. 2; *Notes, Theological, Political, and Miscellaneous*, ed. Derwent Coleridge (1853), pp. 220–21.
6 Second ed., Hartford, 1787, pp. 141, 164, 204.
7 "Coleridge's Quotations," *Athenaeum*, 20 Aug. 1892, p. 259.
8 CPW, 36:27, 115:164, 338:77; cf. CPW, 71–72.
9 CPW, 110:19, 315:1, 316:31, 376:3, 468:55. *The Old Man of the Alps*, where the word appears dissyllabically in "the churning-plant of sovereign power" (250:85), seems to me to be more likely Wordsworth's poem than Coleridge's.
10 CPW, 378:29n; *Friend*, 26 Oct. 1809, p. 175; B.M. MS. Add. 34225, f. 7.
11 B.M. C.126.h.15(1), Sir John Walsh, *Popular Opinions on Parliamentary Reform Considered* (4th ed., 1831), pp. 8–9.
12 The quite definite political implications of this innocent-looking passage are made clearer by a description of Italy in *On the Constitution of the Church and State* (1830), pp. 21–22: "With the single exception of the ecclesiastical state, the whole country is cultivated like a garden. You may find there every gift of God—only not freedom. . . . All the splendors . . . could not soothe the pining of Dante or Machiavel, exiles from their free, their beautiful Florence. But not a pulse of liberty survives."
13 John Cartwright, *The Commonwealth in Danger* (1795), pp. 97–117; John Thelwall, *The Rights of Nature* (1796), p. 6n (3rd ed., p. 5n).
14 CPW, 141:314, 158:16. The reading in CPW of "Murderess" for "Murderers" is in error; see CL, 286.
15 "Coleridge on George Washington," *BNYPL* (1957), LXI, 88.
16 See MC, 5, 10, 14 May, 4 June 1794; *Annual Register*, 1794, Chronicle, p. 15 (revised ed., 1808, p. 28); SPJ for 1800, p. 222.

Chapter IV

1 CPW, 84:7, 85:7, 86:(2)12. Cf. CPW, 29, 47–49, 58, 63, 64, 68, 98, 174, 175; Southey and Robert Lovell, *Poems* (Bath, 1795), p. 4; Southey, "Hymn to the Penates," *Poems* (Bristol, 1797), pp. 210–11.
2 CPW, 71:12; Oxf. Bodl. MS. Eng. letters c. 22, f. 149.
3 *Cambridge Intelligencer*, 31 Dec. 1796; see CPW, 163n.
4 CPW, 23:55, 115:171–72, 149:15–17, 162:45, 163:56.

5   *Imagination and Fancy* (1845 [for 1844]), p. 288. The italics are Hunt's. The Electress of Bavaria retired to "a small pleasure house" with her fiddler, Frantz Eck.—MP, 16 Sept. 1799, p. [2b]. If Coleridge wrote the Latin declamation at Jesus College entitled "The Desire of Posthumous Fame Is Unworthy of a Wise Man," he attacked ambition, presumption, Cromwell, and Suvorov's massacre at Izmail all together as early as March, 1792; see "A Prize Declamation," *Chanticleer*, Jesus College, Lent Term, 1886, I, No. 2, pp. 29–32; W. F. Prideaux's Appendix to Richard Herne Shepherd, *The Bibliography of Coleridge* (1900), pp. 89–92. Oddly enough, Hunt quoted from the poem in 1835 to show how the ice-palace of the Russian empress had realized the "poetical description of the palace of Kubla Khan."—*Leigh Hunt's London Journal*, 28 Jan. 1835, II, 25.

6   John Livingston Lowes, *The Road to Xanadu* (corr. ed.; Boston, 1930), pp. 29, 33, 379–82, 470; CN, 240.

7   See Christof Hermann von Manstein, *Memoirs of Russia*, ed. David Hume (1770), pp. 250–53; William Coxe, *Travels into Poland, Russia, Sweden, and Denmark* (1784), I, 484–519; William Tooke, *View of the Russian Empire* (2nd ed., 1800), I, 44–45; R. Nisbet Bain, *The Pupils of Peter the Great* (1897), pp. 282–85; and the fuller discussion in Woodring, "Coleridge and the Khan," *EIC*, IX (1959), 361–68.

8   BL, I, 12. See John Beer, *Coleridge the Visionary* (1959), pp. 145–46.

9   CPW, 440:21, and see F. L. Beaty, "Two Manuscript Poems of Coleridge," *RES*, VII (1956), 187.

10 *The Eighteenth Century Background* (1940), pp. 168–204. In a MS of *Joan of Arc* written before he knew Coleridge, Southey had denounced "Mitred Hypocrisy" (Harvard MS. Eng 265.3, III.43).

11 Paul Kaufman, "The Reading of Southey and Coleridge . . . Borrowings from the Bristol Library, 1793–98," *MP*, XXI (1924), 319; in general, Kaufman's article has been superseded by George Whalley, "The Bristol Library Borrowings of Southey and Coleridge, 1793–8," *Library*, 5th s., IV (1949), 114–31. There are complete transcriptions of the catalogue and borrowings in the Arthur Beatty Wordsworth Collection of the University of Wisconsin.

12 *Collected Papers*, ed. H. A. L. Fisher (Cambridge, 1911), I, 1–161.

Chapter V

1   *Life and Correspondence*, ed. C. C. Southey (1849–50), I, 221.

2   CN, 81, 161. Miss Coburn (CN, 81n) thinks the principle comes from the Bishop of Llandaff's reply to Paine.—Richard Watson, *An Apology for the Bible* (1796), p. 356.

3   CL, 752; CPW, 359n; George Whalley, *Coleridge and Sara Hutchinson* (1955), p. 10.

4   Mary C. Park, *Joseph Priestley and the Problem of Pantisocracy* (Philadelphia, 1947); Sister Eugenia [Logan], "Coleridge's Scheme of Pantisocracy and American Travel Accounts," *PMLA*, XLV (1930), 1069–84;

J. R. MacGillivray, "The Pantisocracy Scheme and Its Immediate Background," *Studies in English . . . University College, Toronto* (1931), pp. 131–69. For an anecdotal view see Henry Gunning, *Reminiscences of . . . Cambridge* (1854), I, 280–301.

5 *Lectures on History* (2nd ed., 1793), II, 124.

6 EOT, 35; CPW, 50:37, 53:71, 1023:1; and "Absence: A Poem," line 73, as given by R. D. Mayo, *Bodleian Library Record*, V (1956), 315.

7 CPW, 69:5, 71:7, 75:27–28, 92:15–21, 130:151.

8 W, 144–45; William Crowe, *Lewesdon Hill . . . with Other Poems* (3rd ed., 1804), p. 45.

9 CPW, 161n. Cf. 161:31; CN, 199; LL, I, 83–84; CL, 307.

10 *Poems on Affairs of State* (1710), I, 13–23. For the restoration of monarchic usage, see *The House of Nassau: A Pindarick Ode, ibid.*, II, 325–37, and *The Rising Sun; Or, Verses upon the Queen's Birthday*, III, 457–68.

11 CPW, 163n. For Coleridge's annotations on proofsheets for the edition of 1797 (now B.M. Ashley 408), see *Poems*, ed. J. D. Campbell and W. H. White (1899), pp. 91, 105.

Chapter VI

1 See *Parl. Hist.*, 1794, XXXI, 955–58; MC, 16, 18, 20 June, 23, 26 July ("Bits of Ribband—to Grown Children"), 1 Aug., 4, 16 Sept. 1794; 6 Aug. 1799.

2 *Shakespearean Criticism*, ed. T. M. Raysor (Cambridge, Mass., 1930), I, 136.

3 "The Concept of the Political Leader in the Romantic Period," unpub. diss., Northwestern Univ., 1951.

4 The details, to be found in the *Nouveau Larousse* and in Ferdinand Brunot, *Histoire de la langue française*, Vols. VI and IX, are summarized by J. M. Thompson, *The French Revolution* (London, 1944), pp. vii, 121.

5 Walter Moyle, *An Essay on the Constitution & Government of the Roman State*, ed. J. Thelwall (Norwich, 1796), p. 7n.

6 B.M. MS. Add. 34225, f. 6 (cf. CPW, 132:9–12n); Harvard MS. Eng 265.3 (III.310).

7 S. T. Coleridge, *The Watchman*, ed. Lewis Patton, Yale Univ. diss., I, lxvii, II, 485–86.

8 BP, I, 323:330. See R. D. Havens, *The Influence of Milton on English Poetry* (Cambridge, Mass., 1922), p. 515.

9 Besides Havens, see Humphry House, *Coleridge* (1953), pp. 63–67.

10 28 Sept., 5 and 12 Oct., 9 Nov., 7 Dec. 1793; 4 Jan. 1794.

11 CL, 151, 164, 191; W, 111–13; EKC, 37; Lewis Patton diss. (Yale, 1937), II, 497.

12 See Bowles, *Sonnets and Other Poems* (1794), p. 112; (7th ed., 1800), p. 118; CL, 318.

13 Quoted in William Beloe, *The Sexagenarian* (1817), II, 318.

14   EOT, 108. See W, 21; EOT, 47n; Terrett, p. 73; *An Answer to "A Letter to Edward Long Fox, M.D."* (a pamphlet of December, 1795, in which Coleridge first accused Burke of setting fire to the temple of Freedom), p. 8.

15   Priestley, *The Doctrine of Philosophical Necessity Illustrated* (1777), pp. 99, 110.

16   W. E. Gibbs, "An Unpublished Letter from John Thelwall to S. T. Coleridge," *MLR*, XXV (1930), 86.

17   See CL, 140; *Poems*, 1796, p. 180 (Coleridge's note: "When *Kosciusko* was observed to fall, the Polish ranks set up a shriek"). CPW omits this note, alters the mechanics as usual, and promulgates other errors: e.g., this sonnet did not appear in the 1803 volume.

18   See J. P. Collier, Preface to *Seven Lectures on Shakespeare and Milton* (1856), p. xxxvii.

19   See the "College Commemoration Sermon—Oct. 6ᵗʰ 1799" (B.M. MS. Add. 35343, ff. 31–63); CL, 532, 636; J. A. Colm[e]r, "An Unpublished Sermon by S. T. Coleridge," *N & Q*, CCIII (1958), 150–52; R. Sprague Allen, "The Reaction against William Godwin," *MP*, XVI (1918), 225–43; C. Kegan Paul, *William Godwin* (1876), I, 17, 119, 362; George M. Harper, *William Wordsworth* (New York, 1916), I, 387. For a later development see Lucyle Werkmeister, "Godwin on the Communication of Truth," *MP*, LV (1958), 170–77.

20   *Coleridge, Critic of Society* (Oxford, 1959), pp. 14, 42.

21   *A Wiltshire Parson and His Friends* ... (1926), p. 20. It was Bowles who taught Coleridge that pity "is at least as powerful an incentive to virtue as logical argument," according to Lucyle Werkmeister, "Coleridge, Bowles, and 'Feelings of the Heart,'" *Anglia*, LXXVIII (1960), 63.

22   CPW, 85:2–3, 87:2–3. The transferred words appear in an intermediate form of the sonnet to Bowles, drafted for the 1796 volume, at Harvard: fMS. Eng 947.8.

23   See CL, 564; W. L. Bowles, "Recollections of the Late William Linley, Esq.," *Gentleman's Mag.*, III (1835), 574–76. See also *London Mercury*, XXIII (1931), 561, 564.

24   But see D. V. Erdman, "Newspaper Sonnets Put to the Concordance Test [Part II]," *BNYPL*, LXI (1957), 611–20.

     Believing the sonnet of 1795 an early version of the one to Stanhope printed in 1796, Dykes Campbell noted an echo from the sonnet to Burke in "untainted by Corruption's bowl." (CPW, 89; JDC, 575) In later poems Coleridge writes of "Corruption's slimy track" and "Corruption's wolfish throng." (CPW, 146:439, 151:19) "Friend of the Human Race" in Coleridge's known sonnet may be put beside "Friend of Humankind" in this one. Erdman has given further intelligent reasons for believing Coleridge the author of this sonnet and of another to Stanhope in the *Cambridge Intelligencer* of 21 February. The question is still open. It is ironic indeed if Coleridge suppressed his authorship of these two mild utterances and let through the Jacobinical effusion of 1796. The evidence concerning his authorship that E. L. Griggs has considered conclusive against the first sonnet applies equally against the second; in a letter to George Dyer postmarked 10 March 1795, Coleridge exclaimed: "I shall soon transmit to the Morning Chronicle 5 more Sonnets to Eminent characters—among the rest, one to Lord Stanhope!—" (CL, 155–56) but the exclamation point could possibly mean that he is sending still another sonnet on Stanhope, this time in the avowed series. If Coleridge did not write these two newspaper sonnets, he as well as Stanhope may have inspired them, for they repeat or develop several motifs from his other sonnets to heroes: the glow of the patriot sun after its setting; hailing a contemporary with ardent hymn; abstaining from corruption's bowl; and at least a suggestion of the union between science and political reform. Negative evidence, like the appearance in the first sonnet not of Coleridge's usual word "Freedom" but of "Liberty" (which serves for a rime with "sky"), may be more significant than the evidence of internal similarities, both because of a common current language of political verse and political reference and because of the likelihood that newspaper sonneteers would borrow from a stronger writer. Yet it might be noted that the sonnet to Stanhope by John Towill Rutt contains a different set of clichés altogether (Ghita Stanhope and G. P. Gooch, *The Life of Charles, Third Earl Stanhope* [London, 1914], pp. 143–44).

25   CL, 787; JDC, 576; BE, I, 286; E. L. Griggs, "Notes Concerning Certain Poems by . . . Coleridge," *MLN*, LXIX (1954), 28–29; Erdman in *BNYPL*, XLI, 617–18.

26   B.M. Ashley 2850, p. 52. Misquoted by T. J. Wise, *Ashley Library*, VIII (1926), 86.

27   Cottle, *Early Recollections* (1837), I, 202n; CL, 568; for anticipation of Coleridge's contrasts of Pitt with Fox, see Horace Walpole's letters to Sir Horace Mann, for example that of 2 Dec. 1783. In "Lord Moira's Letter," MP, 20 Jan. 1798, identified as Coleridge's by a letter from Stuart (noted by Erdman), Fox is praised for his temper, morals, and intellect, all opposite to Pitt's, and his allegiance to radical reform, which differentiates him from the supporters of Moira.

Chapter VII

1   *BNYPL*, LXI (1957), 508–16. He presents strong internal evidence. Although not conclusive, the sonnet's absence from Coleridge's published volumes, manuscripts, and correspondence is dampening.

2   WPW, I, 363; HCR, 59; BL, I, 126; JDC, 81; CL, 295, 982; CPW, 977; CN, 1491, f. 61 (where the editorial note puts the arrest after breakfast on 6 Sept.). The Pierpont Morgan Library holds interesting letters by Thelwall concerning visits of 1797 and 1803 with Coleridge

and Wordsworth. Notice also Coleridge's newly available letter of 1801 with a liberal gesture concerning Thelwall's atheism (CL, 667).

3   See D. V. Erdman, "Unrecorded Coleridge Variants," SB, XI (1958), 155. CPW erroneously gives the date of the duchess' poem in MP as 21 (for 20) Dec. Elisabeth Schneider's suggestion that Mrs. Robinson may have shown the poem to Coleridge before 20 Dec. (Coleridge, Opium, and Kubla Khan [Chicago, 1953], p. 350) is strengthened by a note in the MP of 26 Dec.: "The Duchess of Devonshire, from a congeniality of taste, is the zealous patroness of Mrs. Robinson, our Laura Maria."

4   A Letter to Her Grace the Duchess of Devonshire: A New Edition (1784), p. 8. This work seems to be unknown to writers on either Combe or the duchess.

5   The English Ode from Milton to Keats (New York, 1940), p. 248.

6   My quotations come from the text of Griggs, CL, 639–42. Campbell's statement that he left five stanzas unpublished (JDC, 625), which has troubled scholars, probably refers to stanzas 7 and 8, the first draft of stanzas 1 and 3, and the original, canceled lines of stanza 2. See CPW, 356–58.

7   See Carlyon, Early Years and Reflections (1856), I, 175; E. J. Morley, "Coleridge in Germany (1799)," London Mercury, XXIII (1931), 561–62—reprinted in Wordsworth and Coleridge, ed. E. L. Griggs (Princeton, 1939), pp. 230–31. It will be noted that the adverse review of Perdita's Hubert de Sevrac in the Critical Rev. for Aug., 1798, attributed to Coleridge by Garland Greever (see CL, 318), comes too late to be the "abuse" mentioned in Germany.

8   See D. V. Erdman, "Lost Poem Found," BNYPL, LXV (1961), 249–68. That Coleridge hoped to get the poem into the Annual Anthology is clear from Southey's letter of 15 Dec. 1799 (printed by Irvin Ehrenpreis in N & Q, 18 Mar. 1950, p. 125): "If you can procure me the conclusion of Francini & the Hermit of the Alps, by referring to the filed papers—why I shall be glad of them in the volume." Apparently the Morning Post for 3 Jan. 1798 was missing even then.

9   See Albert Philip Francine, The Francines, Originally of Florence . . . (privately printed, Philadelphia, 1917); Albert Mousset, Les Francine: créateurs des eaux de Versailles, Intendants des Eaux et Fontaines de France de 1623 à 1784 (Paris, 1930).

10 See CL, 575, 629, 904; Elisabeth Schneider, p. 86. For a full, generally accurate account, see Robert D. Bass, The Green Dragoon: The Lives of Banastre Tarleton and Mary Robinson (New York, 1957).

Chapter VIII

1   H. R. Fox Bourne unhesitatingly dated the poem "early in 1796."— "Coleridge among the Journalists," Gentleman's Mag., CCLXIII (1887), 474.

2 *The Years of Endurance, 1793–1802* (1942), p. 205.

3 *Patriotism in Literature* (New York, 1924), p. 190.

4 Cf. *The Young Larks* and *The Dromedary and the Rhinoceros: A Fable,* in SPJ for 1797, pp. 54–58, 77–79. Horace Walpole's fable, *The Entail,* appeared in MC shortly after Coleridge's poem.

5 CPW, 171:43–44n. Mechanics varied from one printing to another. The wording differs slightly in the MS, not in Coleridge's hand, in the Henry W. and Albert A. Berg Collection, The New York Public Library (from which I quote with permission), and in the Greenough MS, described by E. J. Morley in *London Mercury,* XXIII (1931), 561.

6 CL, 712, 764. Cf. the serious instructions "On planting Oaks" in Notebook 12, B.M. MS. Add. 47509, ff. 8–12, entered later than 28 May 1807, and his note on the Commonwealth of perhaps the same period: "even wise men, comparatively wise, were eager to have an oak, where they ought to have been content with planting an acorn."—*Notes, Theological, Political, and Miscellaneous* (1853), pp. 176–77.

7 Fox, *Memorials and Correspondence* (1854), III, 20–21.

8 See "The Blasted Oak. Addressed to the Right Hon. William Pitt," MP, 11 Jan. 1798.

9 See *Senator,* XIX, 265–515; *Parl. Hist.,* XXXIII, 735, 1089–1275; *The Times* and MP, 5 Dec. 1797–6 Jan. 1798.

10 *Senator,* VIII, 44. The better-known reading, "wild beasts," appears in *Parl. Hist.,* XXX, 1215.

11 Details from the several memoirs of Pitt may be found in H. K. Olphin, *George Tierney* (1934), pp. 54–57, and in the commentary to the numerous satirical prints on the duel, George, Vol. VII.

12 See D. V. Erdman, L. Werkmeister, and R. S. Woof, "Unrecorded Coleridge Variants: Additions and Corrections," *SB,* XIV (1961), 241–42.

13 *Sämmtliche Schriften* (Berlin, 1784–96), I, 119–20. Coleridge's copy of this edition is in the British Museum.

14 Barham's MS, with his transcription of *The Devil's Thoughts,* is in the Berg Collection of The New York Public Library. Elisabeth Schneider (*Coleridge, Opium, and Kubla Khan,* p. 291) says that the satire by Southey and Coleridge was suggested by *The Devil in Ban: An Idyll,* in the *Monthly Mag.* for Feb., 1799, which is a translation from Voss by William Taylor: but the resemblance is slight. Dr. Erdman has called my attention to a closer analogue, beginning "As the Devil, one morning, was taking a walk," in *Husks for Swine,* 1794.

15 See *Monthly Mag.,* VII (May, 1799), 333–34; LL, I, 148; MP, 8, 16, 17 Jan., 21 Sept. 1799.

16 *Poems,* ed. M. H. Fitzgerald (1909), p. 422.

17 Whalley, *Coleridge and Sara Hutchinson* (1955), p. 22.

18 *The Correspondence of William Wilberforce* (1840), I, 119.

19 Three further stanzas on a dully droned sermon, in a MS in the Berg Collection, continue the spirit of the stanzas against consecration and Wilberforce.

20   See George, VII, 565–68; Erdman's approaching edition of Coleridge's
     writings in the *Morning Post*. In *The Green Dragon* (p. 346), Robert
     D. Bass makes a good case for Banastre Tarleton as the original general.
     Tarleton had been drunk with Sheridan; he had earned a reputation
     as butcher in the American Revolution; and recently he had deserted
     Perdita Robinson after an intimacy of fifteen years, voted for the
     Slave Trade, and accepted from the Tories a military post in Ireland.
     See also Whalley, p. 22n.
21   In explanation of Coleridge's puns on Grenville as Boötes, see SPJ for
     1800, pp. 295–98; and the popular *All the Talents' Garland*. On the
     negotiations with Spain, see MP, 16 Dec. 1799; *Moniteur*, 15, 27
     frimaire, an 8; Hist. MSS Comm., *Dropmore Papers*, V, 432; André
     Fugier, *Napoléon et l'Espagne 1799–1808* (Paris, 1930), I, 45, 85–86;
     SPJ for 1800, pp. 295–304; for 1801, pp. 37–38. Later Coleridge called
     the note Windham's; see EOT, 242–66.
22   See CPW, 353; CN, 609, 634, 947; CL, 588, 632, 727; IS, 294; *Fraser's
     Mag.*, VII (1833), 175–77, 367, 620–21; J. P. Collier, *An Old Man's
     Diary* (1871–72), I, 61–62. The "Inscription on a Gravestone" that
     William Jerdan thought Southey had a hand in (*Autobiography*, III
     [1853], 312) has been identified as the lines on Mackintosh by Lucyle
     Werkmeister in *N & Q*, CCIV (1959), 75n. There are likelier epitaphs
     (CPW, 954–55, 961–62, 971); the lines on Mackintosh are in no way
     to be considered as inscribed on a gravestone.
23   CN, 609, 634, 947, 868; Table Talk of 27 Apr. 1823, IS, 294.
24   CPW, 169:10, 212:21, 302:77. In early versions, the Raven's feathers
     "were wet."
25   See Coleridge, *Treatise on Method*, ed. A. D. Snyder (1934), pp. x,
     71; *Shakespearean Criticism*, ed. T. M. Raysor (1930), II, 307; EKC,
     212, 281.
26   E.g., 3 Jan. 1818, 23 Jan., 23 Apr. 1819.
27   *Diary*, ed. T. Sadler (1869), II, 134–35.
28   Notebook 25, B.M. MS. Add. 47523, ff. 91–92; cf. CPW, 983.
29   *Letters, Conversations and Recollections of S. T. Coleridge* (1836), I,
     89–92.
30   CPW, 446:105, 447:125. The title, but nothing else about Coleridge's
     jeu d'esprit, may owe something to Cowper's *The Distressed Travellers*,
     which had been published in the *Monthly Magazine* in 1808.
31   Facsimile in *The Cornell Wordsworth Collection*, ed. George H. Healey
     (Ithaca, 1957), facing p. 401.

Chapter IX

1   BP, I, 316:255–56. Byron marked these lines "Unjust" in R. C. Dallas'
     copy (reproduced for the Roxburghe Club in 1936). E. H. Coleridge
     (BP, I, 315n) takes the "Unjust" to refer to the whole passage on
     Coleridge, but it is to be noted that the line, "A fellow feeling makes

us wond'rous kind," in his original attack on the poem *To a Young Ass,* was strengthened by Byron in the Dallas copy to "He brays—the Laureat of the long-eared kind." He was acknowledging injustice only to the odes and kindred poems.

2 For help see G. Whalley, "Coleridge, Southey and 'Joan of Arc,'" *N & Q,* CXCIX (1954), 67–69. The authority of such primary sources as Southey's Preface and Coleridge's marginalia is at best dubious and frequently made useless by a tangle of contradictions. The rarity is not a book annotated by Coleridge, but a surviving copy of an early edition containing work by him that he did not annotate: and his notes do not always agree with each other, much less with his collaborators' or other evidence. At CPW, 1029, appears Bk. I, 484–96, of *Joan of Arc,* 1796, with the note Coleridge wrote in 1814 (see EKC, 358): "Suggested and in part written by S. T. C." The wording may be partly Coleridge's, but hardly the suggestion. With "the dingle's depth" and the "aged oak Whose root uptorn by tempests overhangs The stream" in this passage, compare lines written by Southey before he met Coleridge, which were then Bk. I, 372–76 (Harvard MS. Eng 265.3):

> how abhorrent to my soul
> That loved these scene[s] of bliss—the dingles bed
> The primrosed bank where hung the fallen trunk
> In antic wildness & the stream hoarse broke [?]
> Though rolling oer the stones—

Perhaps the passage *after* lines 269–70 on "the lorn widow's groan, And the pale orphan's feeble cry for bread" (CPW, 1028) is Coleridge's, as he reportedly indicated, but those two lines could have been revised by him at most, because Southey had written as the original Bk. I, 121–23, of "the groans of death / The shrieks of agony—the widows cry / The orphan plaints," and, in words given to Joan, a "vast variety of woe." E. H. Coleridge took the annotations from a copy of *Joan of Arc* belonging to Coleridge's friend W. Hood of Bristol, as transcribed by John Taylor Brown in "Bibliomania," *North British Rev.,* XL (Feb., 1864), 70–92 (reprinted in a series called "Odds and Ends," Edinburgh, 1867), or he may have worked from fresh transcriptions made by Dykes Campbell in a second copy now in the possession of Mrs. Dorothy Wordsworth Dickson of Rydal, who kindly allowed me to examine it. One further caveat: E. H. Coleridge's transcriptions from the MSS of *Joan* and *Destiny,* as of all other poems, handle canceled passages with abandon, at least by later standards.

3 CPW, 132:21; B.M. MS. Add. 28096, ff. 26–29.

4 The source, identified by Lewis Patton, is *An Accurate and Impartial Narrative of the War, by an Officer of the Guards . . . containing the Second Edition of a Poetical Sketch of the Campaign of 1793 . . . .* 2 vols. [1795]. The baby frozen to its mother's milk comes from a first-person account quoted in the prose tail-piece, "A Concise Narrative of

the Retreat through Holland, to Westphalia, in the Years 1794, and 1795," II, 103.

5 Pages 140–44. Southey made didactic use of the sepulcher "Beneath the Abbey's ivied wall" in *Mary*, a ballad in *Poems*, 1797, pp. 163–70. For further links to ice-floe, way-wanderer, and pestilence, see CPW, 130n, 131:149, 258:47–48. Any thought that Southey introduced Coleridge to exotic accounts of outlandish travel should be checked by J. R. MacGillivray's discovery of a poem signed "S. T. C." in the Cambridge *Chronicle* of 31 July 1790; it has many Coleridgian characteristics and acknowledges the power of love in "frozen LAPLAND."— "A New and Early Poem by Coleridge," *BNYPL*, LXIII (1959), 153–54. Lapland as the geographical opposite of Africa was just then a poetic commonplace, but this poem, *The Abode of Love*, heralded the approach of a Bluecoat angel already voyaging on seas distant if not yet strange. In a poem *On Commerce* Thelwall made commerce itself "The monster breeding Nile of hideous vice, From whose oft stagnant pools incessant spring A loath'd mis[s]hapen swarm."—*The Peripatetic* (1793), p. 39; reprinted in the *Tribune*, II (1796), 28.

6 *Coleridge* (1953), p. 68.

7 No. 27, II, 279–80, issued two or three weeks after Thelwall's lecture of 16 September 1795.

8 LL, I, 76. Like other references to the poem, George N. Shuster's description of it (*The English Ode from Milton to Keats* [New York, 1940], p. 247) as irregularly Pindarick, not symmetrically Pindaric, refers to its later, altered form.

9 I do not say that the ill-advised change was necessarily a typographical error. The corrected copy of the 1834 edition in the Huntington Library shows that Coleridge had a chance in his last months to correct "to" to "for," and he was not consistent in his casual references to the poem. Yet, if he wrote "to" once as early as 1817, he wrote "Ode on the Departing Year" at least once in 1819. (CL, IV, 791, 970) And H. N. Coleridge wrote typically to John Taylor Coleridge on 20 March 1834: "I have endeavored to collect every thing, & the arrangement & corrections give me much trouble."—B.M. MS. Add. 47557, f. 103ᵛ.

10 CPW, 160:5–161:8. In Mrs. Gillman's copy of *Sibylline Leaves*, Coleridge restored the original reading of "skirts" for "train," but only in deference to Cary, the translator of Dante. See N. van Patten in *Library*, n.s. XVII (1936), 223.

11 Facsimile in T. J. Wise, *A Bibliography of . . . Coleridge* (1913), p. 48.

12 For a description of this Coleorton copy, see B. I. Evans, "Coleridge's Copy of 'Fears in Solitude,'" *TLS*, 18 Apr. 1935, p. 255. The printing history bears up Coleridge's interesting comment in this copy on line 79, "And patriot only in pernicious toils!"—as it read in the quarto, printed while Coleridge was in Germany, and has read consistently since 1808. With reference to "patriot," he glossed: "I wrote it 'patient' —who altered it, I know not; but it seems to me an improvement."

13 Coleorton copy of the quarto, in the Morgan Library. See Milton's Sonnet XII, "I did but prompt the age to quit their clogs." For "Dilatation" Coleridge first wrote, apparently, "Dilution."

14 *TLS*, 28 Sept., 26 Oct. 1951, pp. 613, 677; CL, 865n. Rossiter's weakest evidence concerns the direct influence of Bowles.

15 Coleridge later planned an ode, not to Napoleon, but on General Ross, who burned the public buildings of Washington. See CL, IV, 608. The passages given as fragments on Napoleon (CPW, 1003, 1010) were merely transcribed by Coleridge from other poets, the second from Phineas Fletcher, *The Purple Island*, Canto III, st. 1.

16 Dowden MS, now in the Morgan Library; see CPW, 257n. Coleridge's heading in this MS is "Fears in Solitude written April, 1798, during the Alarm of the Invasion.—The Scene, the Hills near Stowey.—" The motto from Horace was always printed inaccurately as "*Sermoni propriora*," but this is not what Coleridge wrote: see CPW, 106; CL, 864; CL, III, 433; Table Talk for 25 July 1832. Absence of the *r* converts something like "talk more individual" into something like "on the verge of conversation."

17 *North British Review*, XLIII (1865), 287.

Chapter X

1 It would be well if we too could regard the lines (CPW, 64) as originating in the fall of Robespierre. Campbell stated that they "were written in 1792, and addressed to Miss F. Nesbitt" (JDC, 562), but (1) he cites no evidence; (2) the Nesbitt interlude occurred in 1793, not 1792; (3) no MS of either year is known; (4) line 14 quotes Southey's *The Retrospect*, impossible before 1794; (5) the poem was apparently new to Southey when Coleridge sent it 21 Oct. 1794 with an explanatory sentence, "I presented a Copy [of *The Fall of Robespierre*] to Miss Brunton with these Verses in the blank Leaf" (CL, 117); (6) its title in the album of verses given to Mrs. Estlin in April, 1795, "Verses addressed to a Lady with a poem relative to a recent event in the French Revolution" (CPW, 64n), can hardly refer to the Bastille of his earlier poem (than which few events in the Revolution were *less* recent), and "I shook the lance" refers to fighting as in the Vendée (1793) rather than to the execution of either Louis or Robespierre; (7) Coleridge dated the poem Sept., 1794, in the volume of 1797 (a date retained in the inertia of 1803)—and not until 1828, in a general pattern of antedating juvenilia, did he set it back to Sept., 1792; and (8) Bowles had originated or renewed Coleridge's interest in Lee Boo (line 10) in the summer of 1794 (CL, 94).

2 Margaret (Mrs. Henry) Sandford, *Thomas Poole and His Friends* (1888), I, 101.

3 Sandford, I, 96–99; John Dennis, *Robert Southey* (1894), p. 92; Jack Simmons, *Southey* (1945), pp. 42–45, 233; EKC, 30; CL, 96–110.

The *Cambridge Intelligencer* advertised the play as published "this day" on 4 Oct. and again on 11 Oct. 1794.

4 *Life and Correspondence,* ed. C. C. Southey (1849–50), I, 217.

5 Terrett, pp. 18–19; CPW, 510:266; CL, 84.

6 Thomas C. Grattan, *Beaten Paths* (1862), I, 282–85; CPW, 496:9.

7 See MC, 17, 19 May 1794. Conversely, the paper on 24 June reported Couthon as charging Bourdon with peddling the lies of Pitt. Thelwall lectured on "a Parallel between the Character of Pitt and Robes-pierre," *Tribune,* I (1795), 254–60.

8 *The Female Revolutionary Plutarch* (2nd ed., 1806), II, 279–311; Ernest Hamel, *Histoire de Robespierre* (Paris, 1867), III, 567; Heinrich von Sybel, *History of the French Revolution,* trans. W. C. Perry, IV (1869), 192–93.

9 See Thomas Rea, *Schiller's Dramas and Poems in England* (1906), pp. 10–12, 24–25; M. W. Cooke, "Schiller's 'Robbers' in England," *MLR,* XI (1916), 156–75; L. A. Willoughby, "English Translations and Adaptations of Schiller's 'Robbers,'" *MLR,* XVI (1921), 297–301.

10 "Three Romantic Poets and the Drama," unpub. diss., Harvard Univ., 1934, pp. 429, 434. I am greatly indebted to the scholarship and critical acuity of this dissertation.

11 MS. II, at Harvard. Cf. CPW, 1114.

12 Allardyce Nicoll, *A History of Late Eighteenth Century Drama* (Cambridge, 1927), p. 62; EOT, 70. Germanized *Osorio* did not become available to Ministerial agents or *Anti-Jacobin* reviewers, who equated Germanic Sturm with London Jacobinism, but a parody of Thekla's song from Coleridge's translation of *The Piccolomini,* in the Ministerial *Sun* of 13 September 1800, was reprinted in SPJ for 1800, pp. 271–72.

13 CPW, 527:202, 531:287, 561:283, 579:341–44, 584:39–56, 585:59, 586:85–95, 596:308–21.

14 See Dora Jean Ashe, "Coleridge, Byron, and Schiller's 'Der Geisterse-her,'" *N & Q,* CCI (1956), 436–38. A few lines entered *Remorse* from *Wallenstein:* see CPW, 853n, and also (as observed by Christensen) compare 857:158–67 with 791:4–20. Was it coincidence unknown to Coleridge that a Spanish naval officer, Francisco de Paula Osorio, had saved his ship *Trinidad* from capture by Nelson at Cape St. Vincent on 14 Feb. 1797, and that an army officer, Manuel Osorio, had been active in the Peninsular War? As a major general this Osorio would lead Spanish forces against South American rebels in 1817. Coincidence or not, one Osorio was an enemy to Britain when Coleridge's villain bore that name, and another was an ally when Coleridge changed the name to Ordonio.

15 For slightly greater detail concerning the revisions, see C. R. Woodring, "Two Prompt Copies of Coleridge's *Remorse,*" BNYPL, LXV (1961), 229–35.

16 See CL, 466–67, 581 ("I wrote 500 blank Verse Lines"—perhaps not of *Wallenstein*), 585, 589, 624 *et seq.;* LL, I, 178; Christopher Words-

worth, *Social Life at the English Universities* (Cambridge, 1874), p. 597.

17   See the frequent references in CL, IV, 589–721; LL, II, 187, 190; *The Reminiscences of Thomas Dibdin* (1834), II, 71.

18   *Shakespearean Criticism*, ed. T. M. Raysor (Cambridge, Mass., 1930), I, 136. For *The Raven* as "A Christmas Tale," see Chapter X.

19   *The Dramas of Lord Byron* (Göttingen, 1915), p. 11.

20   See CPW, 426, 919, 1108; F. W. Stokoe, *German Influence in the English Romantic Period* (Cambridge, 1926), pp. 125–26.

21   *Coleridge: seine Dichtung als Ausdruck des ethischen Bewusstseins* (Berne, 1951), pp. 85–118.

22   Scott's "transprosing" of Casimir on innocence, in *Peveril of the Peak*, was noted by Henry Nelson Coleridge (according to Murray's register of contributors) in the *Quarterly Rev.*, LII (1834), 27.

23   On possible sources see Christensen, pp. 550–60, and the reference in CL, 466n.

24   B.M. MS. Add. 34225, ff. 36–46. E. L. Griggs published a text, dug out of the fragments and variants, in *MP*, XXXIV (1937), 377–85.

25   See J. M. Nosworthy, "Coleridge on a Distant Prospect of Faust," *E & S*, n.s. X (1957), 69–90.

Chapter XI

1   In diction, in the theme of unregarded poet, and to some extent in tone, *A Character* resembles the scattered lines from Burns's *Second Epistle to Robert Graham* printed as Coleridge's in CPW, 1089. But *On the Death of Dr. Swift* is personal, nostalgic, and "romantic" enough to anticipate Coleridge more nearly than Burns does, in tone, fable, and general metaphor.

2   CPW, 451:1–5. E. H. Coleridge missed the following readings in B.M. MS. Add. 34225, f. 10: 14 tongue] tune [?]; 47 wrote] writ; 85 but] scarce. The manuscript scraps of lines 69–74 contain several further variants.

3   *Biographia Literaria*, ed. H. N. and Sara Coleridge (1847), I, 340–41.

Index